BLOODY
CONFUSED!

BLOODY CONFUSED!

A Clueless American Sportswriter Seeks
Solace in English Soccer

Chuck Culpepper

BROADWAY BOOKS
New York

BROADWAY

PUBLISHED BY BROADWAY BOOKS

Originally published in a slightly different form as *Up Pompey* in
Great Britain in 2007 by Weidenfeld & Nicolson.

Published in the United States by Broadway Books, an imprint of
The Doubleday Publishing Group, a division of
Random House, Inc., New York.
www.broadwaybooks.com

BROADWAY BOOKS and its logo, a letter B bisected on the diagonal, are
trademarks of Random House, Inc.

Book design by Caroline Cunningham

Map © Joe LeMonnier

Library of Congress Cataloging-in-Publication Data
Culpepper, Chuck.
Bloody confused! : a clueless American sportswriter seeks solace in English
soccer / Chuck Culpepper.—1st ed.
p.   cm.
1. Soccer—England. 2. F.A. Premier League. 3. Portsmouth Football Club.
I. Title.
GV944.G7C84 2008
796.3340942—dc22
2007050994

ISBN 978-0-7679-2808-3

PRINTED IN THE UNITED STATES OF AMERICA

5   7   9   10   8   6   4

In memory of

Louise, Florence, Jim, and Ed

Contents

Acknowledgments

Look, I hail from a smallish Virginia town, so I can't believe I even know Dave Kindred. I can't believe I have conversations—and e-mails!—with the same great American sportswriter I read in the *Washington Post* while a student in Charlottesville. I can't believe he knows my name and can summon it immediately upon the sight of me, let alone that I'm privy to his towering decency, or that we share the regal distinction of having been Kentucky sportswriters.

So I *really* can't believe that when I covered the 2005 Kentucky Derby for *Newsday*, he suggested that I write my first book, nor can I believe that he arranged for me a meeting with his New York agent.

I mean, come on. I'm from a smallish town in Virginia.

I would have trouble believing that just weeks later I went trembling into the offices at the David Black Literary Agency, had I not been there at the time.

Thanks then to David Kindred for everything, and to David Black himself for his humanity, which I found so striking I felt I should pay the going counseling rate—$175?—and for his exquisitely astute guidance toward this England venture. Thanks to David Larabell and Susan Raihofer of the David Black Literary Agency for their insight and help, and then to a phenomenal English editor Alan Samson, not least for inviting me to the front row at Arsenal.

Next came Doubleday and Jason Kaufman as the unexpected

privileges mounted. Thanks immensely to Jason for navigating my proposal, for the honor of co-working, and for a maestro's calm expertise. Thanks to Rob Bloom at Doubleday for a whole lot of everything that included a whole lot of patience.

There's an extraordinary human being out there who doubles as the world's foremost blue bear in my opinion, and my gratefulness will prove ceaseless for this young Englishman Charlie Allum, as well as for his fellow Portsmouth devotees Dan Pawsey and "Hopkins," whose first name is "Dylan" if we must get technical. These Three English Guys You'd Most Like to Meet in a Pub adopted me during the 2006–2007 season, shepherded me toward the bartenders, and supplied a few hundred laughs. I am lucky to have found them upon this overcrowded orb.

Immeasurable thanks to Randy Harvey at the *Los Angeles Times*.

Thanks to a lawyer named Duncan, a fan named Mary, two exuberant young men named Chris and Jak across the aisle on a train and extraordinary friends named Teresa Malyshev, Jerry Ferguson, Debra Justus, and Isabel Murray.

I've required a ton of encouragement as a person of fluctuating confidence, so the word "encouragement" will dominate from here. I'm steeply grateful to a publishing-industry gem named Lyda Shuster for her decades of friendship and encouragement. I'm steeply grateful to have walked forlornly to a new bus stop in a new neighborhood in fifth grade and found one Karen D. Schell, and for the thirty-five years of stalwart friendship and encouragement that has followed. Encouragement came also from Bill Erdek, who epitomizes goodness.

Sportswriters know the unspeakable horror of writing, so I could mention a hundred. My friend Karen Crouse forges a rare combination of excellence and generosity, plus the you-can-do-it encouragement. Thanks to Lisa Olson, a luminous soul I'm astronomically lucky to know, for her steadfast encouragement, and to Johnette Howard whom I adore with all might, for her outstanding presence and patience and encouragement, and to Susan Reed, for her—yep—encouragement way back when.

Thanks to that glorious baseball writer Susan Slusser for being the glorious Susan Slusser, and for the encouragement.

Aloft in the stratosphere of my cranium, there's one Mary Gwen Knapp, columnist and thinker and colossal heart, not to mention a supplier of encouragement.

Thanks to Kay and Dick Culpepper, whom it would be a privilege to know even if they hadn't birthed and raised me; to Greg Culpepper, an absolutely marvelous sibling; and to Gayle Treakle, the kind of inspiring aunt who would grace every life in a perfect world.

Thanks to Kentuckians, to Oregonians, to New Yorkers, to Britons for their celestial wit, and to the great fans of the club "Pompey," or Portsmouth, for their instructive exuberance. Admiring thanks to all the many people I've met from the nation of Colombia, a people too shining for earthly woes to occlude. Thanks to Tom and Marion Hewson for extraordinary kindness plus Tom's soccer guru-dom, to Lynne and David Gentle for Virginian hospitality in London, to Doug and Sandra Cress for soccer instruction and friendship plus life's largest honor, to Barry Shaw and Rabih AbouJaoude for their many human glories.

And above all, thanks to my hero, Alfonso Avendano Meza. To reside alongside such a singular soul of such humor, buoyancy, kindness, and strength counts as staggering privilege.

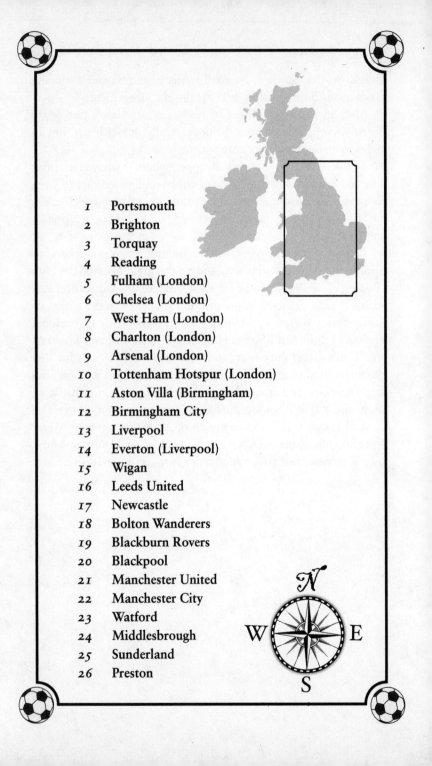

Author's Note

An American brain might not necessarily implode when trying to comprehend English soccer, but it might reel and roil at the complexities of the standings and the schedule. We must be patient with ourselves.

Not only do English professional clubs play on multiple and changing levels, but they play in multiple competitions per season, quite apart from thirty-two teams pursuing one Vince Lombardi Trophy in the NFL or thirty teams pursuing one Commissioner's Trophy in Major League Baseball.

First, England's tiers:

- *Premier League,* or *"Premiership."* Twenty clubs. The top division. The most popular sports league on earth. A thirty-eight-game season from August to May. Each May, clubs finishing eighteenth through twentieth drop to the second tier, while three clubs from the second tier rise to the summit. This is the exciting concept known as "relegation"—foreign to American sport.
- *The Championship* (second division). It's a mysterious name for a second division, but there you are. It has twenty-four clubs. Three rise to the Premier League each May, and three drop to . . .
- *League One* (third division). Again, League One is an ironic name for the third tier, which also features twenty-four clubs. Four suffer relegation at the end of each season, as four join from below.

- *League Two* (fourth division). Here you find the charm of the small stadiums and a relative absence of corporate staleness. There are twenty-four clubs, four of which rise to League One each May, and two of which fall into the oblivion of "conference."
- *"Conference."* A vast array of more than six hundred clubs that teem below the ninety-two clubs in the top four divisions. You see them on TV rarely if ever, but you faintly know they're out there, nobly chasing speckled balls on Saturdays.

For a more beastly cranial exercise, then, there are the number of cups the clubs hunt each season. In certain situations, clubs might speak of trying to win four separate titles in one year. All the competitions exist separately, the outcomes in any one unrelated to any of the others.

An incomplete list that eschews highly marginal competitions to prevent galling confusion:

- *Premier League title.* Goes to the club with the best record across the thirty-eight-game, August-to-May season. Ties are decided by goal difference (between goals scored and goals yielded).
- *European Champions League.* A glamorous, Europe-wide, season-long pursuit that begins with eight groups, then peels the top two teams from each group for a sixteen-club knockout tournament. There's a stark difference between fourth place and fifth place in the Premier League, because each year, the top four clubs in the Premier League standings qualify for this European Champions League, the biggest club competition in the world.
- *FA Cup.* The oldest competition, dating to 1871, it's a season-long single-elimination tournament that in 2007–2008 featured 731 clubs, all English or Welsh. It boasts an adorability when tiny clubs draw mastodons like Manchester United or Chelsea.
- *Carling Cup,* or *League Cup.* It's a single-elimination tournament that features the ninety-two teams in the top four divisions. Gets going in August and concludes in February.

- *UEFA Cup.* It's Europe-wide, and it's rather a fine consolation for clubs that don't reach the European Champions League. The English clubs that finish fifth, sixth, and seventh generally qualify for this.
- *Intertoto Cup.* It feeds into the UEFA Cup, is Europe-wide, and might include an England club that finished eighth or ninth or tenth the previous season. But it's much too perplexing to comprehend.

The top four Premier League clubs from the previous season will compete concurrently in the Premier League, the European Champions League, the FA Cup, and the Carling Cup, which ranks a distant fourth in prestige. A fifth-place club will do likewise save for the UEFA Cup replacing the European Champions League.

As a glittering example, observe Liverpool in the 2005–2006 season. Between October 19 and January 7 in that season, Liverpool alone played twenty matches in five different competitions: twelve in the Premier League, four in the European Champions League, one in the FA Cup, one in the Carling Cup, and two in something called the FIFA Club World Championship, a global event that Liverpool reached because it won the 2005 European Champions League.

In the 2006–2007 season, Manchester United played Aston Villa three times in twenty-one days, twice in regularly scheduled Premier League matches and once because they happened to draw each other for the third round of the FA Cup.

In an epic year, 1999, Manchester United pulled off the "treble," winning the Premier League, the European Champions League, and the FA Cup. In a more recent example, Chelsea in 2007 briefly pined away to win four cups. It won the Carling Cup in February and the FA Cup in May, but bowed out of the European Champions League semifinals in April and finished second to Manchester United in the season that concluded on May 13.

Clearly, England's 849-year head start on the United States as a culture has fostered some serious complexities.

BLOODY CONFUSED!

COMMON SPORTSWRITER
MALAISE

I came down with a dogged strain of common sportswriter malaise on the morning of Tuesday, January 23, 2001. It broadsided me in Tampa, on the floor of Raymond James Stadium, an edifice named for an investment firm and set amid boulevards of soul-murdering strip malls. It struck during my tenth Super Bowl Media Day, an annual event that persists despite both reporters and athletes finding it loathsome.

As about 2,300 reporters surrounded two football teams—one, then a break, then the other—it dawned on me in a howling rush that I had spent a fourteen-year career immersed in a vat of drivel, banality, and corruption, but especially drivel. I had taken the only brain Mother Nature had granted, and I had exposed it to almost fifteen years of listening to stale and preposterous utterances from managers, athletes, and sports-talk radio. It felt as if my brain had stored, as fluid, all the clichés and the fibs and the grotesque marketing and the extravagant nonsense, until one day the organ simply overflowed.

Woozy, I fled up the stadium steps toward the free breakfast buffet.

I cannot recall the precise rote utterance by an athlete or coach or reporter that wrought this cranial convulsion. I wish I could, but I believe the human mind has a mechanism that represses things that aim to turn it into mulch. At Super Bowl Media Day, some reporters seek insight. Some seek piffle. All receive piffle. There's such a debilitating barrage of piffle that it'd be yeoman to pinpoint particular piffle.

I know it wasn't when Baltimore Ravens linebacker Ray Lewis compared his double-murder charge and obstruction-of-justice guilty plea to the plight of Jesus Christ, because I weathered that session dutifully. I doubt it was New York Giants cornerback Jason Sehorn chatting with reporters about his marriage proposal to actress Angie Harmon on a late-night talk show, because I deeply feared that session and did not stray near. It could've been when, for the one thousandth time, across ten Super Bowls, I heard somebody ask a player whether his team could handle Super Bowl distractions, followed by the one thousandth identical answer of "Yes, we can because we understand why we're here." No one had ever said, "No, I don't think so, because some of the guys already have hired seven escort agencies and held three all-night orgies," which would've been mildly intriguing.

I just know that everything around me felt so hackneyed and so marketed, every conversation so artificial, that I could feel the last shreds of individual humanity draining from my system.

This malaise, epidemic among my colleagues, had beset me only in twinges before. For years I had stood in clusters of reporters listening to college basketball players recite the tired balderdash learned in sessions with college PR staffs, and every once in a while I'd feel a sudden flash commanding me to take my own pen and gouge out my own eyeballs. I'd heard almost fifteen years of athletes claiming they'd succeeded even though nobody respected them. That must've killed ten thousand brain cells. I'd heard almost fifteen years of coaches and athletes saying they took it one game at a time, as not a single contrarian in all that time ever dared to say he took it two games at a time. That must've killed a hundred thousand brain cells. I'd listened carefully to almost fifteen years of retired athletes doing TV commentary during games and studio shows or on talk radio, 97 percent sounding roughly like Dan Marino on *The NFL Today*.

That must've made me an idiot.

Athletes crediting a deity for a fleeting game outcome or extolling a deity once in legal trouble . . . commentators extolling purity because some places look pure, even amid the phantasmagorical corruption of American *college* athletics . . . athletes, managers, and commentators saying it's not about the money . . . American Ryder Cup players playing "for my country" . . . the preposterous refrain that the winner of a game "wanted it more" . . . "We just have to focus" . . . "They really have athleticism" . . . "A quarterback controversy" . . . "The people who criticize me don't know me" . . . "David and Goliath" . . . "Cinderella" . . . or the post-arrest staple, invented by PR handlers: "I made a mistake." . . .

It just all crashed in.

Still, after some free-breakfast comfort food—eggs, sausage—the bug went into remission, and even after the dreary Super Bowl game itself—uninspiring Baltimore Ravens 34, uninspiring New York Giants 7—I hopscotched a huge country without complaint, even seeing some poignant things.

At the Daytona 500 that February, the great driver with the gleam in his eye, Dale Earnhardt, died on the final turn of the final lap, and I saw a vast track enveloped in a loving mourn while a gnarled mechanic sobbed into a pay phone. At the annual sixty-four-team university basketball tournament that grips us every March so much that we overlook the phantasmagorical corruption, I saw gorgeous San Diego, always a privilege. At the Masters in April, I saw a single golfer born to an African American Vietnam War veteran and a Thai mother ensure that his Orlando coffee table could hold all four major golf trophies at once, proof that humanity, through careful parenting and tutelage, could tame its own menacing and spiteful invention, golf.

Delights popped up as years galloped by. When the Boston Red Sox won the baseball World Series in 2004 to end an eighty-six-year drought that had become a national cliché, I got goose bumps at the amphibious parade that ran on streets plus the Charles River. At Athens 2004, I saw a female Korean archer score a mandatory 10 on the last chance in the threadbare 1896

Olympic stadium. In October 2005, I saw a football game between Southern California and Notre Dame that beat the best theater. I saw Roger Federer play tennis. I saw Tiger Woods play often.

It's just that the remissions began thinning.

At the very sporting events that filled the daydreams of my sunny Virginia childhood, I'd feel a fleeting and deadening sense of triviality, the sensation tripled during any NBA regular-season game. With access to the very athletes I once yearned to meet as a child, I'd find myself wishing such access unavailable, the feeling tripled at any Major League Baseball game. I grew so weary of Lance Armstrong's defensive preening that his face on the screen triggered a neuromuscular response wherein I'd reach involuntarily for a remote control, even in a bar.

And college sports. Since childhood, I'd loved college sports, that American oddity featuring gigantic TV audiences and filled stadiums with 60,000 or 80,000 or in some cases 100,000 seats. I'd always perceived it as a continent of fine athletic drama dotted with episodic sleaze. Only after about twenty years of learning about universities slipping illicit cash payments to coveted high school athletes, bribing the coaches of coveted high school athletes, treating high school athletes to weekends of lavish dinners and (sometimes) prostitution services on "official visits," fudging the academic records of college athletes to keep them eligible, having tutors do the schoolwork of college athletes to keep them eligible, using corporate sleaze to wring ever more money from the sweat of unsalaried college athletes, and so on, my thick skull awakened to the thought that maybe it was a continent of sleaze dotted with episodic honor.

It got tougher by the year.

In 2002 we Americans endured another tired baseball labor strife that clouded the season with potential cancellation. We had a former Most Valuable Player estimate that half the players took performance-enhancing drugs. We staged an Olympics in Salt Lake City in which a figure skating judge with a fur collar admitted trading scoring favors. At least she's French, we thought—you know, not like us.

In 2003 we had a row over the Augusta National Golf Club's boys-only membership policy, which is its right but also pitiable. We had a basketball player we liked very much, Kobe Bryant of Los Angeles, arrested on rape charges. The number-one sports star of the year? That would be THG, the performance-enhancing drug we learned about that year. To top it all, we had an American coup de grâce in Texas: the shooting death of a college basketball player, followed by his coach's fear that past illicit payments to the player would get exposure, followed by the esteemed coach trying to persuade his assistants to brand the deceased as a drug dealer (thus explaining the good bank balance), replete with the coach saying, "Reasonable doubt is there's nobody right now who can say we paid Patrick Dennehy . . . because he's dead."

In 2004 we had a big, tired hissy fit over Janet Jackson's nearly exposed breast in the Super Bowl halftime show after decades upon decades of cheering cheerleaders with nearly exposed breasts. We had hockey player Todd Bertuzzi sucker-punching Steve Moore during a game, knocking him unconscious and fracturing a neck vertebra. The exhausted, drivelous, please-don't-tell-me-any-more story line of the Los Angeles Lakers finally reached preposterous denouement when the team had to trade the most awesome bloody force in the game, Shaquille O'Neal, because he and Bryant could not coexist. We had a brawl in Detroit during which a fan threw a projectile at a basketball player and basketball players took to the stands slugging fans. I went eagerly to the Athens Olympics and spent the first Saturday night camped outside a hospital with Greek reporters, awaiting in vain two Greek sprinters who may have faked a motorcycle accident in a feat of drug-test avoidance.

In 2005 we Americans spent an entire autumn hearing daily if not hourly about one narcissistic football receiver in Philadelphia. We spent our second straight summer in New York speculating about the intra-team compatibility of one profoundly dull third baseman. I'd begun to realize a twenty-first-century maxim that may have nagged at many fans: sports suck, but I'd hate to live without them.

Then came Friday, March 17, 2005, the nadir de nadirs, when I spent an entire day of this gift of a lifetime watching the congressional baseball steroid hearings.

There you had a daylong view of a committee in Congress. Nobody should ever have a daylong view of any aspect of Congress, where we send some of our most heinous citizens so that we don't have to live among them.

And there we also had a row of grotesquely coddled baseball players who should never speak on television for such duration in any culture concerned for its well-being. One wagged a finger at Congress and said he'd never taken steroids, when by July he would test positive for the steroid stanozolol even though it's remarkably hard to flunk such tests. Another, whose cartoonish muscles abetted his then-record seventy home runs in a summer of 1998 that unleashed poetry about baseball's return to national glory, kept saying he hadn't come to talk about the past. ("Steroids is bad," he said in his opening statement.) Another, invited for his alleged intellectualism and because he previously called steroids a problem in baseball, basically said he hadn't really meant steroids were a problem in baseball. Another claimed translation issues after spending years doing interviews in English. The most credible of all became the one on the end, the handsome former player everyone resented, the first-time author whose just-released book regaled a naive nation with touching steroid tales such as players shooting up each other in their rear ends in restroom stalls.

Then, every once in a while on another base day in Congress, there would come an unspeakable moment in which one congressman or another would, before our very eyes, morph into blubber and start fawning over the presence of the baseball players.

As the first edges of darkness clinched the day as spectacularly misspent, my Tampa malaise had set in again: *Wow. I think I might detest sports.*

From an upbringing decidedly anti-cynical, I had transmogrified into a threat to foist cynicism upon children in my circulation area plus any finding me by accident on the Internet. With no right to complain given all the crummy jobs in the world compared with mine, I figured I'd ride to retirement or death with flaring depression. On the plus side, I had drained some of my vast reservoir of gullibility and reduced the saccharine content in my copy. I'd begun to leave the house for sporting events fancying myself a chronicler of sin rather than of feat, and reassuring myself it's important to cover sin.

Then, in 2006, I happened upon a cure I'd never imagined and that my numerous ambivalent colleagues hadn't tried. I merely and unexpectedly moved to another country for the oldest reason in the book—love—and alighted an ocean away from *SportsCenter* playing morning highlights that recur until you want to primal-scream. When Virgin flight 46 from JFK to Heathrow landed, I would step out into not only another country but the country with the world's most popular sports league, soccer's English Premier League, or Premiership, a league so dynamic it compels Bulgaria and Burkina Faso, stokes the curiosity of half of China and big chunks of Colombia, and prompts young men from Mauritius to think up Manchester United songs that denigrate Liverpool.

I would inhabit London, the central nervous system of Planet Earth circa 2006.

After eighteen mostly wondrous years covering five Olympics, twenty-five major golf tournaments, four Wimbledons, eleven Super Bowls, ten Kentucky Derbys, one Sunday night romp up the Champs-Elysées in July 1998 with a bunch of French people who might've abhorred soccer but seemed to enjoy winning, seven baseball World Series, seven Rose Bowls, five Sugar Bowls, five Fiesta Bowls, three Orange Bowls, basketball from Hawaii to Alaska to Kentucky to Athens to Sydney, nine Indianapolis 500s, three Daytona 500s, and one tractor pull, among other events, I found myself purged of free media credentials, free media shuttle buses, and free media buffet lines. I bought tickets as do real people. I went to stadiums and sat as a fan among the completely irrational other fans. I breathed amid the wisest, savviest old fan culture on earth. I relearned arts forbidden in press boxes, including applauding, cheering, and even jumping up and down like a buffoon.

And crucially, I came upon a league chockablock with facts I didn't know, legacies that hadn't grown exhausted, and astounding fan noise I couldn't wait to comprehend.

I felt confounded at mysterious words such as "Hotspur" (that's the nickname for the North London club Tottenham Hotspur), "Everton" (that's an actual and first-rate club set in Liverpool), and "Sven-Goran Eriksson" (he's the dour Swedish former coach of England's national team). I pictured "West Ham" as some gumdrop village somewhere in the countryside, when it's a storied club in gritty East London. I feared I would mispronounce the words "Arsene Wenger" in public, for he's the revered Frenchman who manages Arsenal, the globally revered North London club. I could not for the life of me define "bung," but I felt relief when I learned that's an illicit and illegal payment, because illicit and illegal payments had a ring of familiarity from American college sports. I had only just learned the home city of the mystically titled "Aston Villa." (It's Birmingham.) Only after marveling at the sublime TV talent of soccer's foremost studio host, Gary Lineker, did I learn he'd actually played the game and played it for the national team, belying the habit of former players of becoming unenlightening cliché-spewers. I suddenly learned that in addition to the Premiership, the European Champions League, and the FA Cup, clubs played for a fourth annual trophy formerly called "League Cup" but by now named for a Canadian beer (the Carling Cup).

I knew nothing of the specific fraudulence of any player or manager. I certainly knew no criminal records. I knew nothing of what constituted a banality by English sports-talk standards. It was like starting over.

It was like childhood, with beer.

2

FUMBLING AROUND
IN DAYLIGHT

I made an incompetent football vacation through England in late
August 2005 as a precursor to relocation. Somewhere in my
denseness, I yearned to join those Americans who exude upper-
most coolness by holding their own in England soccer conversations, with sportswriters Doug Cress and Mike Penner the first
such beings I ever knew. With a fresh thirty-eight-game, August-
to-May season having begun on August 13, I surveyed the schedule from home in New York and spotted a golden nugget even I
could recognize as enticing: Chelsea versus Arsenal, two behe-
moth London clubs, on Sunday, August 22.

I began making my plans for Highbury, Arsenal's stadium so
storied it endured even World War II bombing. Having read Nick
Hornby's best-seller *Fever Pitch* in 1994 in a halting attempt at
soccer competence and Euro coolness, yet having never seen
Highbury even given four Wimbledon assignments, I fancied myself almost debonair that I'd get to see Highbury soon. I told my
friend Jerry, a New Yorker who started liking Chelsea before it
became a Premier League mastodon, that I might even see Chelsea play at Highbury, what with everybody on vacation in August. I briefly liked myself.

Of course, as I rode in a taxi on FDR Drive along the East

River one day, Jerry telephoned with a polite bit of instruction. While American sports schedules always list the visitor first— Washington at Dallas, Arsenal at Chelsea—English "fixtures," as they call them, always list the home club first. Thus, the match would occur at Stamford Bridge, a place of which I'd never heard and certainly never read about in any landmark book.

What a grand beginning.

Upon arrival in London with nine allotted days, I found an atlas and traced a map of England. Then I began doing the heavy research required to fill in twenty dots on the map. I learned the location of the long-mysterious "Aston Villa." With dogged effort, I found the location of the club Wigan, in the city of Wigan. I soon knew the answer to the befuddling question "Where is Middlesbrough?"—it's in northeast England, not far from the coast—becoming one of the first Americans in history with that distinction. I made little dots for previously mysterious places like Bolton, Blackburn, and the briefly elusive Charlton, which seemed to do business on the eastern side of London. I woke on a Saturday, went for some astronomically priced coffee, and scanned the slate of matches.

Choosing Charlton to start, with tickets available for the humdrum clash with Wigan, I left Barons Court in West London around 1:00 PM, rode a numbing sequence of Tube trains and incompetence through the inconceivably vast capital, and did reach Charlton's ground in southeast London by 4:15—or during roughly the fifty-fifth minute of the match. There I learned two things about England.

It's capitalist, yes, but it does practice some limits. Despite available seats, the woman in the club office would not sell me a ticket even though I wished to pay full price to witness maybe thirty-five minutes—plus added time!—of the glory of Charlton versus Wigan. Polite and even faintly pitying, she appeared as if she'd never heard such a request. That differed from the United States, in which any corporation would take most any chance to rip out the cash from your wallet, as well as the lining, the credit cards, the tattered pictures of family members, and the hide off the cover. To an American, if somebody actually turns down money, it's a really touching teardrop scene in *Babel*.

And then I learned that if you loiter outside a soccer stadium during a match, you're likely to join some tourists snapping photographs, which struck me as bizarre.

I did get my first real-life peek at the Premiership, though, when a nice security guard let me place my left eye between two fence posts at the side gate. I saw a goalkeeper and decided he played for either Charlton or Wigan. Within moments, I walked away down Floyd Road amid a flood of Charlton supporters mildly elated over their 1–0 win and pretended that I too had taken in the grandeur.

In fact, it would take me eight calendar days and four Premiership days to find my way into one soccer stadium. I would go futilely to Stamford Bridge that Sunday, because as an American, I reckoned that if you're willing to pay enough and plunge even further into debt, you can get anything. I would turn down a sidewalk offer of a ticket for £48.50 because some police officers warned me it might be counterfeit. I'd resist the temptation to take a train to Sunderland way up in the northeast on the following Tuesday night. I'd turn up at Highbury for a Fulham match on a Wednesday night inanely thinking tickets would be available, and I'd marvel that I'd never, ever seen a stadium so intimately tucked into its neighborhood, and I'd gaze at an elderly woman sitting in her living room blithely watching the news just barely across a narrow street from Thierry Henry, the Arsenal supernova.

But I wouldn't get in, of course.

Luckily, from one angle at Highbury, I did get an excellent glimpse of an entire stand containing other people watching, so I got to see other people see Arsenal versus Fulham. They looked enthralled.

My Premiership wisdom accruing dramatically, I reckoned I might not get into Manchester United's Old Trafford that coming Saturday, as that globally famous stadium tends to sell out early, so I took a Friday stadium tour in the rain. With eight fellow tourists, including a Hungarian father and son who repeatedly violated the tour rules and even walked out to the edge of the "pitch" (English for "field")—I thought they might even practice some penalty kicks before the kindly female tour guide reined them in—I learned a lot. I learned that the legendary manager Sir Alex Ferguson has occasional quibbles with the press. (No.) I learned the fascinating bit that certain people apply for ambulance jobs so they can wedge into the rotation of those assigned to the stadium tunnel on match days. That alone calls for a soccer documentary perhaps titled *I Just Hope They Learn Some CPR*.

Mostly, though, I went mouth-agape at the Manchester United dressing room. I simply could not believe it, and still don't. It had nice hot tubs over in the distance, I suppose, and it would've passed my mother's rigid cleanliness test, but the digs of the world's most famous team lagged startlingly shy of the plush pro dressing rooms I'd frequented with brain-deadening regularity in the United States. I might even dare call it spartan if that would not offend Sir Alex Ferguson. In fact, this dressing room would qualify as a tenement next to the posh locker room of even, just as one example of many, Florida State football.

And Florida State is just a *university,* albeit one that grasps the God-approved need to spend money on lavish locker-room carpeting. Carpeting replete with huge Seminole insignia. Huge Seminole insignia onto which you're not allowed to step, even mistakenly. Step on it, and a student towel attendant about half your age will come up and upbraid you.

No, really.

But then, in our measured culture, we know that any new baseball or football stadium locker room must boast luxury so that we can lure in more of the athletic gods who'll bring us the methadone of victory. In the case of Barry Bonds, our locker rooms might have an easy chair for strategic napping, although the easy chair might not be quite so swish as widely reported. Even the bathroom stalls might be wide and comfortable enough for two hunky star players to fit into one, broadening our sentimental notions of team unity by injecting each other's rear end with a steroid.

A player's locker will have the amenities of a fine closet. It will remind him yet again of his rightful place at the apex of the cosmos, just in case he needs more reminding. It will feature a shelf on which the god might store vital items like his cologne, his chosen religious ornament, and his souvenir from the day he hit that game-winning home run. It may have compartments for the necessary and furtive storage of his performance-enhancing drugs. To the edge of the shelf he might tape photographs of his children or his wife or his mistresses in various towns (a slight exaggeration, as he'd seldom showcase the mistresses to nosy reporters, who'd never report on the mistresses anyway). His locker will boast little walls on each side that cordon it off from the other lockers, plus nice hanging implements for his fine apparel.

From what I could see, Manchester United players get a shared bench and a hook on the wall.

I do remember the hooks as red, so there's one decorative touch.

Standing in that locker room, jaw headed south, I just couldn't believe the athletes had not staged some sort of revolt in response to these shabby conditions. All that arrogance, all that self-centeredness, all that certainty as to their indispensability—and I refer to the Portuguese heartthrob Cristiano Ronaldo alone—yet no beef about dressing-room conditions?

It refreshed me and pointed again to the cultural importance of keeping locker rooms closed to the media. U.S. professional sports leagues have mandatory policies about opening their locker rooms to reporters for certain periods of time both before and after games. This stirs more interest in the sport, and more interest stirs more money, and we have shown a certain fondness for more money. Thus do American athletes turn up constantly on TV, in front of their lockers, often shirtless or wearing only a towel, spewing rehearsed lines into gaggles of microphones as twenty reporters surround them and jockey for position and absorb the bony elbows of cameramen. Of course, we consider this normal. Perhaps if at Manchester United we'd see the exhilarating bull-in-a-china-shop striker Wayne Rooney on TV after each match, standing before his pathetic little red hook, the club would feel embarrassed and feel moved to do something to placate the poor tycoon.

As it happens, only tourists get to see this tidy slum, and some of them barely notice as they're plotting their bid to skirt the rules and walk out onto the pitch.

It's just as well.

I wandered through the museum and learned that apparently Manchester United won the three most coveted competitions— the league title, the FA Cup, and the European Champions League title—at the same time during the same spring of 1999. I had not realized this even as a sportswriter, but that's forgivable given I spent May 1999 chronicling three-year-old colts in Kentucky, Baltimore, and the Long Island–Queens border.

Then I took my dressing-room astonishment and left the building, noticing some DIE GLAZER graffiti just across the road that honored the new American owner, Malcolm Glazer, the owner of the NFL Tampa Bay Buccaneers, reviled partly out of fear he'd bought Manchester United with a lot of debt and would curtail the pursuit of top talent. I wondered why that hadn't been part of the official tour.

That Friday night I pored over the Saturday possibilities for my Premiership debut and noticed something that grabbed my full and freshly rehabilitated sports attention. There in the papers were two teams that had just celebrated "promotion," part of a concept known simply as "relegation," a concept literally foreign to myself and my culturally barren country. Each year in the distant wonderland of English soccer, three clubs from the twenty topflight (that is, Premiership) teams suffer relegation into the second tier because they had the malfeasance to finish eighteenth, nineteenth, and twentieth. Each year, in turn, three clubs from the second tier, a twenty-four-team league mysteriously titled the "Coca-Cola Championship," earn promotion to the first tier, or Premier League. Wigan and Sunderland had just earned such promotion, and they would appear on the same field. As far as I could tell that pitch would be in the city of Wigan. I decided to celebrate their promotions with them.

So I debuted, at Wigan, on August 27, 2005, and while there's no need to insert violin music right here, I felt happy. No American I knew had ever been to Wigan to my knowledge. No American I knew had ever heard of Wigan. My parents and grandparents had told me umpteen stories through a Virginia childhood with nary a mention of the existence of any Wigan. With Americans sharing a common inability to view a map and spot, say, Louisiana—this helps explain why it took us four days to get food to starving Americans after Hurricane Katrina— Americans certainly could not point out Wigan. Or even Preston. Let alone Bolton.

After riding a train about forty-five minutes west-northwest from Manchester, I disembarked at Wigan, population 81,000, and walked out of the becoming center city toward the stadium, into a zone of strip malls as dreary as all Houston. I marched with serious intent to the JJB Stadium ticket window and thought it a mite intrusive when the woman behind the glass asked for some identification, when my name appeared on the ticket, and when she asked, "Home or away?" I had never heard such a personal question from behind a ticket window. I hailed from a land in which they'll sell us nameless single-game tickets so long as we seem to have a modicum of apparent human features, such as a wallet and at least one hand for reaching into it. I hailed from a land in which "segregation" is invariably a bad word conjuring bygone times of shocking idiocy.

What a jolt, then, to learn that home and "away" (visiting) English fans sit segregated, that two sturdy lines of security officers in fluorescent yellow adorn the edges of visiting cheering sections, and that the word "segregation" has one definition that's not macabre. Even while it predates the 1980s, it's among the array of policies that have helped rid the stadium experience of the brawling hooliganism of the 1980s. While American stadiums do have cheering sections, especially for college sports, we all know they're not strictly demarcated. It's commonplace for pockets of the enemy tribe to sit among hordes of the home tribe with min-imal fisticuffs. This gives us the opportunity to revile others right up close. We reserve the right to go to Yankee Stadium in the Bronx and sit in the upper deck with hordes of New York base-ball fans and pockets of Boston baseball fans so that we can ruin a luminous Sunday afternoon annoyed at the IQ-depleting "ban-ter" that ricochets, *for three to four hours,* between the majority New York fans and the minority Boston fans. This usually in-cludes such profundities as (follow carefully please) *Yankees suck, Yankees suck.* This makes us so proud and suspends our wonder at the trite inanity of our political debates. We reserve the right to pull for a home American football team, then grumble because those three frigging visiting fans two rows ahead kept standing up and cheering their improbable victory. This gives us a conver-sation piece at awkward family gatherings where we can use up some of the interminable time by explaining how we almost, *al-most* told those clowns to shut up.

Come to think of it, stadium segregation is an ingenious con-cept, galvanizing competing noise and prolonging life in general. It must count among the reasons Britons live six months longer, on average, than do Americans. It is the handiwork of an expe-rienced nation with an 849-year head start on our little concoc-tion across the Atlantic.

On a sunny day inside JJB, with the Premiership angels singing overhead in my estimation, I sat amid bafflingly large chunks of empty seats but smack next to one couple.

In America it's considered proper to have a chat with two other people when you're, say, the only three people within a large cluster of empty seats. In England it's not.

So as the public-address speakers played pop music, I said to the woman next to me, "Do you know this song?"

She looked dumbstruck by such forwardness and said, "No."

That concluded our afternoon's discourse.

"F——ING MOVE!"

Kickoff approached at Wigan, and most of those nearby seats simply refused to fill. I thought it surprising that Wiganites would not revel in Premiership status after their inspiring three-decade vault through the concentric circles of lower leagues. I reckoned August must find most Wiganites on vacation (just another reason Wiganites and other Europeans outlive Americans). I remained ignorant of such century-old trends as Wigan being a rugby town.

Among the 17,222 others that day, three shaved-headed guys did take the seats just behind me. They looked a bit scary to me at the time, but that's probably because in America our parents and our grandparents often condition us to think of life as an incessant attempt to avoid getting mugged. My dear maternal grandmother, for example, might've unwittingly invented the concept of carjacking. Through the 1970s, whenever we'd leave her house in Virginia Beach, Virginia, at night, she'd tell us to make sure to lock the car doors because people tended to try to rip open your doors and steal your stuff when you idled at red lights. I would digest this advice despite never once seeing a single awake human at any traffic light in any of the eternally comatose Virginia cities between her house and ours in sleepy Suffolk.

Besides, within the first minute of action at Wigan versus Sunderland, one of these three guys hopped up and down with his hand on my shoulder for leverage because Wigan had just scored through a penalty in the second minute after one Jason Roberts had gone down under duress from one Gary Breen. This began a long sequence of embraces with strangers in the soccer grounds of England. Whether I cared who won or not, whether I attended a match as a curious tourist or a wishing fan, I have hugged people I didn't know and never would see again, pretending to rise to their level of elation. In America we'll chat with a stranger all game long, but we'd never hug him after a favorable play. We're simply too young as a culture to have evolved to that level of self-assurance. We stand off and high-five them, then we reach upward and downward to the other rows giving and receiving high fives, as if we had something to do with the act of exceptional talent that just transpired on the field. In England nobody seems to chat, but many people do hug.

The sunny day at Wigan did bring Wigan's first-ever Premiership victory, by that precarious 1–0 from the penalty. The day brought several first-time realizations. I never knew that husky male voices in soccer grounds croon—to their players!—the American ditty written either by Jimmie Davis and Charles Mitchell or by the Rice Brothers, "You Are My Sunshine," once listed as Country Music Television's number seventy-three country song of all time. This blew me away. August 27, 2005, did mark the first time in my life I had ever heard the word "f——" matched with the word "sake," and it came from a single throat that observed a referee's snap decision from a quarter-mile off and hollered, "F——'s sake!" Despite roaming the globe a lucky amount, I had never known that f—— has a sake until alighting at Wigan. I suppose everyone and everything has a sake, so f—— deserves one as well.

And then, at the end of Wigan's victory at dear old JJB, I did hear a rendition of John Philip Sousa's magnum opus "Stars and Stripes Forever," the official national march of the United States by decree of our esteemed and grotesque Congress, only with the lyrics rewritten so that the many words of the original song had been distilled to two, sung while pointing at Sunderland fans:

Going down, going down, going down
Going down, going down, going dowwwwn . . .

Thus did Wigan fans correctly forecast Sunderland's relegation that would occur in May 2006, while I felt reassured that after my homeland had gained so much energy from English imports like the Clash and the Sex Pistols and the Buzzcocks and the Buggles and the Psychedelic Furs and the Pet Shop Boys and the Beatles and David Bowie and Elton John and Rod Stewart and Oasis and Arctic Monkeys and the Smiths, and the Smiths, and the Smiths, my country had given the British Isles some songs to sing at soccer matches.

Wigan had proved a grand adventure, but I figured Newcastle might stir my senses even more. For one thing, the stadium held 52,387, I read, as opposed to Wigan's possible 25,138. I'd found an available ticket by dialing Newcastle's number in proper sequence, showing unmistakable progress in accessing Premiership stadiums. I reached Newcastle on Sunday morning, waking up just as the train crossed the river into the station, a beautiful first sight of a lovely city. Renowned as a party town, Newcastle sits high in the northeast, where England starts to think about becoming Scotland.

On a luminous day, the visitor would be Manchester United, which, as a newfound American expert on this stuff, I knew had won three titles in 1999, plus a bunch of other cups. The little chart I made of every season since 1992–93, in fact, showed Manchester United winning eight of those years. Meanwhile, Newcastle had maintained a keen, passionate following despite starting its fiftieth straight season without a major title—its eighty-first without a league title—and it's amazing how you can travel one-quarter of the way around the world and still wind up among Cubs fans.

Bounding out into Newcastle for my first time, I proceeded to the gleaming modern stadium tucked appealingly into the city, and it took me only thirty-five minutes of circumnavigating the enormous structure to locate the proper gate for entry. After a beer and revulsion at a meat pie I spotted going into a nearby mouth, I plopped down in the upper deck next to a freckled woman who looked about thirty. Some reflex within me craved conversation, but she never once acknowledged my presence on the earth.

Instead, I heard her utter only three things during the match. The first: "Move!"

From the upper deck, high above the city of Newcastle, she commanded her feckless Newcastle United players to move rather than stand around as spectators against the Manchester United defense. Her advice seemed sound, but it did conjure something I'd found achingly sad since 1995. One night then, in a basketball arena in Chicago, from the upper press box, I suddenly took notice of a middle-aged man in the upper rows, screaming at the referees. I became momentarily, profoundly depressed, and I mean seriously, incontrovertibly glum. I don't know why I never glimpsed this kind of thing carefully before then, but suddenly I saw the fanatic in all his twin strains of powerlessness: not only did he cut a preposterous figure, mustering anger over calls he could not possibly see as well as the three referees granted access to the actual floor with the players, but he yelled at referees who probably couldn't have heard him in an empty coliseum and absolutely couldn't have heard him through the clamor of 19,999 other people. It's mind-boggling, yet commonplace and universal. This capacity to excoriate referees and players who can't possibly hear us might be one of the few things that bridges our troubling disparities as a planet.

The second thing she uttered: "F——ing move!"

This proved beyond a doubt my theory that the Newcastle players could not hear her instructions. Sure enough, Newcastle did not f——ing move and did not f——ing score that day— an offside negated their one "goal"—and even a know-nothing American could spot that Newcastle's best hope lay in a combination of hoping for a goal-less draw and praying for a Manchester United "own goal," which even I knew entailed a team accidentally scoring for the opponent.

The third thing I heard her say: "F——ing wankers!"

That plaudit went toward the sliver of Manchester United fans over to our right in the upper deck, people who, curiously, could not hear her either. It also helped summarize my novice's afternoon. I had never—*never*—heard the English word "f——" used in so many creative forms, despite prior residence in New York, despite spending an inordinate chunk of life near sports fans, and despite seeing almost every Martin Scorsese film. At Newcastle that day I heard it as a noun, verb, adjective, adverb, conjunction, preposition, pejorative, subjunctive, and maybe even a gerund. I heard it hollered without compunction within earshot of children, which would be taboo in the United States. Eighteen months later, two kindly lads who supported the wee Brentford club off the western edge of London would teach me that some English fathers teach their children that there's stadium language and there's language for everywhere else, but at this point I felt stunned.

I might overstate, but Newcastle fans seemed to possess an uncanny, almost innate sixth sense. They seemed to spot doom just around every corner, even when doom hadn't necessarily revealed itself to others. If keenly observant, you might have detected that they had undergone some sort of phase, perhaps a half century, that may have included a certain lack of cups. They embodied what the great English tennis sage and clothing designer Ted Tinling once said after Martina Navratilova blew a U.S. Open final to Steffi Graf: "At 4–2 in the second set, Martina saw vultures no one else could see."

Newcastle fans' version of this prescience conjured their alien cousins in Boston and the North Side of Chicago. I thought of that haunting night in Chicago in autumn 2003, when that fan interfered with that catchable fly ball, that left fielder melted down, and you could sense the entire operation quake even with a solid 3–0 lead and only five outs to muster. I'd spent the last twenty days of October 2004 in Boston as the Red Sox won their last eight games to quench their eighty-six-year drought. I'd heard great celebrations and great sounds and felt great goose bumps. I'd stood on Lansdowne Street behind Fenway Park after

Boston's 10–3 game 7 win over the Yankees in the American League Championship Series and watched it fill so swiftly with revelers that it truly frightened me. In as meaningful a story as I could ever remember reporting, I'd interviewed bereaved relatives of lifelong fans who'd lived normal life spans but died during 2004 without ever seeing the moment.

I understood that Boston fans and Chicago fans and Newcastle fans participated in something weirdly privileged. By nurturing their interest and keeping it keen through a long wait, even by wallowing in their gloomy endurance—preening over it, in many American cases—they stood the chance of a payoff that would trump any title by the Yankees or Manchester United.

For that reason, plus the loveliness of the city in general, Newcastle United zoomed onto my list of prospective favorite clubs. When I learned that about twenty thousand showed up just to watch the twenty-five-year-old English striker Michael Owen sign his contract—they must have sensed that, while playing, he might actually move—that enhanced the appeal all the more. When I'd carefully study the 1995–96 season, in which Newcastle led the standings by twelve points in March but suddenly came to impersonate a sinkhole and somehow cratered below Manchester United by May, that added still more.

But on that first Sunday, in the sixty-sixth minute of Manchester United's 2–0 win, I saw something non-Newcastle and brilliant. I saw Wayne Rooney score. By now, I picture him making a pugnacious barrel up the pitch, leaving Newcastle players—who couldn't or wouldn't move, anyway—strewn around like carcasses until he stood alone, scored deftly for a 1–0 lead, and hurried over to a corner spot below the visiting supporters. In actuality, Manchester United goalkeeper Edwin van der Sar punted, defender Jean-Alain Boumsong failed to clear the ball, and Rooney scrambled to it and rammed it in past Shay Given. Pretty soon, Newcastle fans commenced filing out even before Ruud van Nistelrooy's add-on in injury time for a 2–0 final. As they left, they carried the distinct look of having seen this match before.

Only on Monday would I learn that TV cameras had recorded Rooney's celebration and that some resourceful videotape editors had slowed down the scene to allow for accurate reading of his lips as he shouted toward his admirers in the upper deck.

He called out to them, "F——ing beauty!"

He thus garnished my Newcastle and Premiership debuts poetically and sent me back to the United States that August 2005 with a fresh ration of f——ing knowledge.

4

IS THAT REALLY

CHELSEA'S PITCH?

Six months later . . .

Ten days after moving to London in February 2006, I went to see the club called "ChelseaTheyBoughtTheirTitle." Two generous lawyers invited me. I had heard much about ChelseaTheyBoughtTheirTitle and marveled that when English people around the country spoke of this club, they seldom settled for the proper terminology, "Chelsea," but always opted for the more demanding elocution of "ChelseaTheyBoughtTheirTitle," almost as if they were manifestly incapable of pronouncing "Chelsea" without affixing "TheyBoughtTheirTitle."

Chelsea, by then, epitomized the swanky London decade. It played in a swanky London neighborhood, in semi-swanky Fulham on the edge of utterly swanky Chelsea. Long a mainstay in English soccer and occasionally a powerhouse, Chelsea had become a full-on powerhouse in 2003 by that most time-honored of methods. A magnate had bought it—Roman Abramovich, Russian oil, born in 1966, one of the twenty richest people on earth—and had used that money in one of the noblest places a man can use it: on salaries that would enable the fans to watch their club beat the living hell out of the loathsome other clubs.

On this day, Saturday, February 25, 2006, Chelsea would

play some straggler from the south called Portsmouth. I knew very little about this Portsmouth, save for some vague reckoning that it probably sat by the water. We had a Portsmouth in my home state of Virginia, close to Suffolk, Norfolk, Hampton, Windsor, Southampton, Sussex, and Virgina Beach, as we're incapable of thinking up our own names save for the odd "Virginia Beach," which we concocted on our own by standing on a beach, then noticing we were in Virginia. In the spectacular wastefulness of the teenage years, I'd spent many nights among friends in Portsmouth, the Virginia version, driving around and around and around and around and around with no destination, much like NASCAR. I even lived in this derivative, Virginian Portsmouth for a year at age seventeen when our parents moved us from adjacent Suffolk while they finished our new house. I spent much of the year wallowing in spite that they'd moved us twenty-five minutes from our friends.

I often wonder why anyone has children.

For the 3:00 PM kickoff of Chelsea versus Portsmouth—if I'd gone alone one year prior, I might've mistakenly taken a train to Portsmouth—we met at 12:30. From the station the London lawyer, Duncan, an understated and kindly sort of about forty, began shepherding myself and Jerry, my great friend for twenty-five years, a New York lawyer, and one of a smallish assortment of Americans who prefer the Premiership to American sports. Duncan led us through a maze of streets away from the stadium hubbub, to a fine gumdrop of a pub I could not find again if you gave me three hours and one London A-to-Z map guidebook already turned to page 99.

The pub half-teemed with Chelsea fans, but with the real deals, the long-sufferers, those who knew Chelsea before it changed its name to ChelseaTheyBoughtTheirTitle. These people had weathered lean decades before striking Russian oil. They had not just straggled in from Tokyo or Chicago or Mayfair professing satellite TV devotion after Abramovich helped turn Chelsea into a global brand. Even Jerry had signed on in the 1990s, safely before the Roman Empire.

In a small ring of six Chelsea fans, then, I stood for more than two hours, talking, listening, learning, and drinking enough beer to stagger a large farm animal. We chatted about the leaner Chelsea years, about the astounding fitness of rugby players, about some upcoming exposé of an alleged gay orgy among Premiership players, about how Americans watched women's soccer during the 1999 World Cup but Britons never would, about how they'd love to have Wayne Rooney on Chelsea, about how most Britons can't abide the NFL's abundant halts. It was sublime, this pregame. To a wayward sportswriter, these hours proved so magical, so alleviating of life's puny worries, that I realized at once I'd spent two decades missing something.

Now, American sportswriters do tend to arrive two or three hours before game time—or thirty minutes before if atomically inept like myself. We enter the press box. We put down our laptop bags. We convene in little groups. We gossip about other sportswriters or about things we know to be true of athletes or managers but can't get into the newspaper. We have a pregame meal, often of food that will kill you faster than will other food—or, as at Cincinnati's stadium during the 1990s, of food that might kill you before sundown. We drink sodas. We do not drink alcohol—it's forbidden—even though that would be one hell of a lot healthier than sodas. We're at work, so there's stress.

American fans, meanwhile, relish the tailgate, an extraordinary invention that is among the top five reasons for the United States to exist. It arguably trumps even the nation's grand achievements such as the interstate highway system, the university system, the washing machine, the skyscraper, the Wright brothers, the first credit card, and certain forms of the rabbit corkscrew. Tailgating, of course, finds its essence in college football, finds its quintessence in the South, and finds its epitome at the genteel and elaborate Grove, a patch of ground at Ole Miss in Oxford, Mississippi, another city name we borrowed due to the inability to think up our own.

I once saw West Virginians tailgating in a Holiday Inn parking lot just north of Detroit on a cloudy December 23 at 19 degrees Fahrenheit. Their bleak surroundings gave me an initial wave of sadness, but on closer inspection I spotted their grill and their hardiness and I felt a second wave, this one of awe. As they tended to their sausages, I tended to branding them heroes.

Something about the American tailgate had always seemed important to me. On autumn Saturdays all over our huge country, fans will drive into stadium parking lots some six hours or nine hours or, if blessed with sleeping quarters, twenty-four hours before kickoff. Almost invariably, a wife or two (or more) in garish school colors will bound out of the passenger seat. A husband or two (or more) in even more ghastly school colors will assist. A table will unfold and stand nobly behind the vehicle, and the wives will unveil their Thursday-Friday creations—masses of cold cuts, potato salad, finger sandwiches, barbecue. Sometime during these opening moments of the weekly symphony a cooler full of beer might appear, or a separate table might buttress a bourbon bottle next to a vodka bottle next to a Bloody Mary mixer next to soda mixers next to, in some cases, a bottle of red wine just in case someone stops by with the really weird wish of protecting his arteries. There might be plastic glasses and paper plates and plastic cutlery. Many tailgate areas will feature a grill and the peerless smell of charcoal. Gristle will metastasize. Some tables might even boast a heated dish full of swimming meatballs next to a tiny glass brimming with toothpicks.

If there's a heaven, it looks something like all of this. In heaven, everyone will have an automobile—fuel-efficient, of course—and everyone will pull up to an eternal tailgate with cold cuts and bourbon and what-all. Nobody will worry about the food's health effects because everybody already will be dead.

In the moments before Chelsea versus Portsmouth, I realized I'd missed a thousand pregame conversations, walking past a thousand pregame tailgates toward the press box, gazing at their food, inhaling their smoke, and squinting at the school colors on fifty-year-old men who never got over the cruelty of having to *graduate* and, you know, *leave*.

Somewhere in the neighborhood of guidebook page 99 in London, I had a mild epiphany.

The so-called pregame, I reckoned, usually beats the hell out of the game itself, especially considering that during the pregame the game still maintains all magical possibilities. So we may just have it backward when we frame things in terms of pregame and game, like some undercard leading up to some main event. Maybe in the grand scheme of life upon this violent and wretched planet, we should see the middling game only as something that provides fodder for the next glorious pregame, when again we can converse with old and new friends. If the pregame really pales next to the game, then why did we scramble away from the pregame so late that day that we missed the first two minutes of the game? If the game is so important, after all, then why do so many intelligent people on both sides of the ocean prepare for it by drinking themselves into a state where they'll be unable to re-member two-thirds of it?

In fact, during that pregame I learned from Duncan a sacred truth about soccer. In the relatively limited soccer I'd watched—World Cups and Olympics mostly—I'd never once mulled the nugget Duncan spoke. Duncan explained that in his two adult decades attending Chelsea soccer both home and away, only once could he recall arriving at his seat with a bloodstream uninhab-ited by beer products. And that particular game, he recalled, just looked all wrong, all wretchedly misshapen.

Never again had he erred so thoughtlessly, and never again would I endure one of my occasional beerless soccer matches without wondering if they just looked wrong. Luckily, I remain for now too dim about soccer to tell.

So after the glory of the pregame, we headed for the sigh of the game. We somehow got through the typical English old-stadium floor-to-ceiling turnstiles, which call to mind a minimum-security prison. Having reveled at Wigan and Newcastle in that little slice of magic you feel from that first view of the green pitch, I entered Stamford Bridge to find . . .

The pitch . . .

The pitch looked like some forlorn, abandoned field in east Texas. Mud ruled. Whatever grass dared to pop its merry head above the surface of the earth seemed to have undergone a tram-pling from some urban herd of cattle. It became possible, when beholding this pitch, to feel sorry for the blades of grass that did jut to the surface. They'd come out on a Saturday and they'd found no friends. Some did convene in little clumps. In the great race to destroy or preserve a field, seemingly half the money in the world couldn't beat the English winter and the obligations of playing in the European Champions League—a separate, continental tournament for top clubs that some fans crave more than the actual league title. ChelseaTheyBoughtTheirTitle, this palace of talent and fine roster furnishings, mauling the league that season, had a decrepit pitch that day.

That's what I remember about this mundane match during ChelseaTheyBought's march toward a second straight Premiership title, because I just kept looking at the pitch. I'm sorry. I did know that the perfunctory 2–0 win over Portsmouth gave ChelseaTheyBought three points, making sixty-nine points for the season with a staggering fifteen-point lead and eleven games remaining. I knew the Chelsea manager, José Mourinho, whose name I mispronounced by using an "h" sound on the first letter in "José," inserted Eidur Gudjohnsen in the sixtieth minute, and that Jerry said he liked this Icelandic bale of energy, and that I marveled to myself at a league with Icelanders given our startling lack of Icelanders back at home.

I remember our stadium section seemed infested by tourists such as, say, us.

I really felt no sense of Portsmouth, that it held nineteenth in the table, that it did not so much teeter toward relegation as seem to have booked passage downward already. I knew neither that Portsmouth had lost in January by 5–0 at Birmingham City nor that it was inexplicable that season that somebody would lose by 5–0 to Birmingham City. I just knew that I felt a vague sense of the malaise that used to brush up against me during the 1990s.

In that time, as a sports columnist in Lexington, I followed University of Kentucky basketball during one of its heydays. Roughly fifteen times per winter, the schedule would bring a perfunctory game. Kentucky would play, for example, Georgia. Now, when waking that day, you'd know Kentucky would beat Georgia. Walking to the arena, you'd know Kentucky would beat

Georgia. Inside the arena, Kentucky would beat Georgia. And afterward, we'd conduct forgettable interviews to glean forgettable quotations about how Kentucky had beaten Georgia.

Yet still, despite only a one-in-ten-thousand chance of any surprise or intrigue, that arena would fill to twenty-four thousand. People who knew full well Kentucky would trounce Georgia would pay good money to see Kentucky trounce Georgia, then listen to radio shows detailing Kentucky's trouncing of Georgia. It was the same with Chelsea versus Portsmouth circa February 2006, and it's the same all over the world. This kind of sleepwalk occurs especially in sports in which some clubs have money advantages, such as Major League Baseball or the Premiership. Even I knew Chelsea would beat Portsmouth by about 2–0, and so I went and watched Chelsea beat Portsmouth by 2–0.

In the numbness of predictability ever more common to sport as it becomes ever more business, the day winds up living on only in other ways. There's the marvel of talking to people from another sports culture in a pregame pub. There's the beer, the elixir of choice for a country 849 years older than my own as the most effective way to cope with the daily horror of life. And there's Duncan's wisdom about how a game might look wrong if not mixed with said beer.

And there was that pitch.

5

A TWELVE-INCH DIGIX
IN CAMDEN

As an arriviste set to choose a new favorite club, I knew it'd be
bad form to glom onto a juggernaut, and English soccer has four
juggernauts. Everybody acknowledges these juggernauts. Everybody acknowledges the financial advantages of these juggernauts.
Nobody talks much of a salary cap that might validate the ac-
complishment of actually being a juggernaut. What with the English being such refreshing and devout realists, nobody places
much stock in fairy tales. Everybody accepts that these four will
finish first through fourth in the standings, and that one of these
four probably will win the FA Cup, the yearlong domestic tournament that runs concurrently with the league season and involves 731 clubs from all divisions. Yet everybody remains rapt.

I couldn't choose Chelsea as my club in the year 2006, for
that would have shown all the maturity of this nine-year-old kid
from my childhood who chose as favorite teams the Miami Dol-
phins, the Oakland Athletics, and the North Carolina State Wolf-
pack. Why such geographical disparity? Because those teams
happened to win the titles when he was nine. But forgive him. He
was nine.

Likewise, I knew I'd loathe myself as one profoundly dull individual if I chose Manchester United, which by now would re-

semble rooting for Wal-Mart. If you didn't glom on pre-Alex Ferguson, you lap at the shores of shady.

Further, I could not choose Arsenal, even though to those Americans with the first clue about the Premiership, Arsenal's the coolest of the kingdoms. First off, it's the second-best club name in the world behind Aston Villa, better than any of ours even with our 300 million citizens and 12 million illegal residents and 3,718,695 square miles. As a special bonus for Americans, the name "Arsenal" conjures weaponry, and we adore weaponry, reserving our highest presidential approval ratings for presidents who bomb the hell out of some fourth-rate military power. Our teams tend to go by the name of the city in their address or, for an extra dose of good and dreary marketing, their states (see Arizona Cardinals of Phoenix, or Florida Marlins of Miami). And then there's Arsenal's usual style of play, which sometimes deserves, as accompaniment, Mozart. I've heard many people regard Arsenal as a second-favorite club, in direct violation of the teachings of my soccer guru Tom, who forbids having second-favorite clubs. I knew Americans who chose Arsenal as a first-favorite club in 1995. By signing on in 2006, I'd not only qualify for JCL (Johnny Come Lately) status, but I'd have missed three titles, including an almost inconceivable unbeaten season in 2003–2004 (26–0–12). There's little so unctuous as retroactive gloating.

As well, I could not quite choose Liverpool, even though it's the cherished club of my soccer guru Tom, and even though among the four mastodons it seems to possess the largest heart.

Half-English, half-American, and thus uniquely qualified for soccer guru-dom toward a clueless American, Tom came upon Liverpool hereditarily. He can recollect discussions with his father about how Liverpool victories enhanced existence almost mystically. He can recall actual physical illness in May 1989 upon a single shocking added-time goal by Arsenal against Liverpool, which shifted the entire nine-month league title from the latter to the former. His nimble memory bank can link certain Liverpool victories to certain life crescendos, such as meeting his marvel of a wife, Marion. He has taught his four young children that the words "Manchester United" constitute profanity. I felt the Liverpool tug from the Liverpool influence of having a Liverpool soccer guru, in the way parishioners often tilt toward the worldviews of beloved pastors.

Not only that, but it floors me to this day that two New Yorkers, Richard Rodgers (1902–79) and Oscar Hammerstein II (1895–1960), sat down in the mid-1940s and wrote the closing number for their 1945 Broadway show *Carousel* and that sixty years later, in Istanbul, Liverpool players down 3–0 at halftime in a European Champions League final against AC Milan of Italy got motivation from hearing their fans croon "You'll Never Walk Alone," a Liverpool staple since the 1960s, and that they proceeded to rally and win on penalty kicks after a 3–3 draw.

So, wildly curious, I took the four-hour train from London to Liverpool on March 25, 2006, just to be in the midst of Liverpool versus Everton, a rivalry—called a "derby," bafflingly pronounced "darby"—between two major clubs whose stadiums sit across a city park from each other. I did so even though the sweet woman on the telephone the previous Monday had ushered me through the two-part dance that's mystifying to an American: she said they had tickets available, but she said she could not sell me one because I lacked a ticket-buying history. What an affront to the ruthless churn of capitalism. For any match of historic venom—even Liverpool-Everton, known to have less venom than most—a club might sell no tickets to strangers, the better to minimize potential brawls. So, with no chance of seeing the game in the flesh, I still walked excitedly toward the celebrated stadium tucked into a gritty neighborhood, Anfield, that gloomy spring day, and I hung out in various pubs through Liverpool's 3–1 win, and I waited postgame like some crush-struck teen for the Liverpool players to emerge, pretending I belonged. And before all that, I stood pregame for thirty minutes just outside the stadium at the Hillsborough memorial, which commemorates the ninety-six people killed on Saturday, April 15, 1989, when Liverpool fans flooded into a stadium tunnel in Sheffield. I watched an elderly man with a cane hobble toward the stadium gates, halt, turn, and touch a name among the ninety-six fallen before ambling on in.

I easily could've chosen Liverpool as my team—Liverpool of the big heart and my soccer guru Tom, after all—but offspring must claim their own identities to sustain the evolutionary progress of life. I sought some version of *it*, you know, *it*: the real, organic English soccer experience, and if *it* didn't exist anymore in a day of gargantuan TV contracts and stadium luxury boxes, then something with shades of *it*.

There was another reason I hadn't jumped at Liverpool. Two weeks prior, on the Saturday night of March 11, I'd piddled around in my friends' house in Camden, North London, with the BBC's *Match of the Day* as background noise. At the time, I thought *Match of the Day* was some nifty highlight show that synopsized the goals and near-goals and dreary managerial comments of a given Saturday; actually, it's the four-decade-old weekly religious service for a nation, and the strains of its theme music garnish the childhood memories of English adults. As *Match of the Day* played, I committed blasphemy and paid only scant attention to the twelve-inch Digix TV in the basement guest room.

Suddenly, though, I heard this great crowd noise blaring from the set. The noise so clearly unleashed by what happened shockingly in the draining seconds of Portsmouth versus Manchester City gave me goose bumps even through a screen in Camden, and even though I knew nada about either squad except that Portsmouth wore blue and played on brown sod at Chelsea. Why bother with sport? Here's the number-one answer: because you might hear this kind of noise. It might swim your ear canals and rustle your soul and electrify your skin and maybe even prolong your life.

For myself, following sport is largely about the hunt for that noise.

The noise forged at Portsmouth's Fratton Park during that match on March 11, 2006, can prove elusive in the world. It requires a whole bale of ingredients. You need a crowd that cares more deeply than most. You need an intricate set of sporting circumstances. You often need some sort of shocking turn in the game or race. A comeback maybe. Sometimes a drought will help: imagine the noise coming someday when the parched finally behold a title at Newcastle.

Sometimes you can go a long way but still miss the noise out of your own chronic ineptitude, and it can bother you for the remainder of your life. I know. In one of the most famous home runs in baseball history, a hobbling Kirk Gibson of the Los Angeles Dodgers blasted a shot off one of the most impenetrable ninth-inning pitchers in history, Dennis Eckersley of the Oakland Athletics, in the first game of the 1988 World Series. It turned a sure 4–3 Oakland win into an indelible 5–4 Los Angeles win. It's *still* shocking. And myself? Rather than staying put in my very own press-box seat with the ideal view, I scurried downstairs early to beat the elevator rush so I could wait just outside the Oakland clubhouse to hear the winning pitcher's comments. As I stood outside the locker room and watched on a small TV as one would in, say, Bangor, Maine, Gibson hit that home run, and my winning pitcher (Dave Stewart) no longer had won. The noise in that stadium must've been something. I wish I knew. Similarly, many observers equipped with ears claimed they'd never heard stadium noise to rival the night in Sydney when Cathy Freeman won the Olympic 400 meters. And myself? I had the ingenious and contrived idea of watching the race from the Sydney park where aboriginal Australians had set up shop for the Olympics so as to make known their mistreated plight. That noise sure sounded like it might've been something through the dilapidated TV in their tent.

On *Match of the Day,* I missed the first playing of Pedro Mendes's searing goal at Fratton Park because I'd been unpacking a suitcase. The noise alerted me to watch further replays. Crowds usually disappoint with the general human incapacity to sustain noise, but this noise had serious sustenance. You could hear that the Frattonites had begun chanting, "We are staying up, we are staying up," and even I could discern that they probably meant the club would avoid relegation, optimistic as that seemed. The show cut from the Fratton scenes to the *Match of the Day* panel, and I remember their grins at the Portsmouth exuberance, grins not of belittlement but of impression, so much glee emanating from nineteenth place in the twenty-team standings.

Portsmouth, after all, had not won in the calendar year 2006. It had arrived at March 11 with a measly eighteen points from twenty-seven matches since August (twelve points for four wins and six points for six draws). It had stayed afloat in the Premiership for three straight seasons, with a fourth clearly not forthcoming. That 5–0 loss to Birmingham City had brought the requisite Grand Canyon of nadirs. That eyesore had given way to more benign losses to Newcastle, to Manchester United, to Chelsea after a gritty effort on a crummy pitch, and to Aston Villa. A February draw with Bolton brought the lone lonely point of the calendar year.

Well, a second point did beckon against Manchester City. Portsmouth had drifted into this apparent 1–1 draw with spirited play but squandered chances. Mendes had scored at sixty minutes with a curling projectile from twenty-five yards. Manchester City's Richard Dunne had headed in a Joey Barton corner in the eighty-third minute. Time had waned. Added time had drained. Fratton Park had roiled headlong into that Zantac time "90+3," a strange concoction that means the ninety minutes of regular time plus the usual three of "added time," or "injury time." Manchester City had almost finished clearing a corner. And Manchester City's Bradley Wright-Phillips had hustled toward the ball to clear it further and secure the draw.

Even a year on, I still cannot quite grasp just how Mendes flicked the ball away from Wright-Phillips and maintained control. It still seems partly magical every time I type in "Pedro Mendes" and "Manchester City" on YouTube.com (after which I give thanks for the parents of the inventors of YouTube.com). Every time, Wright-Phillips, from the hubbub around the goal, rushes out toward the ball. Every time, Mendes, from about the midfield line, rushes in. Every time, they converge about forty yards from the goal. And every time I click "Play" or click "Watch Again" or click "Watch Again" again, it still baffles me how Wright-Phillips goes from farther in than Mendes to farther out,

Mendes goes from farther out than Wright-Phillips to farther in, and the ball decides it wants to hang with Mendes.

Every single time, then, Mendes cocks his right leg and sends the ball blasting to the top left corner of the net. The ball smooches the net cords and bounces down. Goalkeeper David James, who in summer would sign with Portsmouth, kicks it upward in disgust. Mendes rushes to the front row of fans. A security guard urges Mendes to be careful but seems to smile. The place absolutely reverberates with a bedlam almost unattainable upon the earth.

Even as somebody who couldn't get to Portsmouth without a map and certainly couldn't name any of its players, I had this thought: *Oh, to have been in attendance.*

Sitting over in America flipping TV channels in many a wee hour during a misspent life, coming across recorded Premiership matches that filled hard time on cable, I always did marvel in brief spurts at English soccer crowds, before I'd flip on over to some brain-deadening tedium like *Eyes Wide Shut.*

Three things always struck me: singing, creativity, and endurance.

The very idea of tough, gruff, blue-collar men singing throughout a game remains alien to Americans. It probably owes to our masculinity issues as a young nation that we often rate singing as just a mite fey. We don't sing much at football stadiums or all that much in general, and it just might help explain why we're so stressed. "When you sing, your consciousness is raised," Frosty Westering said one day in September 2003. Frosty, then seventy-five, coached Division III football at Pacific Lutheran University in Tacoma, Washington. By one of Frosty's unusual credos, his players sang habitually—before games, after games. During my three-day visit as a reporter, three of them gave me a ride in their pickup truck while singing Peter, Paul, and Mary's "Leaving on a Jet Plane." That would sound kooky to some Americans, but then there's this other thing: Frosty had four *national* championships in the small-college divisions, not that he cared all that much. During warm-up exercises before the Division III national championship game in December 1999, his players actually sang

"The Twelve Days of Christmas." Imagine warming up for a title game and hearing the other side sing "The Twelve Days of Christmas," then proceeding to get run over, annihilated, *totaled,* by 42–13.

So the singing in England grabbed me especially after my Frosty experience, as did the chanting, even though I never could understand any of it through the TV and can't understand four-fifths of it from my seats in the stadiums themselves. The very idea you could start up a brand-new chant based on events you've just witnessed—*brand-new!*—then have that chant infiltrate your section, then have it spread to the entire stand or even throughout the stadium, just boggles the American mind. I'm sure it has happened here and there in the New World, but I'm also sure it hasn't happened much more than here or there.

Third, I always marveled at the sustenance of English cheering. In some stadiums—Liverpool's Anfield, for one, and in other European nations—it seemed to carry on all the time. As a nation more than eight centuries behind evolutionarily, and with such poorly developed lungs as a result, we seldom approach such durability of noise, and then only at college games, seldom at professional events. While we do manage the occasional memorable crescendo, I'm pretty sure we've never had one stem from the hopelessness of next-to-last place, as at Fratton Park, a situation that would've coaxed only about five thousand Americans to the stadium to begin with.

Yes, Portsmouth had barged right onto my short list.

6

MY VERY OWN
RELEGATION WEEKEND

Despite our wealth of American sports leagues, we lack any relegation process in the United States, and that's probably among the reasons that in 2005 we ranked forty-eighth in life expectancy, ten spots behind the United Kingdom, just to name one of many superiors. Relegation, a balm for tedium, surely prolongs life. Whoever invented relegation deserves to rank a smidgen of the way to Dr. Jonas Salk in the pantheon of humanity. While Dr. Salk, by discovering a polio vaccine, found a way to enhance life for those who might have gone paralyzed otherwise, the inventors of relegation found a way to resuscitate cities, towns, and villages that would have lain dormant, as do many in, well, the United States.

In the dying Septembers of American baseball seasons, the residual Aprils of NBA seasons, and sometimes even the fading Decembers of NFL seasons, our woebegone teams usually go unnoticed except by next of kin. Like plankton or a decrepit tire, they have sunk to the bottom to remain unseen by most. Anybody who actually knows whether they occupy fourth or fifth place counts as exquisitely observant, as an eccentric social outcast, or as someone who writes about sport for a living, thereby often qualifying in the first two categories. Some clubs, like the

Colorado Rockies of baseball (before their rise in 2007), reel in the dungeons for so long that it's perfectly possible to forget they exist. It's a rite of Americana that in the stadiums of perennial competitive sediment such as Tampa Bay (baseball) or Atlanta (basketball) or Kansas City (baseball), among many others, you'll see small, telltale clumps of fans sitting around large swatches of empty seats.

Why do the people in these clumps attend these games? They might've gotten drunk and accidentally bought season tickets six months prior. They might've relocated from the city of the away team and endeavored to support their old favorites. They might be the center fielder's cousin's dentist's niece. They might be doting parents whose eight-year-old son supports the visiting Yankees because he has seen the Yankees on TV seventy-three times and has detected that the Yankees win all the time while the home club wins about 42 percent of the time at best, so he has begged his beleaguered parents to take him to see the Yankees. They might've gotten free tickets because they won—thus lost—a raffle at work. They might be old men who love baseball because, as the peerless American sportswriter Dan Jenkins put it, baseball supplies ample breaks and old men do have to piss a lot.

Or they might simply have succumbed to the tedium of twenty-first-century American life and opted for the stadium because it was the only thing left that didn't look like a chain store in a strip mall.

They might be asleep. They might be comatose. They might be dead.

A snapshot of these souls registers immediate meaning in the skull of a born-and-raised American. It's the dregs of the season. It's the imbalance of the baseball salary structure that sends a franchise lacking a huge cable TV contract, like the Tampa Bay Devil Rays, floating to the bottom for every single season of its existence save for 2004, when it finished next to last and only the awake or the deranged noticed.

Even while it's a boring capitalist system that leaves Tampa Bay adrift, it's a deadening socialist system that allows a franchise to finish in last place year upon year upon year yet remain in the league. It tells the Detroit Lions they're still an NFL franchise, against all reason and national honor.

From time to time, a snide American sportswriter here or there has noted that a certain American team here or there merits relegation—cheap laugh, if that—but there's never been any real push to implement relegation. In fact, as John Kerr, the men's soccer coach at Harvard University, and the first American to appear in the English top division (four matches for Portsmouth in 1987–88), explained to me on the telephone one day, relegation would be impossible in the United States because of the country's sheer size, the logistics, and the costs.

Imagine, then, the pleasant shock of alighting in England one late winter. Imagine you've just jetted in from some deprived planet with no relegation. Imagine starting out by thinking relegation sort of cute, nothing more. By April, you see the front of a newspaper section, and you see a little box containing the top of the table, but next to that, a little box containing the bottom of the table.

Huh.

Relegation, it turns out, is not some scarcely followed gimmick, but an entire, consuming, yearlong emotional construct. Relegation is so many things. It's a hobgoblin whose leer from the shadows casts melodrama over an entire season of clubs lurking near the "drop," as they call it. It's a magic potion that lures the eyeballs to the bottoms of standings just as much as the tops. It's a phenomenal beast capable of wreaking fear, envy, shame, insecurity, desperation, horror, humiliation, and class resentment—in other words, just about everything that makes sports worth the time.

As a bonus, the chase for seventeenth place can give everybody something to do when the chase for first yawns.

As a second bonus, relegation can help you sometimes if you've just arrived in a new country and you're wretched at decision-making and you're worried that choosing one of the sixteen underling clubs as your favorite would mean not getting to choose any of the fifteen others.

Having seen the player who turned out to be Pedro Mendes

score that crackling goal on TV in March, having heard the Portsmouth fans, having gained goose bumps through a TV's small speaker, I decided to devise my own relegation weekend.

On the morning of Saturday, April 15, 2006, the first dregs of standings I'd ever studied carefully looked as follows:

16. Aston Villa . . . . .36 points
17. Birmingham . . . . .29 points
18. Portsmouth . . . . .29 points (trailing on goal difference)
19. West Bromwich Albion . . . . .28 points
20. Sunderland . . . . .12 points

With my newfound knowledge and wisdom, I carefully deemed it pointless to watch Sunderland and congratulated myself on my astuteness, for I had learned such intricacies in only *two months*. I knew I had to concentrate on places 17 through 19 with one eye cocked toward Aston Villa just to make sure it cleared.

On Saturday afternoon, April 15, I would debut at Portsmouth's Fratton Park for the visit from Middlesbrough, which sat fourteenth. Able to purchase a ticket because Portsmouth and Middlesbrough aren't bitter rivals, I would let Portsmouth Football Club charge my credit card for the first time, as if to thank it for the inadvertent goose bumps of March. On Sunday, April 16, resorting to an inane American optimism that somebody would let me in, I would turn up at Villa Park hoping to see Aston Villa of Birmingham and Birmingham City on the same pitch while their fans raged in glorious mutual hatred. On Monday night, April 17, I would go to West Bromwich Albion for its match with eighth-place Bolton.

Now, in the United States, if on three successive days of a holiday weekend you went to see the eighteenth-place team play the fourteenth-place team, followed by the seventeenth-place team playing the sixteenth-place team, then the nineteenth-place team playing the eighth-place team, and if you had no prior allegiances to any of those teams, and if you spent the hefty Premiership ticket cost on tickets and the hefty United Kingdom train cost on trains, and if you even stayed in a hotel one night, people might call you names.

"Loser" comes to mind.

Meanwhile, in older, wiser England, blessed with its greenery, its pubs, and its relegation, I recorded more goose bumps per hour than during any ten New Year's Eves, without even getting any at West Brom.

First, on Friday I called Fratton Park, where tickets remained for the Middlesbrough clash. I admitted to being an American tourist, and the woman on the phone sort of apologized in advance for the stadium. This struck me as a cultural difference, coming from a country in which we bathe in nostalgia and revere grimy old stadiums where, to quote Boston radio sage Eddie Andelman on baseball's Fenway Park, the last strains of bubonic plague adorn the men's room walls. In this woman's voice, I heard no pride in resisting the urge to go posh that had gripped England ever since it molted out of the hooligan 1980s.

Studying a bit, I learned that Portsmouth harbored perhaps the most bizarre manager/coach story I'd ever heard. Apparently, and you just won't believe this, it had a manager, Harry Redknapp, who once quit the club in 2004 and went to manage its most reviled rival, its very Lucifer, Southampton, requiring stout security forces when he returned to manage against Portsmouth, until, twelve months later, in a staggering turn of sporting history, he *returned*. I figured I might come upon the single most bewildered set of fans on the planet. Come Saturday noon, I boarded the South West train in London for the eighty-eight-minute trip southbound.

Having been only to Newcastle, Wigan, and Chelsea, but having seen plenty of other stadiums from the outside and peeked through their gates at slivers of grass, I felt astonished at the sight of Fratton Park. Here it graced the global, wildly lucrative Premiership, yet there are Texas high school football teams with grander stadiums—in fact, many Texas high school football teams, what with Texas being altogether insane. To circumnavigate the stadium, to idle around lost per usual, to seek the office where I could collect my ticket, I had to pass through a brick-walled alley so shockingly narrow it'd present great inconvenience to any sumo-wrestler Portsmouth supporters, who'd have no choice but to walk the other 98 percent of the way around the stadium. From the outside, the whole place resembled a ramshackle rodeo ground my father and I visited in Cody, Wyoming, on a vacation in 1999.

I loved it.

Inside, of course, the field looked green, and there's nothing like that green. Those of us in the South Stand settled in close together and rubbed elbows plus the occasional triceps or shoulder blade in the devout nonluxury seats. A kid three seats down had a stadium meat pie, and I briefly studied this alien creation, which contained some sort of horrifying brown liquid that appeared quite possibly radioactive. I thought I'd retch. Portsmouth sat eighteenth in the table by then, but the section was crammed, with no seat backs visible. Three women sat to my right and never spoke to me; to my left, a row of men never spoke to me except to point me to one of their seats so they could take mine and sit together.

The atmosphere rocked so hard. Eighteenth place sounded like second. The city of Portsmouth and the club go by the nickname "Pompey," for ancient reasons with various explanations, and the fans chanted, "Play up, Pompey, Pompey, play up!" to the tune of the "Pompey Chimes," or the same sound major clocks or church bells make at the top of the hour. Even I knew from some light reading that this tradition dated to the 1890s. They continually chanted something like "Blarney," or "Blurney," or "Blarmey"—something I couldn't glean and felt too embarrassed to learn by asking, so I checked my program to see if they were referring to one player's surname. They were not.

I had stumbled into the latent stages of a whiplash resurgence. At the end of December, Portsmouth sat eighteenth, with seventeen points. At the end of January, Portsmouth languished in nineteenth, with seventeen points. On the morning of February 25, when I barely noticed it at barren Chelsea, it seemed even more hopeless, time expiring with eighteen points, to twenty for Birmingham. Then came Mendes's goal—and immediate, absurdist, wondrous cries about staying up—but then, with Mendes's goal as fulcrum, a win by 4–2 at West Ham in East London, a win by 3–1 at Fulham in West London, a 2–2 draw with Blackburn at home, and a pinch-me 1–1 draw with Arsenal at home three nights before my debut.

That meant eleven points from five matches, a resurrection from bleakness to within a shout of the coveted seventeenth place, with the Middlesbrough tussle as riveting a sporting event as dotted the planet. That eighteenth versus fourteenth could be riveting simply amazed a Yank. The first half went goal-less, but somebody named Gary O'Neil scored in the fifty-fourth minute after somebody named Benjani Mwaruwari rampaged up the right and slid him the ball, but it's the remainder of the game that lodged in my memory. For those last ten or fifteen minutes, as I recollect, the Middlesbrough menace threatened the Portsmouth goal with repeated flurries. Greenwich Mean Time inarguably slowed. Seconds dawdled, then crawled, then moved like sludge as the ball ricocheted hauntingly around the box before the Pompey goal and the woman next to me screamed, "Get it out of there!" Even having stumbled into this scene in April 2006 all detachment and no clue, I became almost unbearably nervous.

Through all of this the antique stadium itself, with a clever malice, offered no digital clock, at least not one that I could locate despite looking around repeatedly. Only one anachronism of a clock—with hands!—garnished the facade over to the left at the rowdy Fratton End section, and that thing didn't tell us much and seemed even to delight rudely in my unawareness at how much time actually remained. Once I thought I saw it smile like the devil. I thanked goodness I'd never left my seat and held my single beer and avoided the bubonic plague, not only because about fifteen other people would've had to stand to let me out, but because I'd have come back even more baffled.

I suffered for my prospective future squad.

Finally, about seven hours later in my estimation, the referee blew a whistle, and Portsmouth had leapt to thirty-two points, clear of Birmingham by three and firmly into seventeenth place. I joined my new stranger friends in a rousing rendition of "We are staying up! We are staying up!" I felt semi-Himalayan goose bumps. I remained in my seat and watched the players go into the tunnel. Then, as I walked toward the aisle, I saw two children, a boy and a girl, each probably eleven or twelve, descending, no, bouncing down the stairwell to the right. I shall never forget them. "We are staying up! We are staying up!" they shouted in a delirious two-voice chant.

In the United States, we don't have children beyond the age of ten all delirious over late-season forays into seventeenth place. If we did, we'd probably recommend their families get a visit from Child Protective Services.

7

SUNDAY CONTEMPT

Naturally, we're inured to longer trips in the United States, partly because we're geographically huge and partly because longer trips help us fulfill our God-given duty to squander oil products at a pace exponentially more rapid than any other countries. I once saw a basketball game in Mississippi on a Saturday and an NFL game in Green Bay, Wisconsin, on a Sunday. It's believed to be the only Mississippi-Wisconsin weekend in U.S. history, and I'm deeply proud of this honor. Another time, because the office begged when it really didn't have to, I flew ninety minutes from New York to Indianapolis on a Saturday morning, drove three hours north from Indianapolis to South Bend, saw a football game between Notre Dame University and the U.S. Naval Academy, returned to Indianapolis by 2:00 AM, woke by 6:00, caught a twenty-minute flight from Indianapolis to Cincinnati, connected to a five-hour flight from Cincinnati to San Francisco, took a one-hour taxi (traffic) across the San Francisco Bay to Oakland, and saw a Sunday afternoon NFL game between the Jets and the Raiders. Covering an afternoon basketball game in Nashville, Tennessee, then driving four hours through wee-hour snow flurries to St. Louis for an NFL playoff game, when the boss didn't even ask for the playoff game?

Really, who wouldn't?

It's always a bit of a geography lesson, then, when you mention to an English fan your Saturday at Portsmouth (on the south coast) followed by a Sunday at Aston Villa (midcountry), a collective three hours by train. They look amazed. Seems it's just not done all that much. Throw in the fact that Aston Villa played Birmingham in a derby on Sunday, April 16, 2006, with tickets profoundly unavailable to the tourist, and such a weekend seems downright misguided.

Luckily, I major in downright misguided, so I rode the Sunday morning train to Birmingham, watching bald guys drinking cans of Carlsberg and marveling at how, through long evolution, English stomachs had come to consist of corrugated steel. Approaching Villa Park in a taxi from the city center under a partly sunny sky, I knew I'd probably add to my growing list of games experienced from outside stadiums. Yet again, I'd stand in a parking lot wondering what just happened to cause that crescendo I just heard, or stand in a pub among strangers wondering why I didn't choose a pub among strangers half a block from home. In my grand tabulation of matches experienced from outside the stadium, I already had Charlton, Chelsea, Arsenal (before it moved to a new stadium), and Liverpool.

Add Villa, and I'd have only fifteen parking lots to go for an even twenty.

But we have this wonderful, horrible saying in the United States, and it goes like this: you never know. So on I went. Sure enough, when I proved unable to ask directions on account of maleness and took twenty-five minutes to circumnavigate the stadium and find the ticket office, the security guard at the door explained that I could not purchase any of the remaining, available, unused, advertised tickets. He explained that Aston Villa versus Birmingham was a derby and you had to have a ticket-buying history with the clubs. He recommended a pub up the street. It didn't even help when I showed him my U.S. passport, hoping in vain to convey runaway ignorance and exact some pity.

Right at thirty minutes to kickoff, as I trudged back into the parking lot—I believe I had taken on a bit of a forlorn look—I heard a whistle from behind. I ignored it, presuming the whistler aimed elsewhere, but then the whistler whistled again.

I turned to see an approaching brother and sister, ages twenty-two and twenty-one, with faces profoundly unvisited by the aging process. They said their father's business trip had prevented his attendance and that they'd sell me his ticket for £20, provided I was not a fan of Birmingham City. I said that until recently I'd lived in New York and had not known of the existence of a Birmingham City, and that I certainly did not wish to adopt Birmingham City on a sudden whim while standing among thousands of home fans at Villa Park. They grinned, took my £20 note, and walked me around the stadium toward the Holte End, asking me questions about New York. They said their parents had taken them to the United States maybe four times, but always to Orlando, and I found these youths so decent and polite and exquisitely parented that I considered not even one single wisecrack.

Thereby did I enter the Holte End for a match between Aston Villa and Birmingham City with little to no idea as to the severity of the contempt therein. I mean, we Americans have rivalries. We have had, through the years, Redskins–Cowboys, Raiders–Broncos, Yankees–Red Sox, Florida–Florida State, Kentucky–Louisville, Ohio State–Michigan, and then, the most beautifully, irrationally contemptuous of them all, Alabama–Auburn. We boast frothing contempt in almost all the fifty states. We know the value of a good, controlled, in-stadium hatred. Even while we feign gentility and perspective, we know a stadium improves on any day when it's seething, roiling, and curdling with disdain.

I'd seen disdain.

I'd just never seen . . . oh . . . my . . . God.

Aston Villa 3, Birmingham 1, even with its insignificance to the Premiership title, with its sixteenth place defeating eighteenth place, bolted into my all-time top ten sporting events. It's up there in the neighborhood of Rulon Gardner, the ninth child of Wyoming dairy farmers, defeating Hercules from Siberia in the Greco-Roman wrestling at Sydney and then telling us that moving Aleksandr Karelin called to mind moving a cow. It's not far from the 2000 Super Bowl between the Rams and the Titans, or the 2001 Wimbledon final between Goran Ivanisevic and Pat Rafter, or the two famous Kentucky-Duke basketball games of 1992 and 1998.

In the Holte End that Easter day, wave upon wave upon wave of goose bumps washed over me, especially after halftime. The noise made echoes, and I'll never forget feeling the entire stand inhale during those pregnant milliseconds that precede most goals and help make soccer uniquely orgasmic. By that I mean the millisecond just after the seasoned viewers have made a realization. They have realized their side will score, but they have not yet had the time to exult. They're inhaling, I suppose. There's that moment tucked in there, and I find that moment almost matchless upon this troubled coil, not least because you know euphoria's coming in the very next moment.

From the first half, we had only a Villa goal, at ten minutes, in the opposite goal, after which the brother in the brother-sister tandem grabbed me, hugged me, hopped up and down while I stood like a log, and then apologized to me, for I must've looked startled. Then we had a Birmingham equalizer. Twice after halftime would come the magical mass inhalation. It cropped up in the fifty-sixth minute just before Gary Cahill hurled himself skyward, contorted himself parallel to the ground, stretched out his right leg, and yanked the ball into the opposite corner of the goal. And it materialized again in the seventy-eighth minute, when Juan Pablo Angel fed Milan Baros unmarked on the right, and Baros blasted a shot. Both times I felt the quirky silence followed by an outpouring that would blow the doors off a house. The back of my neck reveled.

All along, I kept hearing things about this guy Steve Bruce, and while I'd never heard of Steve Bruce until the previous month, I got the distinct impression he might rank among the worst people in global history.

(Point of information: Steve Bruce managed Birmingham City.)

And the songs.

I'd never heard such a range of songs. To a Briton, they probably rated old-hat, but I didn't know whether they were old standbys or instant creative concoctions, so I just found them incredible, even if I understood only about 37.5 percent of the lyrics. Added oomph fueled the songs, as clearly the Holte End knew that Portsmouth's 1–0 win over Middlesbrough had pushed Pompey to thirty-two points and shoved Birmingham firmly into the relegation zone at twenty-nine, and clearly the Holte End would greet a Birmingham relegation almost as affectionately as one would a newborn child. On that day I learned of yet another of relegation's knacks, how it ladles upon a match an entire new layer of songs.

To "Guantánamera," the song about the Cuban peasant girl from Guantánamo and the emblem of Cuban patriotism, written probably in 1929, we had:

> Down with the Baggies
> You're going down with the Baggies.

I gathered the word "Baggies" might have something to do with West Bromwich Albion, that other Birmingham-area club facing relegation.

To "Beer Barrel Polka," the concoction begun when Czech musician Jaromir Vejvoda wrote the music in 1927, we had:

> Down with the Baggies
> Down with the Baggies, you go.

That one managed to mesh an abiding loathing with playful mirth, and I loved it thoroughly, even though for all I knew the worst thing I could say about Birmingham was its name's not as pretty as Aston Villa's.

Later on, the Holte End opted for a ballad, a version of Vera Lynn's 1939 ballad penned by Ross Parker and Hughie Charles:

> Someday we'll meet again,
> Don't know where, don't know when.

I found this almost staggering. The Holte End as lounge act. Imagine.

But a ditty at maybe the seventy-first minute latched itself onto my memory, not to unfasten anytime soon—odd given I couldn't understand the lyrics. Suddenly, before my very ears, the Holte End crooned a phenomenal version of the Monkees' 1967 hit "Daydream Believer," one of the few songs I'd actually liked from the ballyhooed 1960s that preceded my adolescence. I asked my host for the lyrics that we'd just heard but that the Monkees had never imagined. Maybe two or three times, he repeated to me the phrase "sad bluenose bastard," but I just couldn't understand him, and so, with his hand shaking a bit— he was a nervous viewer who doubled over and smoked during matches—he carefully spelled it out:

Cheer up, Stevie B,
Oh, what can it mean
To a sad bluenose bastard
And a s—— football team.

I felt retroactive goose bumps.
I felt awe.
I'd spent my life in stadiums, but I'd just never . . .
Later I would e-mail those lyrics to about twenty American sports friends. Many wrote back amazed. Others wrote back envious. It probably seems mundane to the average English fan, but everyone deserves a religious experience at their first hearing of "sad" combined with "bluenose" combined with "bastard." After about thirty-five years of studious attention to American sports, I felt I'd wandered into a new realm, in which teams could get relegated and fans who disliked them could make up songs about it, even to "Daydream Believer," a Monkees song that during my teen years became a remake by Anne Murray.

Exiting Villa Park, we saw police chase some would-be brawlers across a field, the lone moment of near-violence I've seen even as I hail from a country in which many still think it's somewhat dangerous to attend English soccer (just one from our vast national reservoir of misconceptions). I felt actually intoxicated, but by oxygen alone. Owing to the cruel but understandable English stadium policies, I'd been unable to have a beer at my seat, reason enough for colonies to secede from a motherland had we not seceded already. Or, viewed differently, who needs beer when you have relegation and "Daydream Believer"?

After all, only relegation could've brewed that scenario from May 2005 at the Hawthorns on the northwest edge of Birmingham, of which I learned the next night. Just before West Bromwich Albion and Bolton played a goal-less, thrill-less, and largely song-less Monday night draw that completed my relegation weekend, a kindly man of maybe sixty began edifying me by answering my questions. This occurred in the concession area as I drank a beer and he ate a terrifying meat pie. He explained to me that "Baggies" came from West Bromwich players wearing baggy shorts beginning about a century prior. He said that in all his days attending soccer matches, one of the best had to be that day in May 2005, when West Bromwich played Portsmouth on the final day of the 2004–2005 season, and West Bromwich won to secure the coveted seventeenth place, and West Bromwich fans cheered, but Portsmouth fans also cheered, because West Bromwich's win shoved Southampton into relegation, a story that supplied my first inkling that Portsmouth fans might rather despise Southampton. He said of soccer, "It's really the heart of England."

Then, after some time and a bit of familiarity and comfort, he gently said, "If you don't mind my asking, what is your opinion of your current president?"

8

MEDIA-INACCESSIBLE

ENGLAND

Still in observer mode, I'd begun to notice some things.

I'd never lived in a place in which a team could win more than one major cup in one year. In the United States, we keep it simple, probably because we're a young culture with still-forming brains that become further impeded whenever we hold congressional steroid hearings. In the NFL, our biggest league by far, thirty-two teams pursue one Vince Lombardi trophy, which goes to the winner of the Super Bowl and gets its name from a great 1960s coach who fulfilled many of our national militaristic, quasi-pathological fantasies by screaming at—and scaring the hell out of—his players. In baseball, in the NBA, people play for one title. They give trophies and junk for conference titles and division titles, sure, but there's only one champion.

I'd just about grasped the idea that Premiership clubs play for up to three championships:

- The league, a thirty-eight-game regular season
- The FA Cup, a concurrent yearlong tournament with every club in England
- The European Champions League, an also-concurrent year-

long tournament with the previous season's top clubs from all over the continent, including four per year from England

Or, if they don't reach the European Champions League, the next three—or four—finishers qualify for a second-tier European tournament called the UEFA Cup. I'd even grasped that all these entities keep separate, that FA Cup matches don't count in the Premier League, and so on.

All right, fine, got it, but then Jerry informed me there's yet another cup involving all twenty top clubs. I'd never once heard of this fourth cup named "League Cup," or "Carling Cup," an also-concurrent six-month tournament of the top four divisions. Whew. Almost immediately upon arrival in England, I had watched Manchester United and Wigan playing for this fourth cup. Some observers made light of the fact that Manchester United might not boast about winning this cup, being Manchester United, thus seeking bigger cups.

By April 2006, I still had never once heard about the Intertoto Cup. It would be a year before I would start to read about Blackburn pursuing a spot in the Intertoto Cup, and at that time I simply could not believe somebody out there pursued yet another cup. I could not comprehend the Intertoto Cup and decided to allow it more time. It might require even another year, absorbing the vagaries of the Intertoto Cup, which apparently involves much of Europe.

Plainly, it's a bit harder being a big-time manager or coach in England than in the United States. In addition to all the usual issues all managers face, the English manager must dabble in energy conservation as he attempts to win two or three or four cups at once. In filling out his roster in a given week, he might have to sacrifice Wednesday night for Saturday afternoon or Saturday afternoon for Wednesday night. In the case of a decent man named Steve Coppell, manager at Reading, he might even come right out and state misgivings about achieving the amazing feat of a UEFA Cup qualification from the first top-flight season in 135 years of existence, worried it will dilute the efforts Reading brings to other pursuits.

Having read that, I almost tumbled out of my train seat and into the aisle, for we just don't dwell in that kind of realism in the United States. We'd expect our coach to say something along the lines of, "We'll worry about that when we get there, and if necessary we'll recruit some ragtag players from the area, coach them into shape, upset four superior teams on the path to a storybook title, and become a really bad sports movie about the value of hard work that's really trite and clichéd but does well at the box office."

English realism vies right up there with multiple cups among jolts to an interloper. Only two days into my Premiership indoctrination, on a train from Wigan to Newcastle, I read the following quotation from Sam Allardyce of Bolton: "Our target is sustainability, to become a Premiership fixture like Charlton. We don't want to get to the next level"—he meant the four mastodons—"because we know we can't, we're not daft. We could have finished fourth last year and missed maybe the only chance we'll ever get."

We'd pillory somebody making such a statement for its failure to tread in daydreams. As an American, I had to read it thrice to digest.

Further, I'd begun to take note of the phenomenal English loyalty, the phenomenal English eyes, and the phenomenal English stomach.

* *English loyalty.* I'd seen plenty of fan loyalty to American teams, just not quite the depth of loyalty as in England. Somewhat more than Americans, English fans seem to have their club insignias swimming in the bloodstream as if affixed to the platelets. Where the idea of having one's ashes scattered on one's favorite field seems reasonably normal in England—the subject came up as part of my tour of Old Trafford—it's a concept we've only lately picked up in the United States, even if we did trump England when a Philadelphia fan ran onto the field to scatter his mother's ashes *during a game.* English loyalty to club is so profound that England seems to have far fewer people who sort of like this club or sort of like that club or sort of

like that other club over there. My soccer guru Tom makes it sound as if professing love for other clubs results in a hiking of one's already astronomical taxes.

- *English eyes.* Off the bat, I detected telescopic strength, as if it correlates with hereditary beer consumption. From even half a stadium away or more, these evolved lenses could spot perceived handballs in a benevolent attempt to assist the referee with his work. At times early on I thought the English felt it some sort of duty to assist this beleaguered referee with his thankless work by going to the stadium and pointing out the handballs. I found this a routinely beautiful commitment to civic service.

- *English stomachs.* I'd witnessed the strength of American stomach linings, as at car races and the Kentucky Derby (whose official drink is the glorified glass of bourbon called the mint julep), and I'd witnessed in short bursts the sturdiness of English stomachs, but I'd just not got the extended, day-to-day look at the true Herculean measure of English stomachs. I hadn't lived and traveled and followed soccer among these mighty organs, hadn't comprehended their true durability against the torrent of challenging beverages and other shocking mistreatment poured into them.

Still, the paramount cultural difference between following American sports like a ravenous hyena and following the Premiership like a ravenous hyena would be, weirdly enough, media access to players' dressing rooms for pre- and postgame interviews. American reporters in the big three sports have routine access; Premiership reporters have almost nil. It causes a fundamental distinction in the sports-following experience. American fans watch athletes with great personal familiarity (even when misconstrued); Premiership fans watch their athletes with a certain mystery.

The two lands just *sound* different.

By the end of the 2005–2006 Premiership season, I realized I'd never heard the voice of Wayne Rooney, a major star, having sat too far away to hear him yell, "F——ing beauty," at Newcastle and having heard only others speak incessantly, between his April 2006 injury and the June 2006 World Cup, about his frigging metatarsal. When I thought about this, it startled me, for I'd come from a chatterbox culture where you might absorb a quotation from your favorite athlete every single day for six months during the season, either by hearing it on TV or radio or by reading it in a newspaper. Where they're always talking to us even if they're annoyed at the prospect. Where it's perfectly normal to sit with your breakfast cereal watching the morning highlight shows and think nothing of the fact that you're watching an athlete standing in front of his locker shirtless, trying to say something numbingly insignificant into a phalanx of maybe ten microphones. Where brave beings known as "sideline reporters" interview coaches even as the coaches head for halftime; even though the coaches never say anything remotely interesting, the custom persists like gout. Where, in certain circumstances, players receive fines for skipping media sessions. Where signs adorn the walls outside players' dressing rooms, restating league rules about the necessity of letting in the reporters starting at fifteen to twenty minutes after a game.

In baseball, the American reporter will have about three hours of access to the dressing room before games and roughly another hour afterward for the rehash of feats and blunders. That doesn't count playoffs or big-media games, in which there'll be organized pregame and postgame press conferences (often transcribed and printed) in addition to the dressing-room access. For the NBA, the reporter will have pregame access, postgame access, and daily postpractice access during the season, even though he or she seems to have less access than he or she did twenty years ago, prompting him or her to complain. An NFL reporter suffers by contrast, because that reporter has only postgame access on Sundays, then some practice-time access during the week; this access varies slightly from team to team, and some stars provide no access at their lockers but do give deeply unsatisfying ten-minute access in a press conference setting. That doesn't include Super Bowl week, when the two teams combine for a one-hour session with selected players on Monday, three-hour interview sessions on Tuesday, Wednesday, and Thursday, and another hour with each coach on Friday, enough to jostle a rational brain into madness.

Daily access to the American coach or manager is a national given, written into the Constitution by the Founding Fathers in 1787. In general, coaches and managers appear on TV more than the president, a fact that always pleases about half the country. Players often hide in training rooms fixing phantom injuries just to avoid the daily media. Even the 119 big-time universities have regular weekly coach press conferences for football and basketball, regular coach-and-player postpractice access on Monday through Thursday, and multi-person media relations staffs. That doesn't include championship events, which include daily access, with the players and the coach sitting at a long table in front of a room of reporters.

This regular national flood of access became one of our manufactured national crises, simmering for years but reaching its hysterical apex in the early 1990s. Then we had a dreaded "national conversation" because, of course, that blob of reporters bolting through every game began to include more and more women entering domains where men change clothes. We hemmed. We hawed. We argued. We shouted—especially on talk shows. We remembered our Puritan roots and all the joys they had brought us, even though we couldn't really think of any. We had some athletes who pleaded religious convictions and asked to meet women outside in the hall for interviews, but that didn't work. We had some athletes who saw women and *then* got undressed. We had some athletes who said and did lewd things to women. We had one legendary woman who, responding to a lewd gesture, said to an athlete, "It looks like a penis, only smaller." We had elected officials suggesting new laws, for ultimate horror. We had fans perceiving athletes as victims. By now, we still might have beautiful female reporters getting asked out by athletes or athletes' wives staring contemptuously at beautiful female reporters, but the whole thing has subsided to a normalcy.

All along, through the whole fatuous ordeal, there existed the easiest solution in dilemma history.

Ancient civilizations called it the "towel."

So imagine my surprise at the sound of England. From time to time, here's a Premiership player speaking after a match, seeking and achieving banality. More often, we hear from zero of them. Here's the manager, usually reliable for TV camera commentary, then maybe press conference commentary, but certainly no second round of questioning in the dressing room while surrounded by fifteen reporters and doling out the less-rehearsed, better stuff. Here's an interview in a newspaper every once in a while. Here's Sir Alex Ferguson opining that England's national team plays timidly because it fears derision from the English press, when in fact added access might blunt some of that derision, because you're less apt to deride somebody you know a bit.

And then here comes a fine trickle of summer books in which the players get to tell their side. In fact, here's one book in which a Premiership player provides a melodramatic account of the day he learned one club wanted to offer him £55,000 per week rather than £60,000. He recalls how he gripped the steering wheel of his luxury vehicle, trying to cope with the horrifying news: "I was trembling with anger."

Never mind the fact that if he finds £55,000 per week unmanageable, it's a really bad idea to give him £60,000 per week. I believe this inane passage from Ashley Cole's book alone, on balance, might justify the English approach of limiting player availability.

9

TWO MONTHS TO

CHOOSE

While still in lame deliberation as the season waned, I enhanced my budding understanding of the Premiership . . . in Colombia. You can hear all about the foremost league's global tentacles, but there's something about seeing them up close. At a dinner in Bogotá on an April vacation, one of the fellow diners heard "England" and asked immediately if I'd ever seen Aston Villa play, and I briefly found that odd until I remembered the Aston Villa squad features the Colombian Juan Pablo Angel. On TV on a Saturday morning, I quickly came upon Arsenal versus Tottenham, which wowed me more in this completely exotic place than it ever did in the United States. And at a family party in a barrio near the airport in Cartagena, on Colombia's north and Caribbean coast, I ate sancocho and drank beer out of little green bottles and saw something unforgettable to myself: six boys, probably fourteen or fifteen years old, out on a dirt street, in a neighborhood in which the electricity later would go out because a storm happened to brush by meekly, with nothing to carry them through the humid afternoon except six pairs of shorts and one soccer ball. No shirts, no shoes, and no posts, so they used rocks. Still, they had themselves a fine Sunday, swaggering over their goals and cooing at bypassing girls and maybe even pretending to be Juan Pablo Angel, as I thought of all the childhood Sundays I spent in Virginia loaded with options yet choosing to sit in the air conditioning affixed to the couch like a trapped muskrat.

Meanwhile, on Saturday, April 29, 2006, at Wigan, my old haunt, Portsmouth won 2–1 on Matthew Taylor's penalty in the seventy-first minute and finished yanking survival from the esophagus of relegation. After accruing seventeen points in its first twenty-seven matches, Pompey had hogged twenty from its next nine. The pitch at Wigan teemed with a seventeenth-place celebration of some two thousand Portsmouth fans, quite a total given Wigan's geographic presence up near Iceland. Pundits called Taylor's goal a "multi-million-pound penalty" (estimated cost of going down: £30 million), called the Portsmouth manager "Harry Houdini," and quoted owner Milan Mandaric saying, "In my seven years at Portsmouth Football Club, this has to be the most emotional moment." In yet another of life's blunders, I missed it out of indecision, yet I felt some sort of kinship with it, as if that might be the *it* I sought. As my first partial season concluded, it certainly had a chance to be *it*.

As a new season began, on August 11, 2006, I made a self-imposed club-choice deadline of October 31 and set about testing the persuasive first impression of Portsmouth, born of Mendes's goal and of having once lived in a Portsmouth, albeit spending that time miffed at my parents. I had it down to Portsmouth, Aston Villa, and Newcastle, with outside chances of Reading, Tottenham, and maybe Everton. I wanted to take the decision as seriously as an idiot interloper could take it.

Portsmouth had attributes besides Mendes's goal and a sister city in Virginia. I found the nickname "Pompey" appealingly plucky, and I liked the presence of about twelve explanations for the nickname's origin. I liked that people chanted the same "Pompey Chimes" that fans chanted 110 years prior, so that I might one day chant the Pompey Chimes and imagine it was 1898 and everybody was wearing only black-and-white clothing, thereby connecting me to history. Further, it dawned on me through careful research that Portsmouth was a seafaring town with a navy heritage. Not only had I come from a seafaring (if sleepy) metropolitan area with a navy heritage, but the idea of Portsmouth made me think of my maternal grandfather, a tugboat captain with a gruff demeanor and a big heart and mammoth forearms. He'd tell my brother and myself these wondrous stories from navigating Chesapeake Bay, wondrous not least because he knew how to wink, and even as little blond towheads we could sense the high percentage of fiction. I still remember the boat hit by a German vessel during the war and "sawed half in two," and how he held on to the railing of his half so tightly as it bobbed, barely afloat, that his fingerprints remained in the metal even to the day of the tale. Opposing fans might mock Portsmouth fans with the "Guantánamera" version, "Town full of seamen/you're just a town full of seamen," but that'd make me all warm and fuzzy.

Studying the season's early stages and roaming some, I noticed that Aston Villa had hired manager Martin O'Neill, whose BBC World Cup commentary I'd found salient and unafraid and instructive; I even got the I'd-like-to-play-for-that-guy vibe, a vibe that seldom visits sportswriters, who know too well how the coach species bears striking resemblance to that of the cobra. By contrast, O'Neill seemed rather a sage, learned professor of soccer. But then, you can't choose a club for one manager, I thought. I saw a match at Reading, half an hour west of London, because I wanted to see how the first crest into the first division in 135 years of existence might look, and it was good enough and spirited enough, but not grimy enough. The stadium seemed new and clean and far too suburban. I sought more soot. I cast a studious eye on Newcastle, accursed, still digesting Michael Owen's gruesome World Cup injury, but the story line seemed rote to me after a childhood and early adulthood spent listening to wailing accursed baseball fans in Chicago and Boston. I liked "Tottenham Hotspur" because it figured in one of the great and charming mysteries of English soccer—why do people say "Tottenham Hotspur" and "Bolton Wanderers" and "Blackburn Rovers" in common parlance, but only "Portsmouth" or "Everton"?—and I did feel a certain sympathy when Tottenham missed out on the

European Champions League in May 2006 because their players got food poisoning from a Marriott buffet, but it just didn't quite click.

Strangely, I got an added Portsmouth tilt from a gory play very early in the new 2006–2007 season. On Wednesday night, August 23, at Manchester City—the other Manchester club besides Manchester United—in only the second game of the thirty-eight, Portsmouth's wondrous Pedro Mendes futilely chased a ball as it scurried out of bounds, five minutes past halftime. The play had died. Mendes merely would retrieve the ball. Then, sickeningly, as Mendes neared the line, here came some Ben Thatcher of Manchester City—first I'd ever heard of him—flying toward Mendes. Not content with a gratuitous tackle, which would've been merely stupid, the Manchester City player rushed in with a venom suggestive of some steroid rage, throwing a forearm to Mendes's head that knocked Mendes unconscious. Mendes remained unconscious as he rode off on a stretcher. He had a seizure. He received oxygen. Gary O'Neil called it "the worst thing I've ever seen on a pitch." Mendes woke in a hospital on a drip. Thatcher apologized by writing a letter, which beats a phone call or media interview, but he received a paltry eight-game suspension. He wouldn't have seen the light of the pitch for two seasons if I ran the league or the world.

I run neither, but seeing this play every half hour on the sports channel had the unintended effect of endearing me further toward Mendes and Portsmouth. At the same time, I tried to ignore that Pompey opened the season with five straight shutouts—"clean sheets," they call them—crushed Blackburn by 3–0 and Middlesbrough by 4–0, and hurried out to an eye-popping first place by September 17, with thirteen points to twelve for Manchester United and twelve for Chelsea. I didn't want to choose a club based on one luminous month, and besides, my soccer guru Tom had warned me of the triviality of early standings, a notion bolstered by manager Harry Redknapp when he said, "We are trying to finish above our highest previous finish in the Premiership, which is thirteenth. We've had a good start, but we're not getting carried away." I tried to ignore the start, but probably failed.

Even the BBC's soccer corruption special of September 19, 2006, which implicated Redknapp, deterred me only momentarily. For one thing, the whole ruckus taught me the definition of the word "bung," unquestionably fulfilling a public duty toward uninitiated residents from far-off lands. I came to understand that a bung amounted to a sort of illicit payment, and having come from a land of plenty that abounds with illicit payments, I felt a moving and emotional bridging of the cultures. I came to perceive our similarities as greater than our differences and gained newfound hope for the world.

The program showed Redknapp having an allegedly illegal conversation with an agent about a player from Blackburn. Luckily, by moving, I had emptied my tank of misgivings and started anew. Returning to fandom in a new country, I could re-activate my fanatic's rationalization gland and use the first of my available set of allotted rationalizations. I simply reasoned that I still could choose Pompey through my old saw of remembering that following sport means following sin. Weary from my homeland, I knew sports fandom had grown ever more confusing.

Besides, in a way, Redknapp sort of reminded me of a horde of gloriously sinful great-uncles from my mother's side who drank straight whiskey and swore in perpetuity and brawled in saloons and made excellent company. Harry even *looked* somewhat like they once looked, whether or not he did any of the above.

Pompey had cooled off beginning in late September, but I eyed the long term, the rest of life, the till-I-die-wherever-I-might-reside, and the crowd and details of Pompey promised the best potential for recurrent goose bumps. From late September to late October, Portsmouth lost to Bolton, lost to Tottenham, beat West Ham, lost to Chelsea, beat Reading, and collected one new fan, one more obscure droplet in the vast harbor of fandom.

With a fresh coat of Pompey, I headed for Fratton Park on November 4 for the match with Manchester United. I knew full well that the match transpired 194 miles north in Manchester, but I wanted to see if Portsmouth during a match felt anything like the ghost-town-like Washington, D.C., area during any televised Redskins game. I made a ceremonial walk to Fratton Park, past the arterial devastation of the neighboring KFC and the McDonald's, through the crosswalk, past the Safe Storage, to the 108-year-old edifice.

As the match began in Manchester, I walked through No Sumo Wrestlers Alley to the Pompey store, listening to the match on the broadcast in the store as the only patron. Armed with a list of Pompey pubs I'd actually looked up and printed in a lapse into efficiency, I walked all over the neighborhood, often alone in entire blocks of row houses, row houses being rather exotic to us Americans in our idolatry of yards, which play an invaluable role in our employment of 12 million illegal immigrants. I wanted to feel the barrenness during a match, to sense everybody inside watching the match. Yes, it did seem beautifully barren, even if I lacked the first clue whether everybody was inside watching soccer or inside cleaning out the refrigerator or outside at some horrendous mall.

The first three Pompey pubs I chose practically echoed with emptiness, for while they had TV in two cases, they lacked the proper cable package to air the Premiership, alerting me again to one American superiority: seldom does a sporting event appear on some channel outside the basic cable package. Finally, I found the Devonshire Arms, which aired the game but proved so packed I barely could wedge in. More, I definitely could not fit in. I felt embarrassed, even presumptuous. Wearing black as usual, I thought everybody looked at me as if I didn't belong, even if nobody even so much as looked at me. How dare I take up rarefied space. Here a pub teemed with people who'd emerged from the birth canal tattooed with the sprightly blue-and-yellow Pompey insignia, people who in some cases had stuck close through the horrid late 1970s, or fifteen straight second-division seasons between 1988 and 2003, people who loathed this Southampton. To myself, Southampton remained an American high school football dynasty from the boondocks on the other side of the boondocks near my hometown. I hated neither that Southampton nor this one. By the time I looked up, Manchester United led 3–0. Nobody much groused. Everybody seemed fairly realistic.

10

CLUELESS

The transition from silent objectivity back to irrational fandom requires time and metamorphosis. Luckily, there's no therapy involved, and the medication costs only £2.80 a pint even though they have to import it from Belgium.

There's a slow molting of two decades spent in American press boxes where an announcer always intones, "Attention, ladies and gentlemen, a reminder: this is a working press box, and there will be no cheering allowed." After sitting quietly through athletic drama for twenty years, jotting down stuff with a fervor, never breaching decorum except to giggle with your buddy Joe through an entire Indianapolis 500 that's so loud nobody can hear you anyway, the body forgets how to cheer. When you observe people as they do cheer, they start to seem unhinged.

So I rode the South West train service the ninety or so minutes from London Waterloo south to Fratton Park on Saturday, November 11, 2006, wondering if I could summon the motor sensory skills required to clap, and pretty certain I'd lost altogether the capacity to clap while jumping up and down. I had been a spectator in seats outside the press box precisely twice in my last ten American years, including once at a classic NBA playoff game with four lead changes in the last thirteen seconds while I stood there, arms folded, analyzing. Well, the train rolled in toward Fratton, and through the train window on the left I beheld again my new soccer home in all its mighty grayness. There it stood, as it had since 1898 when five Portsmouth men hatched the club from the vestiges of the local Royal Artillery club. It looked either majestically dingy or dingily majestic.

As Portsmouth readied to play Fulham at 3:00 PM, Pompey stood a heady fourth in the standings, with its nineteen points trailing only Manchester United (twenty-eight points), Chelsea (twenty-five), and Bolton (twenty), but as my soccer guru had instructed me, early-season standings have no meaning. Fulham stood somewhere else in the table, apparently. Of all the first-division clubs in England at that moment, I'd probably heard less about Fulham than any. I'd never heard an American discussion of Fulham. I'd never heard of an American who knew of the location of the Fulham club, and while I figured out within weeks that Fulham sits in London, I had no clue where in London. The name Mohamed Al Fayed rings familiar to Americans because he lost his son in the same accident that killed Diana, Princess of Wales, but it took me months to routinely connect Mr. Al Fayed to Fulham, even though Mr. Al Fayed owns Fulham. By November 11, I knew no Fulham history except that Fulham employed two American players then—and three by season's end—but that counts as Fulham trivia, not Fulham history. I had no thoughts about Fulham except that as an instant know-it-all American I reckoned that it probably should lose at Portsmouth.

On a mostly cloudy day at Fratton Park, I made it through the gulag turnstile and took my seat in the Milton stand behind one goal, which seemed far less rowdy than the opposing Fratton End behind the other goal. The various stands within English stadiums have names and entrenched reputations, and while the Milton End keeps pretty tame, its appeal is that you can hear the full brunt of the boisterous Fratton End, loudly enough that even an American can understand one cheer in ten. As I heard their indecipherable chants and wondered if there existed some sole person up there initiating them, I also heard two fabulous sounds that distinguished Fratton Park: drums and a bugle.

Now, I once did attend the venerable beach volleyball competition on Bondi Beach at the 2000 Sydney Olympics, and while I don't remember who won or who played, I'll always remember that a lone Brazilian fan had brought along a trombone. These are the people who supply life with verve, I thought, these people who, before leaving the house or hotel room in the morning, remember to bring along a trombone. Sunglasses. Sandals. Wallet. Keys. Trombone. Well, at Fratton Park they had two drummers I could barely see way across the pitch in the Fratton End, plus one guy playing a bugle. The combination sounded just a little like Friday nights in autumnal America, when people gather beneath lights for high school football games while the student band plays. I always loved Friday nights in autumnal America, so I loved that sound, but in the Fratton sound I relished something else. While the drummers' energy never seemed to waver as they lent the match a fine samba, I fixated my ears upon the bugle player. He could play along for a while, hitting the early notes in any song with gusto, but then he'd seem to go breathless, the last notes barely trickling out in tiny bursts.

It sounded as if, at some point, on cue, somebody would begin to strangle him.

It sounded as if the bugle itself would develop some sort of clot along the way, whereupon it would begin the irreversible process of croaking, spewing only bits and pieces of sound in its final gasps before bugle death.

It sounded human.

I decided I liked Fratton Park's humanity, especially that horn's distance from perfection.

I sat next to an elderly man who smiled at me once but never spoke. A few empty seats dotted the area. Portsmouth, fluid offensively early in the season, kept an abiding threat on the Fulham goal, but the Finnish goalkeeper, Antti Niemi, kept rebuffing my adopted mighty blue squad. For some reason, the Portsmouth fans reserved a special loathing for him, shouting some sort of benign epithet I couldn't quite translate. As Portsmouth's collection of *almosts* piled up, I'd act out disappointment from time to time in a sophomoric attempt to fit in, until I realized nobody cared, so I quit the tack.

Gary O'Neil's narrow miss at fifty-two minutes epitomized

Portsmouth's frustration, but by that moment I had a little problem. Near the end of halftime I'd walked up the steps and along the outside fence to the men's room, and I'd waited in line at one of the few places on earth with a shorter women's room line. I'd finally made it into the inner urinary-trough sanctum when play began again. While still in this rustic outhouse, where I did not spot any visible strains of bubonic plague, something happened to elicit a groan from the audience, followed by a silence. Too inexperienced to realize that a Fulham goal would've loosed a fair amount of sound from the nearby away section, I thought this sounded like it could've been a Fulham goal.

Now, I'm from the state of Virginia, where we believe—or at least believed in my childhood—in not making nuisances of ourselves. We're a genteel, meek bunch, known for statesmen (eight presidents, none lately), keeping mostly quiet. Usually, we Virginians can't stand standing out. We'd never ask for any of your food even if starving, and we might not even ask a stranger whether Fulham just scored or not. It's inexplicable and even unbelievable yet true, and it's surely the familiar old impulse that prevented me from asking any of the strangers around me whether a Fulham goal had occurred. I might've feared they would laugh at me. Not only did I not inquire, but of course I saw no scoreboard, nor did I or anyone else pivot to check the gigantic new video screen just about ten rows behind my shoulder blades, for apparently it malfunctioned that day.

That's how I reached my inconceivably inept status of the fifty-seventh minute, when Fulham's Claus Jensen launched a corner that teammate Zat Knight headed, whereupon it deflected off Portsmouth's Dejan Stefanovic and into the goal. Then and there, I believed the score might've just become 2–0, and I spent the next seventeen minutes alternating between thinking that the match had become rather hopeless and that the match still hyperventilated with doubt. My later research indicates that Uncle Harry changed to a more attacking 4–3–3 formation, but I couldn't have discerned that had he changed to a 2–2–2–2–2. Uncle Harry inserted Andrew Cole in the sixty-sixth minute, but I wouldn't have noticed had it been Pelé.

I did sense that when Portsmouth finally scored after so many threats, the method made sense. We—no, they, for one must earn one's "we"—sort of got tired of peppering the goal and finally just crammed in the ball. At the far end of the pitch from myself, O'Neil propelled a corner from my left and Niemi's right, and while "propelled" probably doesn't rate acceptable parlance, the thing just looked propelled. The ball went into the box in front of Niemi and began caroming around while a Portsmouth team meeting gathered in front of Niemi. Eventually, Cole scored. Fulham's manager complained about something.

I applauded, turned to the old man next to me, and expressed undeserved relief, but I still did not know the score for sure. Either Cole had just made it 1–1 or he had halved Portsmouth's stark deficit. That meant that when Lomana LuaLua almost scored at eighty-five minutes, he either almost won the match or almost forced a draw.

Either way, I wished I could see LuaLua score. In the previous spring, he'd become one of the first Premiership players I recognized. I loved his name. I loved that he grew up practicing gymnastics at an army camp in the Congo on the edge of Kinshasa, often on buried truck wheels that passed as a springboard. I loved that he'd practice back flips off high walls, because I'd have never had the intestines to do that. I learned snippets about LuaLua, such as that he'd left 100,000 Congo fans waiting to see him play in an African stadium because he'd forgotten to renew his passport back in England, or that he'd once cleaned toilets in a McDonald's. And I loved that he'd punctuate goals with fabulous somersaults, until one day in April 2006 when he hurt himself in the celebration process and wrought a postgame critique of his gymnastics prowess from Uncle Harry. To me, LuaLua represented the utmost appeal of the Premiership—that fans on the English Channel could revel in the goals and somersaults of a player from the Congo who learned to somersault on embedded truck wheels. No other league can claim such, and to such a degree.

Alas, he did not score, and I did not see a somersault in person, and I did not know whether Fulham led 2–1 or the teams stood 1–1. In fact, I still did not know as Portsmouth's frantic bids to score ended, as did the match itself. As the people turned to leave, I tried to glean from them whether their countenances suggested a draw mode or a loss mode. I could not tell and figured a draw mode and a loss mode might mimic one another after a home match with Fulham. As the Chicagoan Brian McBride and other Fulham players walked over to applaud their traveling fans, I still did not know. I thought of hollering to McBride, "Did you just win or draw!?!?" but decided against. Portsmouth's point tally had either remained at nineteen or crept upward to twenty, with either total surpassing the dregs of late February 2006, when I'd first caught Portsmouth at Chelsea's Stamford Bridge in West London. Gutless and clueless, I walked up the steps past the blank video screen and out of the park. I went around the stadium and out past the nightmarish KFC and the chilling McDonald's across the street. I went down Goldsmith Avenue toward Fratton station and Smiffy's pub just across from the train station and beyond, still unaware whether I'd seen a loss or a draw. I tried to eavesdrop on people's conversations, hoping to ascertain some clue.

Finally, having decided to walk into the town of Southsea and trailing two Portsmouth fans along the sidewalk, I heard one say to the other that a draw hadn't been all that bad. So it had been a draw, and Portsmouth had twenty points, one fewer than Aston Villa at that moment, and there had been no goal while I occupied the loo.

I kept hope, for I knew I could not get any dumber.

1 1

KNOWING TOO MUCH

From what I've noticed, English sportswriters seem to maintain their allegiances to teams much more than do American sportswriters. That's because it's less taboo, but I might submit another reason. It's also because they spend much less time in the company of the players.

Once you've interviewed the athletes and managers more than is generally recommended by health professionals, old fandom blurs considerably. Naturally, you begin to sense those you like and wish well versus those you deem fraudulent and wish, not illness or poverty or genital herpes, but own goals and red cards and fumbles and a general onslaught of humbling comeuppance. You begin to root—quietly, of course, in your own head— for a hodgepodge: the courteous manager over here, oh, but if he doesn't win, you can be happy for that pleasant quarterback with the long history of big-game failure over there on that opposing side. This tendency might've found its crux in the winter of 2007 when a chronically decent man named Tony Dungy coached his Indianapolis Colts to the Super Bowl title after years of flirtation, and all known media swooned, including those who loathed any road trip to Indianapolis. Had you ever conversed with or asked questions of Tony Dungy, you'd have swooned too. That such a decent sort could win almost reaffirms faith that there's some sort of goodness in sports.

And then, opposite the Dungy effect, you may end up regarding a childhood favorite team as loathsome for the undeniable reason that, having talked to your childhood team at length, you've learned they're a batch of self-centered, ignorant, misogynist ogres, replete with loathsome manager.

It happens.

But let's say you interviewed the Watford defender Jay De-Merit in late October 2006 for a newspaper assignment. You sat in the boxes above an empty Vicarage Road—that's a stadium in Watford, not so far northwest of London—on a Monday for two hours, fifteen minutes. Let's say this interview became more a conversation, and a sterling one at that. You reheard his story about flying to London as an anonymous schlub/Chicago bartender with no contract and few contacts and working his way from the ninth division to the seventh to the second to the first, even scoring a goal at Cardiff in the May 2006 play-in game that catapulted his team from the bizarrely titled "Championship" to the Premiership. You heard him laud the English capacity to make light of most anything. You heard him speak of loving life in Camden, North London, where he might see somebody in an impeccable business suit chatting with somebody who'd been pierced so many times he appeared to have stuck his head into a tackle box. You heard how DeMerit described the Premiership to American friends at home, how it's as if somebody took the entire NFL and shoehorned it into his home state of Wisconsin, pushing the clubs right up next to each other and galvanizing the passion. You heard him describe playing in the Premiership better than you'd ever heard it described. In the "Championship," he said, you might see a guy coming toward you and then think to act, but in the Premiership, by the time you've had that thought, he's on you.

So let's say that this Jay DeMerit from Green Bay rocketed onto your ever-changing top five of favorite athletes interviewed, and that you decided he must've had wonderful parents, and that you even considered yourself a fan of his grandmother, who holds down a spot in the Wisconsin track-and-field hall of fame.

Now, weeks later, here comes Watford to play Portsmouth at

Fratton Park, and you're supposed to wish this guy a potion of thumping defeat and profound embarrassment? You're supposed to see him and his mates as the bloodsucking enemy inveighing against the goodness of your side—you know, as you saw it during the preteen years? Of course not, and so you can end up hoping your team will collect the three points while also hoping this one defender on the other side will have himself a good day.

Fan-wise, this forms the very definition of lameness. I believe in retrospect they should've shredded my ticket rather than accept it at the gulag.

On a mostly sunny day at Fratton Park, I pined away only somewhat for the colossal Ohio State–Michigan game of that same day and yearned only slightly for my homeland and the prospective celebratory burning of furniture in the Columbus streets. Meanwhile, over on the southern edge of England, my dear friend Teresa, a fellow recovering Virginian who turned Parisian and is as fun as ten of most people, joined me for Portsmouth versus Watford, a plus in every regard including that she suddenly began talking later about the "Blue Army" chant, which alerted me at last to what those people had been chanting way back in April when I'd heard "Blarmey" or "Blarney." She could not sit with me, so I erroneously told her to pay close attention to number 8 on the Watford side, because he seemed one of the more likable humans. She later said she could not be sure about number 8, but that number 6 seemed to be American and seemed to have the surname DeMerit. We also noticed, as did everyone at Fratton Park, that number 6 stuck out his head in the thirty-second minute, connected with Ashley Young's corner, and gave Watford a 1–0 lead.

It made me mildly happy and docked me Pompey points within my own cranium.

Portsmouth held down fifth in the Premiership, one point behind the three-way logjam of Arsenal, Aston Villa, and Bolton, and it would really help to beat Watford, which held down nineteenth with nine points, ahead of only Charlton's eight, so I sought a 2–1 win. Again, I could not see any clock, but used my cell-phone clock to realize it had grown awfully late in the first half when Nwankwo Kanu tied the match on a rebound from David Thompson's cross, jarring the roof of the goal above a horizontal keeper, Ben Foster. Teresa said Foster didn't impress her much, adding to the grand tradition of instant-expert Americans. The clubs went into halftime drawn 1–1.

The second half seemed endless, as if played in a tub of goo, and I'd failed to calibrate my cell phone, much as I failed to notice when two Portsmouth penalties apparently went uncalled. Later, DeMerit would make himself available to reporters per usual and say, "I think in the box, referees tend to look at [famous] players a little bit more. You can't change those things. Darius [Henderson, his teammate] just needs to work on making himself a household name and becoming more familiar and recognized. He should go on *Strictly Come Dancing*—he is a good-looking guy, he might be able to get on there. I will suggest it to the manager."

No sportswriter would pull against such a being, but then, I did cheer in the eighty-ninth minute even while unaware it was the eighty-ninth minute. I did sit—and stand—pretty close to where DeMerit dragged down the star Kanu in the box and where the referee deemed a penalty. I did feel bad that such a fine soul had such a thorny moment, but I did prove myself capable of standing and clapping nonetheless, just for the chance to break this draw against the gnarly Watford squad and get the three points the morning had promised.

I had started on my way back to fandom, starving for the three points and drained of compassion, willing to steal the food of three points from a profoundly decent soul.

LuaLua took the penalty, and as Foster sprawled one way— can't remember which—LuaLua banged it right down the middle, securing a 2–1 victory when, moments later, the referee magically called a halt to the proceedings. Aidy Boothroyd, the fine Watford manager who reads biographies of John F. Kennedy and Abraham Lincoln, among others, had upbraided the referee on the pitch afterward, though I missed that spectacle. Soon, DeMerit would write on his website that not only had Kanu sort of made "a meal" of their intersection in the box, but that he had made an entire "Denny's breakfast bar." Portsmouth had barged past Arsenal et al. into a heady third place, even though my Premiership guru Tom had told me not to pay attention to such things before the new year.

All seemed pretty routine, except that after LuaLua had scored his goal, he had run over to the corner right in front of myself and even closer to Teresa, and he had accepted hugs from teammates but had done nothing spectacular in celebration—no somersaults, no forward roll, not even a headstand. I had to explain to Teresa how she'd missed a potential somersault. I felt disappointed as a know-nothing newcomer who needed a somersault to help me access the game, but I presumed LuaLua hadn't somersaulted because Uncle Harry might've admonished him for injuring himself that other time. I remembered Uncle Harry's classic cranky quotation of April 12, 2006: "LuaLua went off and did his treble back somersault with pike and twisted his ankle. It wasn't the cleverest thing he has ever done." That must've caused the restraint, I thought, because I had not read any of the tabloids that morning, not until Teresa and I stopped off at a convenience store on Goldsmith and some headlines screamed up at me.

In one tabloid, LuaLua had noted that he might not like to play for Portsmouth anymore. He had noted that he might think about playing elsewhere because he had noticed certain fans posting messages about his late son, Jesus LuaLua. Jesus, aged six months, had died of pneumonia the previous January 20, whereupon his father's coaches in the African Nations Cup didn't tell the father because they feared he'd return home. And some message-board geniuses, in criticizing LuaLua, suggested his son's death might've come as some sort of penance.

Now, ever since the Internet arrived and office productivity declined, we Americans probably have led the world in message-board sins. (We're so proud.) We know message boards for the frothing, roiling vats of lunacy (and worse) they can be on their best days. Very often, they're the best free entertainment still remaining in a money-grubbing society. I used to place a regular feature in a college football column, "Deranged Message Board

Posting of the Week." I'd remember which teams had lost ingloriously the previous weekend, and I'd scroll through their sites, salivating. My all-time favorites include the Ohio State fan who greeted a young player's emergency surgery with "What does this mean for the offensive line," but there's even an inarguable all-time champion American lunatic, spotted by David Whitley of the *Orlando Sentinel*. In early 2002, Alabama had been cheating again, as one of its moneyed fans had given $150,000 to a high school football coach so that the coach would steer a star player to Alabama. The NCAA had slapped Alabama with major penalties, including a two-year ban from bowl games, the season-ending prizes for good seasons.

One Alabama fan responded: "This is our 9/11."

To which Whitley jokingly claimed to have seen an Auburn post: "This is our 12/25."

The Alabama post is staggering beyond all human comprehension, but I'm still not sure it trumps for vileness the direct reference to a specific baby's death. So while I'm nobody's idea of a prude, for a moment at the convenience store on Goldsmith, I completely lost perspective. I felt just sick. I don't know why; it's naive to assume another country lacks a maniac fringe just because you rate it more civilized in general or just because its people tend to shoot each other less often than in your country. For a millisecond I thought I'd chosen the wrong club, but that's a rash American for you. We're always trying to view things in stark, simple terms so we can flex our moralizing muscles, whereas English fans, in their older culture, probably just saw the story, shrugged with disapproval but not horror, and thought something along the lines of: *Life is absurd.*

Uncle Harry helped me with his postmatch comments. He suggested an idea that hadn't dawned on me (and what a shock): that those posters did not count as Portsmouth fans. Then Jerry reminded me by e-mail that some Chelsea fans had written death threats to Reading players that very week after goalkeeper Petr Cech suffered a skull fracture at Reading. You just try not to let it ruin your day at the pitch.

After all, fandom's harder than it looks.

12

AWAY FAN

It can take several away matches for a manifestly inefficient American to navigate the maze of buying away match tickets in England. For one thing, there's the matter of figuring out that visiting clubs don't handle the visiting tickets until match day. This can be hard to learn and requires intricate research, such as reading the club website. Before achieving that rocket-science knowledge, it's entirely possible to ride a train all the way to Newcastle knowing tickets remain available, walk around St. James' Park for about forty minutes, then find oneself in the home ticket office, which doesn't sell the away tickets. In some stadiums, they sell remaining away tickets at the away gates, but I don't know for sure about St. James' Park because I never found the away gate.

With Newcastle and Portsmouth unembittered toward each other, and with tickets thus open to the public, I bought a home ticket, and as I took my choice seat in a lower section, I felt the immigration authorities should go ahead and deport me for my indiscretion. There sat my people, far, far away, a sliver in the upper deck, lined on both sides by the standard police protection, and I could barely hear the cheers or the trademark Portsmouth exuberance. I probably would've needed the Hubble telescope to spot even the electric-blue wig of Portsmouth fan extraordinaire John Westwood, the lavishly Pompey-tattooed partner in the Petersfield Bookshop who legally changed his middle name to "Portsmouth Football Club." I had betrayed my people, sitting with another tribe while my people sat so far from the action they couldn't even hear when that freckled woman from August 2005 called them "f——ing wankers."

Maybe she didn't, even.

I sat among a noticeably upscale crowd, in which lovely over-fifty women wore lovely coats and hugged friends. About fifteen rows below me, children and even a few adults watched in awe as the players warmed up, and I recognized this as one of the eternal signs of the end of time, for even as a sportswriter I hated to watch teams practice and believed that those who found this tedious drudgery fascinating must be sorely in need of some sort of hobby.

In my backpack I had a brand-new Newcastle scarf, because everybody got one entering the stadium, and I decided to give it to a child as a present. The public-address played the Killers' masterful "Somebody Told Me," and I knew I still lacked my soccer chops when I got annoyed that they interrupted it to read the lineups. The lineups meant nothing to me since, through my eyes, Pompey still looked like an impressionist painting of players, with any individual skills and tendencies still indecipherable. Week to week, Uncle Harry shuffled in the healthy and shuffled out the injured, but I just couldn't follow it expertly enough to know the significance of these moves.

When you fail to notice one week the absence of the leviathan Sol Campbell, so large he seems part man and part topographical formation, you know you're in the forest sans flashlight.

I'd relished my first train ride as an away fan and American convert; it had seemed almost magical to behold. For one thing, we Americans tend to consider trains exotic. We don't ride them much because we inhabit a gigantic country and because train rides require us to be with other people when we'd much prefer to be alone in our cars stuck in traffic and gorging on oil products and getting infuriated at the uninformed rants of one of our vast collection of dim bulbs to whom we've given talk-radio shows. I felt energized as I boarded the train at King's Cross

St. Pancras station on a Saturday night, only to discover that a great portion of London apparently had felt energized likewise, so that a lot of us stood in the corridors for the first two hours, swaying to and fro.

Then again, few Americans would regard a four-hour road trip as taxing. Until you remember the size of England and the astonishment that it ever built an empire from such limited size, it's bewildering to hear somebody refer to four hours as a long haul. To an American, English clubs always seem to play in the neighborhood, or just down the driveway, much like the New York Giants going to Philadelphia or Washington, just down the pike. I think of the NFL's Seattle Seahawks, who play in Seattle, which rests gorgeously on the top upper left edge of the United States, its existence unknown or mysterious to many Americans. In the 2005–2006 season, the Seahawks pulled off one of the great feats of American athletic history, in my lonely opinion. They went 13–3 and reached the Super Bowl despite their usual eight away trips howling with uncommon distance. They flew 2,456 miles to Jacksonville, 2,329 miles to Washington, D.C., 1,723 miles to St. Louis, 2,380 miles to Philadelphia, 1,975 miles to Nashville, and 1,652 miles to Green Bay. Their breather road trips included the 1,110 miles to Phoenix and the mere 679 miles to San Francisco. You know how, when you finish flying six hours, you usually feel dehydrated and slaughtered of brain cells? You wish to scream or undergo physical therapy or regurgitate? You certainly don't wish to ram into muscular humans anytime within the next two days.

The Seahawks looked wretched in the Super Bowl, but then, they'd had to fly 1,935 miles to Detroit.

London to Newcastle: 249 miles.

I'd imagine that were I nine years old, I'd remember every-thing about my first Premiership away trip, so I tried to remember everything about my first one at age forty-four. After all, the Saturday trains of England qualify as living, breathing animals of their own. They're tubes of passion, songs, and information. You might learn the scores of other matches in other tiers from people who hop on midway. You might hear people lamenting

Coventry or, if you're lucky, extolling Brentford. You might sense that the locomotive itself has a blood alcohol level three times the legal locomotive limit.

From London to Newcastle, I remember the nice woman in the concession area who had run out of many alcoholic products but placed my wine half-bottle into a bag of ice so that I could carry this bag of ice back to my seat and balance it on the tray like I'd just bought a new goldfish. I remember passing through Leeds and thinking I might've been a fan there had I popped in only seven years earlier when Leeds neared the top of the world, and wouldn't that make quite a tale after it had suffered relegation *twice since 2004*? And I remember, as ever, the skylines.

I'd come to recognize the true skylines of England, for they're built not by architects and eastern European construction workers but by drinkers. The skylines of England appear on the tables of trains, and they're often impressive. There'll be a smattering of empty beer cans, forming the veritable Greenwich Village of the skyline, the smaller "buildings." There might be some taller beer bottles, say, an overgrown green Carlsberg can here or there, forming the less ostentatious part of midtown Manhattan. Then the big honchos, the empty wine bottles, the Chrysler Buildings, the Empire State Buildings. All together, these cans and bottles will merge on a table, especially late in the ride, a Hong Kong of consumption. I have seen these configurations on many a train, but never so many as on that train northeast on a Saturday night. I listened to a whole gaggle of men loudly solve the problems of English schools.

I'd never heard about Newcastle before August 2005. Some Americans know that Newcastle sits in northeast England, on the River Tyne, not all that far from the North Sea, pretty close to the nonborder with Scotland, but there aren't many. My soccer guru Tom told me that some people in Newcastle identify with Scotland and might root for Scotland against England in soccer. Centuries ago, England and Scotland conducted tragic wars, whose tragic residue spread across the centuries until they wound up garnering Mel Gibson a Best Director Oscar, thereby attaining their tragic zenith. Many Americans would be interested to note that Tony Blair may or may not hail from the Newcastle area, while many others might like to know that Tony Blair was the prime minister of the United Kingdom for ten years, and that the United Kingdom is a nation across the Atlantic Ocean, and that the Atlantic is the ocean near New England and the Carolinas and Florida. Furthermore, some unfortunate Americans might've seen *Goal!,* the movie about an American who reaches the United States the traditional way—by running across from Mexico in the middle of the night so that his family can provide cheap labor to American businesses and lawn owners—then gets discovered in Los Angeles and winds up playing for Newcastle. This movie leads us to believe that a soccer player's life of rampant sex and partying somehow represents an unwise tack. Our hero winds up scoring a goal on a free kick, but it's unclear whether he wins a trophy for Newcastle because the creators of the movie didn't want to stretch the truth any further than they already had.

They did make a sequel.

Newcastle, as it happens, is a beautiful town with a rowdy vibe. A taxi driver proudly told me it's one of the foremost party towns in Europe, and bully for that. Like Red Sox fans before the Red Sox quenched the eighty-six-year drought in 2004, it is real love with Newcastle fans, I suspect. Their fans bargain with life for a payoff that's larger than anything Manchester United supporters will ever feel. When the drought finally does cease, Newcastle will be the place to be upon the earth, greater than Miami Beach, Rio de Janeiro, and Ibiza combined.

On a chilly, beautiful Sunday with cotton-ball clouds in northeast England, fourth-place Portsmouth played seventeenth-place Newcastle, but I knew better than to trust those placements. I don't remember much about the match except that I never got the feeling of an imminent three points that go to a victor. The home squad always seemed faster, fresher, perhaps a by-product of the long, long trip down the driveway our squad had made. I get a mental picture of the Portsmouth goalkeeper, David James, sprawling to make superhuman saves. In the sixty-ninth minute, Newcastle's Charles N'Zogbia, on the left, directed a low cross to the center, and Antoine Sibierski tapped it in. The replay showed that Sibierski should've been ruled offside, but I never noticed any need for an offside call and didn't hear any grumbling because I sat so far away from my new brethren, who no doubt could've detected the offside from there to Barcelona. I sat only among people who did stand and cheer lightly as Newcastle went ahead 1–0, and I stood with them but kept my mouth shut, feeling like an unreconstructed dork.

Newcastle won, 1–0, and denied Pompey a shot at third place. In another twenty years, I'll remember probably only one thing from the day, a moment that would never happen in the United States. As I filed out among throngs of Newcastle fans, behind me there sang a single young-adult, male voice. He kept repeating his chorus in his own made-up tune:

He's big, he's French,
He's often on the bench,
Antoine, Antoine.
He's big, he's French,
He's often on the bench,
Antoine, Antoine.

This guy had thought up his own song about Antoine Sibierski, and he had decided to sing it to all the unsuspecting, exiting masses. He did not care who listened. He did not care to try out for *X Factor,* the British version of *American Idol.* He just sang. We don't have this too much in the United States. We should. Give us another 849 years of existence, and we just might.

13

THE BEST GOAL
IN MY ADMITTEDLY
LIMITED LIFETIME

On Saturday, December 9, 2006, on the south coast of England, not far from the English Channel, at Fratton Park, in the fourteenth minute, Kanu chased the ball nearing midfield with his back to the Everton goal. Everton's Simon Davies chased the ball from the other direction. Davies slid toward Kanu. They converged. As they headed toward opposite sides of each other from where they'd started, both touched the ball, and the ball popped upward, hard to tell just how. It floated lazily over to the right and descended toward Portsmouth's Matthew Taylor, forty-five yards from the Everton goal. Before it could hit the ground, Taylor struck it with his left foot and sent it back upward. I thought he'd struck it casually, almost goofily. I thought he'd struck it in one of those see-what-happens modes. It flew high and flew toward me as I sat in the fifth row behind my fellow American Tim Howard, manning the Everton goal. It sailed to its pinnacle and then gravity beckoned. Here it came, just beginning its descent toward Fratton Park soil, still two-thirds of the way airborne, when there came an instant that would have to rate as one of the best instants you can know upon the earth.

Now, in the interim since I had made my inept away debut, Portsmouth had drawn—which means "tied" in American English—with both Liverpool and Aston Villa. The goal-less draw at Anfield in Liverpool on November 28 had seemed particularly impressive, coming only two nights after the trip to Newcastle. It became the first goal-less draw I ever regretted missing because I, like thousands of other people, just about yearn to see a match at Anfield, and because I, like thousands of other people through the decades, hadn't gotten a ticket. So I still craved a Pompey moment, some game or chunk of game that 19,527 strangers and I could witness together and find unforgettable. A penalty in the eighty-ninth minute against a gritty Watford squad didn't count, no.

So as I still sort of fidgeted with this whole idea of adopting a club, and as I pretty much shrugged at Matt Taylor's ball even as it began its downward slope, the very next instant ranks among the best in a thousand stadiums. I refer not to any moment when the ball thudded to earth, but to an instant when the ball remained airborne. The instant took maybe a hundredth of a second. Wonderful, delectable, available only in the flawed domain of sport, this instant qualified not only as a Pompey moment of a rare kind, but as a Planet Earth moment of a rare kind.

No keen judge of trajectory, and in just my sixth game as an avowed Pompey fan, I had this sudden synapse zip across my brain. It went something like this: *Why, that thing's just about to dive down behind Howard's back and into the goal, and that's about to become the damnedest goal you're probably ever going to see in your whole damned misspent life.*

The instant itself seemed elongated, marvelous, and, no surprise, quiet. It might've been that moment of mass inhalation writ large. I'm fairly certain I threw a gasp in there, but I didn't hear it. It's as if time gave you an extra second there so that you could sense 19,528 people realizing something and maybe 17,000 of them relishing it while the 2,000 or so visitors found it dreadful. It stands out among millions of fellow instants, that instant. Having lived it, I'd just like to wish everyone peace and happiness and one moment in which they see a soccer ball flying precisely from forty-five yards, think little of it at first, lazily monitor its path through the air, notice its descent, and then, somewhere while it's still airborne, become instantly certain it's about to land behind the keeper but in front of the crossbar and in the net.

Why bother with sport?

There's your answer.

Oh, and one other crucial element: it seems helpful if the team you're supporting strikes this ball.

Down the ball dove. By the end, it seemed to have transmogrified to develop eyes and maybe even a little smile, although I couldn't tell. It all but took Howard's legs and tied them into a square knot. He almost couldn't budge. He'd moved too far out to defend this comet, and he looked mildly like a baseball outfielder misjudging a fly ball that sails overhead because he lost it in the lights, and I suppose he looked mildly clumsy, but should we really criticize a goalkeeper for missing something this celestial? I mean, what's the goalkeeper protocol for defending bending forty-five-yard parabolas? I lacked the expertise to know, and I did not *want* the expertise to know.

I just know that as the ball came down behind Howard's lofty body, I spotted the moment when it occurred to him that the gig was up, the play was over, the goal was scored. I saw his body twitch and then try to contort and then relax in concession. I saw him look fairly nonplussed, almost as if something like this happens every once in a while, all the way back to age seven as a tyke in New Jersey. I'd seen something vaguely similar on TV with this Ronaldinho thing for Brazil in the 2002 World Cup in Japan against David Seaman and England, but that happened when I was in New York at a wee hour in a Soho bar and thus could've been an alcohol-induced mirage. Howard seemed less wowed than myself, the neophyte, at how somebody could possibly, without even two seconds to take aim, direct a ball forty-five yards so as to curl over a six-foot-three human being but still just in front of a crossbar. I didn't know for sure, but I thought these players might be even more talented than advertised.

I did know that in the instant that followed my favorite instant, when that thing indeed smacked down and rippled cords in the right side of the net—and to Taylor's left—I got to participate in a mass ecstasy unparalleled on the planet that day. In one swoop, I closed my jaw and bolted upward along with a few thousand strangers in the Milton End and maybe 17,000 strangers in this old rodeo ground, and I got to hop up and down and up and down and up and down, a fine act I presumed bygone in my life, an act people simply don't practice enough. It felt uncontrollable. This had transcended the occasion. In video footage of the goal, I can't necessarily see myself back there, but I can see our entire row going mad. If I slowed down the video and looked carefully, I might well see my own mouth spewing foam.

Meanwhile, Taylor rushed into the near corner like a mad fiend, having just had himself an experience that trumped even ours, that of *generating* such bedlam. And bedlam reigned. Bedlam reigned so much you could sense extra waves forming over on the Channel, and you could fall in love with the old sea town and the old British Navy and the chimes and the drums and the bugle and all Pompey, all at once. Forgive me, but it's not overstating it to say that in that moment I loved England and the Queen and Churchill and the Clash—especially the Clash—all at once. I did not love meat pies, but time remained. Taylor's teammates soon caught up to him for a pileup, and it was all so wonderful that I wondered how the game could proceed.

It did, and we all adjusted to regular life, post-wonder. Well, some of us did. Others of us still felt giddy, if not downright drunk or, in some cases, technically both. The goal played repeatedly on the functioning video screen, and everybody pivoted and looked. At moments it seemed the players could've disrobed and nobody would've noticed. Portsmouth led Everton 1–0, and the segregated Everton section, just a notch over to my left, seemed peeved, as if they couldn't spot the majesty in Taylor's shot. I wondered if seasoned observers saw it as purely lucky. I wondered if, as an American, I relished the goal only because it had a certain bigness. Certainly, I'd rate Argentina's twenty-six pass goal against Serbia and Montenegro in the 2006 World Cup as more skillful and far more impressive, just to name one goal, but something about a howling forty-five-yard masterpiece right in front of you can put you in lucky-to-be-alive mode.

Just before the game, fans had heckled Howard, and he'd held an index finger up to his mouth as if to say, "Shhhhhh," and I found that all plucky and appealing. Now I saw him not only playing with that goal freshly in mind, but with a Portsmouth peppering coming at him. It could've been 4–0 by halftime, and as a signed-on fan, I suppose I should say it could've been 6–0 by halftime. It turned out 2–0 by halftime, and the weird thing was, the second goal qualified as an outright beaut.

Merely twelve minutes after the first goal, Gary O'Neil sent a cross from Howard's left to Howard's right. It went in a line drive—apology for baseball terminology—and it met with Kanu's left foot. Somehow, from the corner of the box, Kanu met this thing on the fly and sent it heading back to his right, where it hurried past a baffled—and hopeless—Howard. There could be no wondering about luck versus skill on this goal, for it was 100 percent skill, 100 percent supernatural familiarity with a ball at the foot—testimony, even, to the childhood soccer games of Nigeria. I felt awed by this goal, Kanu's ninth of the young season, without feeling the intoxicating rush of its predecessor.

The second half played along enjoyably, and David James had to make a few stops, and in a seminal moment some Everton fans to my left somehow spilled out onto the field. I'd never thought of Everton fans as especially rowdy, so it surprised me at first, but I marveled at the speed with which security people collected them and hauled them off to who-knows-where—maybe to some cell with a video screen repeatedly playing Taylor's goal.

Sport ranks among the few things in life that can give you the exhilaration I felt on the walk to the train and on the train ride home. The conductor even allowed some burbling Pompey fan to take the speaker and announce the final score, "Portsmouth two, Everton nil." Pompey stood third in the table, with twenty-eight points. Here I'd signed on to a club partly because of my grand-father's mastery of tugboats and partly because of the dilapidated stadium, but also partly because I thought it might be fun to ride the relegation tightrope, but this club had turned out sort of, I don't know . . . good.

14

I HEAR MY PEOPLE

For Portsmouth's match at Arsenal on December 16, 2006, I showed signs of unmistakable progress since the Newcastle match and sat closer to my people, the blue people. I did not sit *with* my people because my people snapped up all the away tickets either before they became my people or just after they became my people. In so doing, they clearly did not realize they were my people and did not care they were my people, and in general I worried they might not need any more people, or want any more people, especially people who before 2005 had no idea of their existence.

At least my people and I occupied the same tier of the stadium, the lower tier at brand-new Emirates Stadium in North London. At least I could hear my people, who sat in the corner a few sections over to my left, and I could try to decipher my people, such as when they booed Arsenal's adorable little marvel, Theo Walcott, who mysteriously made the 2006 England World Cup team at age seventeen but never graced a pitch. For a millisecond, I could not ascertain or even fathom why. Who on earth would boo Theo Walcott? Isn't he still seventeen? Hasn't he been seventeen for about three years now? What'd he ever do? Did he keep an untidy bench at Germany 2006?

In the next millisecond, I remembered that my people seemed to dislike people who had ever played for some mysterious team called "Southampton," such that it seemed that the Southampton

team must resemble all Lucifer, apparently trafficking in geno-
cide, grand theft, and chronically unseen handballs. We do have
this sort of thing in the United States. I recall a basketball equipment manager for the University of Kentucky, an old teddy bear,
who on the day before the rivalry game would not *occupy the
same gymnasium* as one of the broadcasters from the University
of Louisville. Apparently we Americans once boasted a *Santa
Claus* in Florida—*Santa Claus!*—who tried to dissuade some helpless tot from either Florida or Florida State. We have New York
Yankees fans who, in an unscientific poll outside Yankee Stadium
one night, voted 8–2 they'd rather win zero of the next three
World Series and have Boston win zero than win two of the three
with Boston winning the other.

As sportswriters who do get to see athletes and managers as
human—even if, at times, members of the reptile-human hybrid
subspecies—we tend to make fun of this roiling, frothing, irrational, puerile, bilious, fanatical hatred. This ignores the fact that
without this roiling, frothing, irrational, puerile, bilious, fanatical hatred we'd be unemployed, so I learned to console myself by
noting that releasing the roiling, frothing hatred in a stadium
might just beat all alternatives.

In Emirates Stadium, down near the pitch, I said aloud that I
didn't think I could ever bring myself to boo Theo Walcott.

"Give it time," said my host.

I sat, of course, with Arsenal people, the other people. A
benevolent editor invited me. In the splashy, shiny, brand-new
Emirates Stadium, we occupied the front row, where we could
look upward at the true gods of the age, the plasma TV screens
inside the luxury suites, yet another crucial American contribution to global decadence. The Arsenal people generally regard the
entrenched Portsmouth people like myself as one regards a gnat,
so they teased me and never did strike me with any blunt object.
My host suggested I stand amid these foreign people and cheer
my blue squad whenever appropriate, but I didn't and couldn't,
because I'm from Virginia where we try to keep inconspicuous.

I found the match absolutely riveting, an entire new realm in
soccer viewing, because the field-level view plus the presence of a

big-four club equaled new understanding of the caliber of these athletes.

It's stratospheric.

Other, more seasoned viewers did not find the match quite so riveting, evidence of which I detected late in the first half when the older man next to me fell flat asleep. While marveling at his ability to sleep sitting up among 60,037 when I can't even sleep among 250 on an overnight 767 despite enough wine to deaden a yak, I also understood anew the voluminous tiers of soccer viewers. There are those fumbling through the forest without a flashlight (hello), the mildly curious/somewhat knowledgeable, the knowledgeable, the very knowledgeable, the scarily knowl-edgeable, and then there's this level where you can behold your favorite squad, eleven of the best athletes in the world, and plainly deduce they're having a subpar afternoon while some nitwit next to you sits enthralled.

The guy snored, but only once.

He woke in time to make a wisecrack as I returned from the loo commenting on its immaculate, state-of-the-art loo-ness. He said I thought so probably because we didn't have any loos at de-cayed Fratton Park, and I even got the joke, which I counted as further progress in my seasonal education. It marked the first time I had been personally impugned as a member of my tribe.

I can't remember if he continued snoozing into added time of the first half, because that's when Matt Taylor launched a free kick from the outer-right portion of the pitch I cannot name, and David Thompson's header caromed off the left post to the right, where it found Noé Pamarot, whose header from six yards went high over goalkeeper Jens Lehmann and into the top right corner for a 1–0 lead, Pompey.

I could hear my people exulting even as I remained quiet and gave an infinitesimal fist pump, subtler than subtle, that moved my right five knuckles about one-one-hundredth of an inch. In the strange and inflexible terminology of soccer, Pamarot's goal happened at 45+2, especially weird given Taylor would score at 47. I'm not sure why 45+2 isn't 47, but I try not to ask such things because I yearn to avoid being a nuisance.

I did feel oddly gratified and oddly hopeful at 45+2.

Then, of course, I missed 47 for the aforementioned loo break, giving me my second ill-timed loo break in just two months of fandom. I heard some sort of roar from the corner, and I believe I heard the broadcast piping into the men's room and acknowledging doom. I emerged about to croak with curiosity and spotted a ready concourse video screen, which showed Uncle Harry standing on the sideline with an expression I shall never forget. Shy of a smile but north of a frown, almost concealed but not quite, the expression unwittingly communicated something like this: *Just last January, my squad lost 5–0 at Birmingham, and then just last March we seemed to have secured an unfavorable mortgage in the relegation zone, but we clambered out of that and people called me Harry Houdini, as well they should, and here we're sitting fourth in the table, one point behind Arsenal, and 2–0 at Arsenal, the club I loved as a child.*

I'm not sure, but I think that's what he meant and meant to hide.

He did lead 2–0 because of a sumptuous left-footed volley by Taylor on the left that sang an aria into the right top corner of the goal and no doubt stunned the home crowd into disappointment and quite possibly sleep. I returned to incur the bathroom joke, and not to say I felt any sort of mirth, but the fresh news of Taylor's goal pretty much did light up my soul like all Tokyo. It seemed I cared. It surprised me I cared. I wondered if caring this soon meant we're biologically set up to care and need only a place to plug it in, and I'd happened to plug it in on the south edge of England.

Of course, the problem with caring is that it leaves the door wide open for nervousness, and the problem with that is that when your plucky band of up-and-comers has gone up 2–0 at Arsenal, you're automatically, profoundly nervous. You're getting away with something, and you know it, and you can feel the authorities coming, sirens blaring.

People say the new Emirates Stadium suffers for lack of din, but I do not understand what they mean. It sounded incredible to me. The sound of the urgency and fear streaming from the innards and out of the mouths of 60,037 people (minus, of course, my people) tore into my front-row ears and even provided a glimpse of the real England. Maybe that's because I hail from a nation of relatively quiet stadiums, including one in Arizona where you can view a baseball game from a hot tub. I don't know.

It's just that in the fifty-fifth minute, Arsene Wenger, whom the referee had shipped into the stand as I would learn only when reading the Sunday newspaper, sent in a man named Emmanuel Adebayor. He wore number 25. It grew clear during the ensuing few minutes that Mr. Adebayor probably was the best athlete in the history of the world, with fresh legs to boot. He changed the match utterly and transfused his team's blood thoroughly. After he scored inevitably in the fifty-eighth minute, he retrieved the ball from the net and rushed it back to midfield, anxious to wreak further destruction into our back-pedaling eleven. That gesture had precedent, I'm sure, just not in my experience, and I liked it a lot. What's more, I love the profundity that an American can sit in North London both cheering and fearing the super-human from Togo. It's the world Amelia Earhart envisioned when she forecast, in the early twentieth century, that eventually the entire globe would seem as if one neighborhood.

Mr. Adebayor scored because Theo Walcott went zipping down the right side, with 60,037 people gradually rising section by section as he passed. As the noise built, I thought of the English capacity to see the goal before the goal, because they certainly knew before I did that this loathsome little bastard—sorry, this exemplary young man—figured to skitter that ball across to the danger zone, even if they're not dubiously greenhorn enough to term it the danger zone. As if the ball itself had eyeballs that the cretin Walcott—sorry, that fine young man Walcott—had installed with his foot, the ball dodged two defenders and found its way to Adebayor, who in baseball terminology bunted past a flailing David James.

The crowd began making the most formidable brand of crowd noise in all humanity, that of the home crowd sensing a comeback. Adebayor yanked out the ball and sprinted to midfield. Did we have to continue? Yes, we did, and some two minutes later, well, I may have this slightly mixed up, but I believe every single player on the Arsenal roster, including those from the bench, banged soccer balls in a furious anger at James, who did honorable work to save about twenty-nine of them before Gilberto Silva's low, angled shot toward the left post demanded entry. By my count, that made it 2–2, and the din, even if tame to the seasoned, rattled my intestines large and small.

From ground level, the way Arsenal had attacked its deficit looked very much like science fiction. The Gunners seemed capable not only of outrunning and threatening my blue players but quite possibly of eating them. Impressionistically, Portsmouth began to appear as if it used only nine players, maybe eight. Maybe someone *had* eaten some of them. It seemed so very *28 Days Later*. If I hadn't known we'd reached the twenty-first century in terms of athletic evolution, speed, what-all, I'd have learned it that day. Certainly the score would go to 3–2, almost surely 4–2, quite possibly 5–2, and not-out-of-the-question 6–2. That it ended 2–2 suggested I'd inadvertently chosen a club with moxie.

To the Welsh anthem "Men of Harlech," all Arsenal began singing something I'd yet to hear.

You're not singing,
You're not singing,
You're not singing anymore,
You're not singing anymore.

They sang it to that corner of the stadium to my left, and they sang it to me, but then, technically, I hadn't been singing. I'd been too agreeable to sing during the first half, too nervous during the second, and such a novice anyway that I wouldn't burst into song for one more Saturday.

15

EUROPE

We're all going on a European tour,
A European tour,
A European tour,
We're all going on a European tour,
A European tour,
A European tour,
We're all going . . .

On a dismally dreary December 23 at Fratton Park came the first rewritten "Yellow Submarine" in the challenged life of my eardrums. I thought somebody had just come up with it and had demonstrated a certain puckish cleverness. No, really. As it persisted, I also wondered whether a European tour for Portsmouth meant the next year's UEFA Cup, that semirealistic consolation prize for clubs finishing fourth to seventh, or the next year's European Champions League, that heaven for top-four Premier League clubs. No, really. We all go through different childhoods at different stages on different topics, and this would be my Premiership childhood, imagining Portsmouth could hold down fourth place as of Sunday night, May 13, 2007, the last night of the season.

Back then, who knew for sure? Well, everyone except myself, but on the plus side of my learning curve, I had taken notice of Manchester United's early prowess and pretty much ruled out winning the league. This showed keen acumen. I'd also gazed at

Chelsea and thought second place could prove rather far-fetched. This showed amazing acumen. Europe, however, and all of Europe, seemed freshly possible, even as I felt that old American bafflement from hearing English people say they're going to Europe when we presume they're already there.

Sitting in the rowdy Fratton End for the first time, continuing my sporadic tour of the grand edifice, pressed on the far right side against some sort of decrepit, faded-white, corrugated plastic wall, head next to a steel beam, I came under the impression that my beloved team had become, well, good. That's right: my team was good. I'd chosen a club for reasons that included half-hoping to follow the relegation tightrope, and within two months I'd ended up singing about some European tour. I'd planned to monitor the sludgy chase for seventeenth place and found myself tracking the white-hot run for seventh and fourth. I knew nothing about how or why Pompey had become good and knew not the significance of signing Sol Campbell from Arsenal or David James from Manchester City or Kanu from West Bromwich Albion. About Campbell, I knew only that I presumed with 95 percent certainty he'd scored in the 2006 European Champions League final against Barcelona (true); about James, I knew only that he tried to learn a new word from the dictionary each week, which made me love him pronto; about Kanu, I knew only that he'd scored a bag of goals in the early season, including a scintillating romp at Middlesbrough. I knew nothing of his status as the most decorated African player, nor of the brilliant old Arsenal song that went:

Chim-chiminy chim-chiminy
Chim-chim chiroo
Who needs Anelka when we've got Kanu?

I knew nothing except that whoever came up with that should be proud if not automatically knighted, and yet nine days shy of New Year's Day, and with head and shoulder pressed up against a steel beam, I'd used my whole throat to sing about a European tour. I did not join in singing to referee Graham Poll,

"You woke up / And then you f—— up," because I did not yet know that song and the intricate lyrics simply would require more time. But I wanted this European tour thing. It sounded fun, especially to an American, to whom a European tour often means jetting across the water, tearing through as many countries as possible, talking too loud on metros, complaining about a paucity of ice, making a general nuisance of oneself, and then returning home to settle into a life of quiet desperation.

Under an awful sky so gray it made all other gray blush, through the winter-solstice gloom at this 51 North latitude, where the sun seems to stop by for about ten minutes each day before it whooshes off to somebody else, I sang, and when I sang, I thought European Champions League, not UEFA Cup. I'm an American, and I'm conditioned to expect immediate dominance, not the UEFA Cup, which was so mysterious anyway.

English fans, hailing from an older culture, value fourth place or seventh place and know either can bring fabulous new life experiences in places such as Bucharest or Budapest. American sports differ, of course. In the NFL, by far the top American sport, fourth place is last place, although we do give playoff spots to the best four teams that do not finish in first place. We call those "wild cards," and we used to give out only two of them back when men were real men and you pretty much had to finish first to reach the playoffs, before we started adding more playoffs because more playoffs could give us more money. We had to cope when the number of wild cards grew to four and then six; then we added two more divisions and returned to four wild cards, but we pretty much carried on. By now, because we like to keep things simple, we have eight divisions of four teams each, broken into two four-division conferences. The eight division winners reach the playoffs, as do the two best other teams in each conference. As an American, I sometimes wonder whether the Premiership wouldn't do well by splitting into four five-club divisions, then having four division winners play it off in May. I never suggest this in public, however, so as to avoid the appearance of idiocy.

Having retooled our NFL through the years with only mild

angst, we reserved the full dollop of angst for the alterations of baseball during the mid-1990s. That game, of course, remains in-scrutable to foreign people, such that an immigration agent at the London Waterloo train station once said to me, "I've been watching the baseball, late at night, and what is this thing, the RBI?" I explained the RBI (run batted in) as best I could and never felt more useful to my fellow humankind. Baseball gets credit—especially from itself—as our "national pastime," so a nostalgic resistance movement cropped up when we introduced these "wild cards" during the mid-1990s, because they meant profound change. Baseball went from four divisions with four winners, period, everybody else go home and wait for next spring, to six divisions with six winners plus two wild cards. This fiddled with our innate sense of having to earn something by working hard or by dominating others through hard work, in-timidation, corporate conglomeration, and intimidation from corporate conglomeration. It also meant excruciating change, for the postseason would contain eight teams rather than four. How would we go on if we allowed second-place people into our grand autumn pageant? Could we adjust? Would it mar our fine balance and turn us soft? We wrangled.

I read that Europeans conducted some of the same discus-sions when the European Champions League inflated its number of clubs, but I missed those discussions in a fortuitous turn of luck, as two such discussions in one lifetime might leave a person either incapacitated or yearning for incapacitation.

"We're all going on a European tour . . ."

We weren't in the first half, when even I could glean that our squad looked a mite comatose. Sheffield United served as the vis-itor, and I knew only about four things about Sheffield United. They almost certainly hailed from Sheffield. They'd just won pro-motion last spring. They'd enjoyed a four-game upturn, claiming ten points from a possible twelve to jazz up the match at Fratton. They had a manager, Neil Warnock, whose filter between brain and mouth either had eroded or had come congenitally thin from the get-go. Impolitic thoughts went straight from the mind into the TV microphone and onto the page, and in the American sportswriting business, we have two words for managers like him: "thank" and "you." These people enlighten us and spare us the strain of trying to interpret what coaches might really mean when they say something cryptic, and apparently Warnock had spared a lot of people the guessing game while exhibiting a mad-scientist strain. I don't know whether he embodied the words of Bill Parcells, the legendary NFL coach who famously said that big-time coaches are not healthy humans. I just know that he did not disappoint after Portsmouth versus Sheffield United, when he said he shouldn't comment on Poll and then said, "A referee of Graham Poll's standard should be able to spot it when the ball goes out off a forward's ankle."

His squad had gone ahead 1–0 in only the fourth minute. Down below me and my steel beam and my corrugated heavy plastic and to my left, Derek Geary had made one of the best crosses I'd seen in all my voluminous days following soccer closely. Rob Hulse headed it in from the far post. Fratton Park seemed asleep. The sky seemed to contribute.

By halftime, I figured that if my team indeed rated good, my team would deduce a way to solve this pugnacious Sheffield United threat. Uncle Harry would fire up the troops with something that makes managers "geniuses" in American parlance. Well, forty-eighth minute: goal. And fifty-fourth minute: goal. And sixty-eighth minute: goal. And seventy-eighth minute: almost goal. I read where Uncle Harry had calmly tweaked some things, which to me remained unrecognizable but very effective. I'd say we did what good teams do against upstarts, but I didn't feel qualified to use the word "we."

I enjoyed it all immensely. Benjani Mwaruwari sent a low cross from the right in the forty-eighth minute into that place often called "the area," and Sheffield United's Phil Jagielka's attempt to clear it wound up directing it toward the goal, where Robert Kozluk's attempt to clear it out from Jagielka's attempt to clear it out proved futile and earned him a cruel OG, which is English for "own goal."

Matt Taylor's corner in the fifty-fourth minute came from just beneath me, and I leapt up and dinged my right shoulder on the steel beam when I saw Campbell rise above the defense with that glorious big head primed to connect. The young males around me never did say a word to me, nor I to them, but some stray voice nearby said that would be Campbell's first Portsmouth goal.

The 2–1 lead made me nervous, which made me surprised, but a virtual replica of the previous goal came in the sixty-eighth minute, with Pedro Mendes directing the corner and Noé Pamarot supplying the header. I let out a guttural sort of quasi-roar, proof that fandom can return after two decades of dormancy. Portsmouth had leapt to thirty-two points, six shy of its entire total from 2005–2006, with still the possibility of matching that thirty-eight within the calendar year 2006, and Parcells must be right.

I say that because here we stood, crooning about a European tour, the drum beating, the bugle gasping, just eight months after surviving by four points with the boost of that 90+3 goal on March 11 by Pedro Mendes that Bradley Wright-Phillips almost cleared. It might be the one-millionth example of sport's maddeningly narrow passageways. Yet as these capricious moments in games and seasons decide who wins, they also cement legacies that can grow downright eternal. Parcells himself won two Super Bowls, the first with a worthy mauling, but the second when a difficult last-play field goal attempt from Buffalo's Scott Norwood slid maybe fifteen feet wide to the right. Flutter that ball fifteen feet over, and we see Parcells as still excellent but less cemented. Would we label him great? Not as readily.

Well, here came Portsmouth, seventeenth in 2005–2006, roaring toward its first-ever European Champions League or as consolation its first-ever UEFA Cup. Having shredded Blackburn and Middlesbrough, played well at Chelsea and Tottenham, drawn at Arsenal, and shaken Everton like a rag doll, my team was good. In the recent absence of Lomana LuaLua due to injury, I'd even pinpointed a new "favorite" player. I liked this defender Glen Johnson, who was on loan from Chelsea, even if I felt lost on the vagaries of somebody being "on loan" from somebody else, apparently meaning they'd have to play against their current employer. I sometimes drift toward the sturdy types who seem to do honest, unsung work, and I found Johnson sort of a quiet bulwark who helped see to it that these uppity offenses would not sour Fratton Park's mood. As a grown person, I didn't put his poster on my wall or wait for him at his car or anything, but I did rather like watching him play soccer.

16

AWAY FAN
EXTRAORDINAIRE

On a dismally dreary December 26 in East London, I managed to sit in the away section and applaud the away team. The process of locating the proper gate at West Ham, presenting the ticket, and occupying the away section would fall under the category of mundane for those who emerged from English birth canals. For an American, it's downright nouveau. It laps at the shores of thrilling.

First, I took the Tube. The idea of taking a subway or metro system to the stadium can feel special to an American, even one who has lived in New York. New Yorkers can take the 4, B, or D subways to see the Yankees or the 7 to see the Mets, and those trains lend to the experience a gritty charm and a charming grit. When the left window of the uptown 4 reveals Yankee Stadium shining in the Bronx night, or the outbound 7 turns and pulls up beside Shea in Queens so the whole lit-up construction attacks your eyes, you've grabbed yourself a chunk of magic there. You haven't lived until you've ridden the second car of the 7 subway returning from Shea Stadium in Queens toward Manhattan after the Mets have played the Yankees, treating yourself to the ludicrous barbs that ricochet back and forth between the two sets of fans.

Oh, no, wait, never mind, that part's not all that great.

It's better than driving, though, and other than New York, Boston, Chicago, or Washington, we just lack stadiums embedded in cities with trains that materialize near the gates. The size of the country prevents such gems, as does our unquenchable desire to shower money upon automobile and oil companies. If we travel to Boston in the summer and take the T subway to Fenway Park for baseball, we might return home and rave about it for several days and beam over our T ride as if we've authored the Pythagorean theorem.

To hop on a Tube, then, and to ride a bunch of stops to West Ham, then to proceed down Green Street to Upton Park, feels both phenomenally convenient and borderline Captain Cook. Heading down the street, seeing the many signs in Arabic and marveling at how London became the capital of the world despite its chronic hosting of a cloud convention, I found a sign directing AWAY FANS maybe one block shy of the stadium. This diverted me from the clear and direct route to the stadium and sent me down a street of trademark English row houses. It felt almost like going into quarantine, like I could not be with those other people over there lest I cough on them and give them a bug that would make them develop a man crush on Matt Taylor or start chanting, "I'm Portsmouth till I die." I thought about the people living in those houses, how if I lived in one of those houses, I might get a cup of tea and wave at Aston Villa fans going by, or perhaps invite in some people from Sunderland who would've made an exhausting journey and might be tired, or perhaps buy an audiotape of a large dog and play it and fling open the door just as Arsenal fans happened by.

I figured I'd see much of England there from my window, but I saw nobody on December 26 observing the Portsmouth fans, maybe because they realized Uncle Harry once coached West Ham, but probably because they flatly did not care.

Down the street, around the bend to the right, and up an alley, beside some warehouses and in a concrete, industrial setting that reminded me of northern New Jersey or northwestern Indiana, there stood the away entry gate to Upton Park, amid police officers plus a few police horses. I approached somewhat nervously, slightly wondering if any West Ham fans might stand by and heckle us or perhaps attempt to slug us. That preposterous inkling stemmed, of course, from the old image of English fans still flickering in the brain, a human organ not very adept at banishing old reputations. In the United States, at parties, at dinners, or in casual conversations, Americans routinely label English soccer fans as truculent pugilists, even after twenty years of initiatives that have made England the European model for curbing violence. This misconception is not so surprising, because we Americans don't keep very good track of other countries, partly because we're self-centered but largely because we're too busy working, which, in our defense, did help us invent such boons as the television, as well as such horrors as the television. Besides, regarding English fans as truculent pugilists enables us to indulge in our national pastime of thinking everybody else is so much more frigging crazy than we are.

Nobody spoke to me at the Upton Park away gate—not even a horse—and on I went into the segregated area, surprised to realize we had our own segregated concession stand and our own segregated toilets. I sat among my people and felt like thanking them for letting an interloper sit with them at the cost of merely £26. (Which, in late 2006 exchange rates, is roughly $1,000.) (Not really: about $48.) In gloom that seemed to put a ten-pound dumbbell on the eyelids, we watched as soccer revealed again its vagaries.

Just seven months prior, Portsmouth had celebrated locating the escape hatch, a discovery that happened barely in time. West Ham, meanwhile, celebrated in Cardiff, Wales, where its Hammers played Liverpool in the FA Cup final. West Ham fans, in some cases, probably also celebrated the winning of that FA Cup, what with a 3–2 lead in the ninetieth minute before Liverpool's Steven Gerrard sent a heat-seeking device from about central Dublin into the left side of the net. They'd also finished ninth in the Premiership, eight places ahead of Portsmouth. They liked their squad and their manager. Some Portsmouth fans still regarded Uncle Harry as Judas because he'd returned only twelve months prior from his one-year hiatus in the Hades of Southampton.

When we found them on December 26, they sat eighteenth in the table, their manager had gone already, they had the stress of new foreign ownership, and they seemed rather subdued. Our newly mighty squad further subdued them by pretty much dominating the first seventy minutes and getting two corner-kick, header goals from one Linvoy Primus. I applauded alongside my people and pretended to comprehend the rarity of a Linvoy Primus brace, "brace" being the funky English term for two goals in one match. The goals came from Pedro Mendes corners at 16 and 38 and became Primus's first and second goals since December 2004, a fact I learned the next day. A 2–0 lead at half-time seemed mostly safe, even after a Teddy Sheringham goal in the eighty-first minute left the result at 2–1, and even after the referee announced a whopping four minutes of added time and the woman next to me spoke to me for the first time in the match to say the referee had a serious bias against Portsmouth.

Thereafter, I joined my people in a chant of "Linvoy! Linvoy! Linvoy!" For this curious new English holiday Boxing Day, which is the term for December 26, I got to watch my blue protagonists win while cheering for an admirable and dreadlocked defender from Forest Gate, London, who had toiled his way up after 127 appearances for the lower-division club Barnet. I rode home just a bit giddy and figured this must be how English people withstand the gloomy winter at the 51 North latitude. Football—or soccer. It's really the heart of England.

With three points making a whopping thirty-five, and with zero losses in five matches, Harry Redknapp's Blue Army rolled up north only four days later. On a dismally dreary December 30, 2006, at Bolton, I began jumping up and down uncontrollably in the quarantined upper-deck away section in just the second minute when Andy Cole fed a through ball to Taylor, and Bolton goalkeeper Jussi Jaaskelainen headed out, and Taylor sidestepped Jaaskelainen and scored for a sudden 1–0 lead after only seventy-two seconds against a good squad that hadn't allowed a goal in four matches. I found my reaction strangely involuntary. It was official: I had become somewhat the person I had belittled for years, the fan for whom the caprices of games could prompt helpless hopping. Bolton sat fourth in the table, tied in points with third-place Arsenal. Three points would catapult fifth-place Portsmouth over Bolton and, as it happened when Arsenal lost at Sheffield United, into third place. As we sang about the European tour within the first five minutes, I began to think of my team as not only good but very good. I began tabulating the points and envisioning the thirty-eight, all but adorning my head with a flashing red light of naïveté.

I had ridden the train from the city center with a Pompey couple from Scotland. Using that surely tiresome refrain "Now, in the United States, . . ." I'd noted that, now, in the United States, we'd never had a situation in which a coach left heaven for hell but then came back to heaven. The woman said England had never had such a situation either. There in the distance sat the Reebok Stadium, which dates all the way back to 1997 and feels American. It's shiny with shiny ads. It's suburban and sits next to a giant strip mall with a McDonald's in the middle of the parking lot. The strip mall floods with cars on a Saturday—or at least the last Saturday of the year. Like all strip malls, it's ugly, and it made me wish some other country had invented the strip mall.

Rain fell wrathfully.

Inside, in the spiffy new stadium, the visitors at Bolton occupy an upper deck, completely warded off from the Bolton supporters across a divide and down lower. A visiting fan could venture into the home section only by flying trapeze. I had a beer and my first-ever sausage roll, which did not kill me and might not have even wounded or impaired any organs. I chatted with a Pompey fan who'd stayed in the hotel inside the stadium and found it pleasant. Out in the stadium, a roof protected us from the monsoon that turned parts of the field to slop and turned the sky at one point into a sickly shade of green. Some 22,447 of a possible 28,723 showed up, and I had a whole row to my right on which to hop up and down if necessary. Up 1–0, Pompey began a thoroughly enjoyable sequence of the best passing I'd yet seen, keeping the ball away from Bolton in skillful midfield sequences. Maybe my squad qualified not only as very good but as excellent.

Then Portsmouth goalkeeper David James whiffed on a Gary Speed corner at thirty minutes, resulting in Abdoulaye Faye's equalizing header, and James made a marvelous save on Kevin Davies at forty minutes, but Ivan Campo headed in the rebound for 2–1, and Sol Campbell inadvertently deflected a Davies cross toward the goal at sixty-two minutes, whereupon James deflected but Nicolas Anelka followed for 3–1. Campo garnished his goal with a festive slide.

Two songs I'd never heard summarized my trip back to Pompey earth.

The Bolton fans serenaded us to the tune of the Village People's "Go West" with:

> *One-nil, and you f—— it up*
> *One-nil, and you f—— it up . . .*

And in return we sang "Guantánamera" with:

> *Sing when you're winning . . .*
> *You only sing when you're winning . . .*

I loved that song, but I loved especially the sights I beheld after Cole scored beautifully in the eighty-ninth minute but Bolton stayed in front and won 3–2. First, recognizing James's rare error but reminding him he belonged to us, we chanted him a rendition of "England's number one, England's, England's number one," meaning number-one goalkeeper. This beat to shards the American habit of booing the losing team.

Then, after a visit to the remarkably plush men's room of Reebok, I heard noise still going outside, so I walked back out through the tunnel. There, at the top of the visitors' section, with the home section already emptied, a row of young Portsmouth fans remained at the top of the stadium, entertaining themselves and the ushers. Somehow, in the gloom of a latitude above 50 and above Montreal, on the day of a deluge that really could've marked the end of time, next to a strip mall, after a defeat, they continued chanting and singing and dancing. A young man of maybe twenty-two, shirtless in the cold, played the drum. It looked like a mix of defiance and buoyancy and maybe even, if I may, celebration that we're alive and we get to watch soccer on a Saturday in a good country.

From fans who'd allegedly just lost, it trumped anything I'd ever seen.

17

THE DISTINCT HORROR OF
RAIL REPLACEMENT

An inherent guilt bit me occasionally early on, for I had not suffered for my club. I had not cringed as it fell to the third-tier league in 1961, although I did have the ready excuse of not having been alive at the time. I did not wail as it tumbled again to the third tier in 1976, and I'd completely missed out on the oblivion that followed, between 1976 and 1980, years that included a dip into the unspeakable fourth division. Most Americans don't even realize there's a fourth division, and many would probably believe that Satan resides there, even if Satan does not but the Milton Keynes Dons do.

That dreadful sequence in the late 1970s when the club had to raise £25,000 from fans to avert bankruptcy? I missed that.

I'd missed Portsmouth's astonishing ascent from the fourth division all the way to the first within nine years and its qualification for the top shelf under manager Alan Ball in 1987. And then, resolutely failing to suffer when the 1987–88 team went smack back down, I missed that year, even though that team featured the first American to play in the Premiership, John Kerr, who had played soccer at Duke and would, remarkably, ascend to play four matches in the top division for Pompey.

That one season in the first division bled into fifteen seasons in the second, a time I spent not cursing or suffering or yelling at inept referees who couldn't spot handballs, but gallivanting through life watching sports with forced *objectivity*, unaware of either Portsmouth or Southampton, or that Portsmouth functioned chronically below Southampton, which set up shop up top.

I knew neither the significance of twenty-seven nor the significance of forty-five. While that kindly man at West Bromwich Albion had explained that remarkable Sunday in 2005, the one on which West Bromwich fans cheered for West Bromwich, but Portsmouth fans also cheered for West Bromwich so as to relegate Southampton, only lately had I picked up on the fact that the day curtailed a twenty-seven-year top-division residency for Southampton. Only even more lately had I read the fact that these events placed Portsmouth in a division above Southampton for the first time in forty-five years.

No Southampton fan had ever behaved obnoxiously to me during those forty-five years, mostly because I had never met any Southampton fan, nor even come across any Southampton fan, at least not knowingly. No, I just hummed along and showed up just in time to inhabit the top ten and sing about a European tour. Where many a Pompey fan had mastered the art of seething, I had seethed almost too minimally to mention—really, only when the Bolton fans informed me and others that we'd had one-nil and we'd f—— it up. I couldn't be sure the Pompey throng should let me wear the sprightly yellow crescent of the club insignia, given my wholly unused seethe-o-meter.

Well, on a pristine January 1, 2007, in southern England that soon developed clouds and then rain that turned rapidly biblical, I decided that I had suffered for my squad, for I had endured rail replacement. Rail replacement occurs when there's engineering or construction work on a certain segment of tracks, and the rail companies provide buses to carry passengers to the in-between stations the train temporarily cannot access. There's no discount for rail replacement, and while I'm not qualified to call for a discount given my noncitizen status, I do believe it wouldn't be too much to ask that the bus service provide free cocktails. For my ride to and from Fratton Park for the New Year's Day bout with Tottenham Hotspur proved particularly harrowing.

I'd ridden rail replacement before, but for some reason this would be the more extensive rail replacement, fanning out into the Hampshire countryside, or the real England to American eyes. I saw the greenest green, the gumdrop villages, the movie-set pubs. I saw a horse in a pasture wearing a nice blanket, the charming houses that looked like the Kate Winslet character's in a wretched movie I'd just seen. On the sidewalks I noticed a decided lack of vomit as compared with London, which had just wrapped up its annual New Year's Eve bacchanal, an evening somewhat distinguishable from the bacchanal of its other 364 annual nights. The rail replacement reached Haslemere. It made it to Liphook. It accessed Liss. I believe we did see Midhurst. Since I began riding trains from London to Fratton, I'd always sort of wanted to see both Liphook and Liss, just preferably not with the clock going tick-tock, tick-tock, tick-tock at 2:08 PM before a 3:00 PM kickoff. The bus, in fact, seemed to stop everywhere, and it seemed to discharge passengers who all seemed to have a clue of their whereabouts, so that soon, on New Year's Day in the countryside heading supposedly for the grit of Fratton Park, I became the only passenger. That's right, I had my very own rail replacement service, just myself in the next-to-last row on the left, staring out the window of a huge bus, and the driver, way, way up ahead. I thought to go ask the driver if perhaps we'd reached the end of the line and he had not seen me back there and he was in the process of driving the bus to park it maybe up in, say, London. But I'm male and from Virginia, so I could not bear to ask this question and risk the you're-an-idiot look on his face when he'd tell me I might be able to make it to Fratton by injury time. Besides, this driver, in his clear and ongoing tryout for Formula One, took the traffic circles with such dispatch that I did not wish to distract him. I merely read my newspapers and learned that the Premiership season had just entered the transfer window and that Sol Campbell might just leave. I felt puzzled and thought, *You mean, he can just leave if he wants? Just up and leave?*

Now, in the United States, if a player's still under contract, he can leave, but only if he asks for a trade, and then the club provides the trade. In a trade, his club would send him to another club in exchange for something from that other club. That might be one player of similar quality. It might be two players of lesser quality. It might be five players who pretty much suck at the professional level. Or it might be one pretty good player plus one horde of cash. Or it might be one really good player plus twenty free plane tickets to Maui with a venal congressman from the club's district.

Or, commonly, it might be for future "draft picks," as I several times tried to explain to English fans, who somehow have abided long and full lives without an NFL draft, let alone any other draft of any kind. Explaining to them this bizarre ritual, noting that the Cowboys and Vikings exchanged a record eighteen players and draft picks in October 1989, an American can begin to wonder how the English fill silent air with conversation. Somehow, they've constructed an entire, successful society without giving people a chance to sit in bars and think up prospective trades or call radio shows and suggest trades so preposterously unrealistic that you believe these people should not have the right to vote.

Finally, we merged onto the M3 highway, which seemed pointed toward Portsmouth, and I felt relieved.

Next, we exited from the M3, and went to Havant, and I felt stressed.

It was 2:20 by now, and I saw a little sign indicating HAVANT TOWN FOOTBALL CLUB, and I wondered if perhaps Havant Town Football Club might have a match beginning at 3:00, so I could simply go and see that. I saw a card shop called Havant Forgotten, and I just hoped the driver Havant forgotten to go to Fratton Park at some point during the afternoon.

A young woman joined the bus at Havant, an encouraging sign that the bus line still operated. I thought of my friend and

fellow sportswriter Pat Forde, and how we each often would uti-
lize the phrase "my ineptitude," and how it's a good feeling in life
to embrace this ineptitude, luxuriate in the ineptitude, stop fighting the ineptitude, and accept one's own ineptitude for its in-
evitability. Example: In 1995 the Cleveland Indians made the
World Series for the first time in forty-seven years, so that all the
Cleveland fans with tickets and all the Cleveland fans without
tickets and all the people pretending to be long-suffering Cleveland fans, all converged upon Cleveland and rented hotel rooms.
As we'd often collaborate on travel plans, Pat asked me on the
day before we left for Cleveland if I'd made a hotel reservation,
and I said no, and I asked him, and he said no, and so we spent
the Cleveland part of the World Series not in Cleveland but in
eastern Ohio way over near Pennsylvania, in a fine and clean hotel of a forested rusticity where on the walk from the car to the
building we actually risked being gnawed to death by ravenous
squirrels.

Finally, as the bus driver continued on his determined path
toward a spot on the McLaren Racing Team, I could spot the
swamps of Fratton, the marooned boats in the mud off to the left.
I could see in the distance on the Portsmouth skyline the large
white Spinnaker Tower, the United Kingdom's tallest structure
outside London, and there stood the majesty of Fratton Park, its
lights shining even in the gathering afternoon darkness and menacing cloud assembly of 2:52 PM, with some bulbs, as usual,
refusing to participate.

That rail replacement ride, almost interminable, only preceded another rail replacement ride, the one from the stadium all
the way back to Guildford before hopping the train to London.
I began to ponder that if the first, nervous rail replacement ride
constituted a suffering that might equal, say, one-half of one season in the second division between 1988 and 2003, the rail replacement ride back to Guildford might just entitle me to claim
I'd suffered the equivalent of an entire season in the fourth division between 1978 and 1980. This particular rail replacement
roared through the side roads of southern England on some sort
of different trek from before, and in the dark. It doubled as a re-

frigerated car in which somebody could've successfully stored raw seafood. I realized my new year had begun riding a moving meat locker, and I thanked lucky stars I don't believe in omens. From my perch on the second level, I could see my exhalations. No, really. When an American sports-lover can see his exhalations, he immediately thinks of glorious old NFL films from the 1960s and 1970s, of games in, say, Minneapolis, where players exhaled out through their helmets in big and wonderful bursts of smoke, before we really grew obsessed with comfort and installed in Minneapolis a climate-controlled dome.

This thought of the old NFL often charms us, unless we're on a rail replacement bus.

Worse, every once in a while, some tree would reach out from the side of the road and smack this bus, causing me brief and damaging heart palpitations for which I'll pay later in life. After about three of those, I started to think maybe I qualified to claim one season of fourth-division suffering plus another half-season of third division, perhaps from the early 1980s. The bus seemed to move on for hours, too speedy to be safe but still somehow well south of London. England had seemed to expand geographically. I began to think that for fairness given the exorbitance of train fares, it should drop off each of us at our homes. Finally, we made it onto a train where I overheard some aged Tottenham fans discuss the insouciance of Americans, one even having heard an American mispronounce the "Petula" in "Petula Clark," emphasizing the first syllable ("PET-u-la") rather than the second (the proper "Pet-U-la"). I quietly had to agree that anyone mispronouncing a concept as great as Petula Clark would seem lost in the world, but mostly I felt relieved that my hands had thawed.

In between those two rail replacement penances for past sins, Portsmouth did draw 1–1 with a very good Tottenham club to reach thirty-six points. Portsmouth's Benjani Mwaruwari had scored with somewhat of a fluke at twenty-nine minutes, the ball ricocheting off Tottenham's Callum Davenport, and then one of the greatest names in sports history, Steed Malbranque, had tied the game for Tottenham off a pretty Danny Murphy cross at fifty. Portsmouth's Mr. David James himself had preserved the one point with Spiderman saves on Jermain Defoe and Tom Huddleston. But mostly attention hovered over a play when Noé Pamarot inadvertently kicked Tottenham midfielder Hossam Ghaly and some of Ghaly's teeth flew out. Television replays treated us to slow-motion views of the teeth flying out, and it heartened me to know my country did not stand alone in obsession with violent images.

That idea that you can occupy the southern edge of England during a monsoon while a Zimbabwean athlete scores for the home side, a Belgian-born French athlete scores for the away side, and a French athlete accidentally kicks an Egyptian athlete to cause the ejection of several teeth astonishes me to no end. It almost makes rail replacement joyous . . . but somehow does not quite.

18

AN FA CUP DEBUTANT

If you're an American experiencing your first FA Cup third round—that's the tournament that runs concurrently with but separate from the Premier League season—there's always the chance your new club might play some wee club with the kind of magical name that renders us Americans simply aflutter with romantic thoughts. It could be something like Crewe Alexandra, which upset Chelsea in the third round in 1961, or maybe Grimsby Town, which beat Middlesbrough in the third round in 1989, or the phenomenal Kidderminster Harriers, which beat Birmingham City in the third round in 1994, or Shrewsbury Town, over Everton in 2003, third round. Just one January before my debut, Fulham had lost to Lleyton Orient, and I'd been agog upon arrival reading the tables and finding a team called "Lleyton Orient," a name that suggested some sort of far-flung wonderland, and in fact it does exist in some far-flung wonderland, called London.

For my first FA Cup third-round viewing experience, I got Wigan.

This did give me a chance to sort of reunite with my fellow Wiganites from the Sunderland match of 2005, and as I saw them in the distance, I noticed they numbered about 99, or maybe 101, or maybe 103. When I counted I kept getting confused, as some people seemed to be returning from the loo.

On a dismally dreary January 6, 2007, on the southern edge of England, Portsmouth played Wigan. Fratton Park filled only to about two-thirds capacity, at 14,336, because people often use early-round FA Cup matches to delve into money-saving mode, seeing as how they don't count in the Premier League standings. The Milton End remained so empty that for the first time I could see that its seats spelled out blue letters, "P" and "F" and "C." I chose a ticket in the North Stand so that I could claim the full dinner set of stands. We got under way in a drizzle. Fratton Park seemed beset with a large helping of ennui. The match felt sloppy, whether it was or wasn't. It seemed to occur in a lower gear. There seemed no urgency from the players, really. I couldn't blame the players for fatigue after that Christmastime schedule that had worn out even myself and forced me into questionable eating habits that led to the sausage roll.

Now, if I could grasp this correctly, it seemed the FA Cup third round had engendered romanticizing through the years, but that the romance had begun to ebb owing to the growing presence of, well, money, which has been known to ebb some romanticizing on this planet. Indeed, the four Goliath clubs (Manchester United, Chelsea, Arsenal, and Liverpool) had won every single FA Cup since 1995, such that it seems downright misprinted when you look at the list and see that Wimbledon won in 1988. Money changes everything, as sang the Brains and, in remake, Cyndi Lauper. Why, just look at New Year's Day in the United States. We used to spend it wondrously inert and watching university football teams play bowl games. The day brimmed with wonder, and the games had storybook names like the Cotton Bowl, the Rose Bowl, the Orange Bowl, and the Sugar Bowl. To a foreign person, this can sound all weird and maybe even drug-induced, but of course it's downright inspired. Then we learned we could make a lot of money by taking the top game and moving it to another date, say, January 3 or January 4 or even January 8, where it could stand alone free of viewing competition. New Year's Day went—sigh—from plum to precursor. It has just about flatlined. Yet on January 4, 2006, for example, 35 million

Americans, more than one-ninth of the national population, tuned in to watch Southern California play Texas.

It's a given and a cliché and often a sigh that money keeps blurring the traditions on us, but for me, I'd missed the FA Cup past, so the FA Cup present felt fresh. Enthralled as the day began, I took a sheet of paper like a child again and made myself a chart of the thirty-two matches slated for the weekend, and I found the concepts pretty darned romantic, what with gigantic Chelsea playing wee Macclesfield Town and so on. But there's something else about sporting romance: once you start labeling something romantic and considering it romantic and talking about how romantic it can be, you're automatically straining, and there goes your romance. Sports coverage comes to resemble business coverage, a dreary adversity we thought we'd escaped by seeking sports coverage. I adored the NFL draft as a child for its faraway mystical quality, but then people began analyzing it for weeks ahead of time and televising it for two days, in which we learned how much (yawn) money a draftee would expect, how much of that might be (zzzz) signing bonuses, just about everything but his pharmaceutical cycles. By now, people who follow it for two days probably need some sort of sabbatical or Berlitz course or maybe even a shower. Speaking of business, Chelsea defeated Macclesfield Town by 6–1.

At Fratton Park, things proved much more taut, as the teams slogged away to a 0–0 halftime, and sometime early in that second half I began to have my first-ever conversation at a Portsmouth game with a person next to me, an affable middle-aged woman named Mary. We began with the weather, which had brightened somewhat. Within moments, I feared I had begun to disrupt Mary's viewing experience by repeatedly asking questions about Pompey as her husband watched from her other side. Even while I'd sort of figured this out already, she kindly explained to me that the term "Scummers" applied to Southampton players, Southampton managers, and Southampton fans, and she did not say this, but I reckoned also Southampton trainers, masseurs, water personnel, residents, and the distant family members of Southampton residents. She spoke of this term "Scummers" with such a detached bemusement that I felt sure she never used it in daily life, even as she loved her Pompey and felt gratified to have taken the £2,000 gamble on season tickets way back in second-division days. She sounded almost like an excellent tour guide, explaining that many people in this area used the term "Scummers" while I imagined listening with a set of earphones to be returned at the exit.

As an American, it did rather mar my bliss that Portsmouth did not play Southampton every year, seeing as how they're only seventeen miles apart, so I asked Mary if it wasn't a shame that Portsmouth and Southampton didn't play each other unless occupying the same league among the four divisions, which seldom has happened, or unless drawn together in the FA Cup or League Cup. I was raised on knowing that twice per year the Redskins will play the Cowboys or the Steelers will play the Browns, or that twice or more per year Duke will play North Carolina, or that eighteen times per year (too many for national health) the Yankees will play the Red Sox. I know it's the second Saturday in October without looking if Texas plays Oklahoma in football, and that it's early December when USC plays UCLA in football, and that the winter solstice is coming in a minute or has just now arrived when Kentucky plays Louisville in basketball. We can feel and taste Thanksgiving on those November Saturdays when fans flock to college stadiums to indulge in intra-state or neighboring-state contempt in a gorgeous national symphony of hatred.

Mary answered that, no, it would be a terrible idea to have Portsmouth play Southampton every year, and that she hoped Southampton would remain in the second division, even as it had clambered to fourth place at the time, a threat to gain promotion. I could hear in her words and her voice that this had nothing to do with wishing ill and damnation and cholera upon Southampton. To understand this, she said, I'd have to have seen the last time Portsmouth played Southampton in the Premiership, which would've been April 24, 2005. That day found the "South Coast Derby" at a pitched pitch because Uncle Harry returned to Fratton Park as the Southampton manager, and the mood resembled the ninth concentric circle of hell. I said I'd like to have seen such a thing, and she cautioned me in an almost motherly way that I would not have liked to have seen such a thing. She told tales of riot police and bad vibes and traffic hassles due to the riot police and the bad vibes. Later, I'd read Henry Winter's account of Portsmouth's 4–1 victory from the *Daily Telegraph*: "Two SAS minders guarded Redknapp while another in close attendance wore a jacket marked 'FBI,' which seemed to give this little, local dispute an unexpected global significance." I hadn't even known that Portsmouth played Southampton in the FA Cup itself in January 2005, or that Southampton had won 2–1 on a Peter Crouch penalty, or that Peter Crouch once had played for Portsmouth. I knew Peter Crouch only as the Liverpool player who scored a World Cup goal for England by yanking himself upward using the dreadlocks of Trinidad and Tobago's Brent Sancho just as I had begun to wonder how England might respond the next day should its national team draw 0–0 with Trinidad and Tobago in a World Cup. Thank goodness Brent Sancho wears dreadlocks.

Mary, by now a gem in my book, also told of another FA Cup match, a quarterfinal at Fratton Park in 2004 won 5–1 by Arsenal. She edified me with the common knowledge that Thierry Henry, the French scoring maestro who starred for Arsenal, had become a Fratton Park favorite that day because he admired the home support and concluded by donning a Portsmouth shirt. She said he'd missed two primo goal chances and that the Fratton End had responded with a rendition of "Henry Is a Pompey Fan." She said Portsmouth fans had remained raucous to the end, and while I'd been amazed at Bolton when that row of devotees played drums and danced after the gloomy fact of 3–2, it floored me that a group could sustain support at 5–nil against, dreaming of 5–1, singing about winning 6–5.

I felt actually proud.

As we engaged in the taboo of chatter, Portsmouth seemed bound for a 1–0 win and a place in the fourth round. Andy Cole had gathered a cross from Sean Davis and scored in the sixtieth minute. Then, shockingly, in the eighty-third minute, Wigan's Lee

McCulloch scored to equalize, and Wigan players exulted before the sparse section of some of the hardiest fans extant, Wiganites who'd travel all the way south down the country and clear to Fratton for an FA Cup third-rounder.

I briefly wondered what happens when teams tie each other in the FA Cup, and then I remembered that they play a rematch at the other ground, but just when I thought about a grand return to Wigan, walking past the strip malls near the stadium and feeling proud of such ambitious American architecture, Pompey utterly willed itself a goal. My man Glen Johnson—warrior!—sent a seeing-eye cross from the far right to Kanu, and Kanu headed in the winner. In injury time. To raucous cheers. And a whistle. And the fourth round of the FA Cup.

19

CHEERING FOR A
TOILET-SEAT THIEF

On a globally warmed Al Gore January Saturday, the twentieth, under blue skies with cotton-ball clouds, on the 1:00 PM train eighty-eight miles from London Waterloo station south to Fratton, as men out the train window struck golf balls in shaggy fields, I dug into my usual pile of English newspapers and soon felt gloomy.

In my daily study of a league I'd just discovered, I'd somehow missed that the vile Ben Thatcher, the one who tried to maul our Pedro Mendes back in August at Manchester City, had transferred from Manchester City to Charlton. Seeing as how Charlton would visit Portsmouth that very day, I would have the honor of watching Ben Thatcher play soccer when actually nobody should have to watch Ben Thatcher play soccer anymore in 2006–2007, or for that matter 2007–2008, or maybe even 2008–2009. As a balm for this indignity, I would get to stand among my people as they gave Thatcher "stick," which is English for "taunting," "derision," "profanity," or "bad vibes."

Here, Ben Thatcher had relocated to Charlton when I'd hoped for his relocation to Vladivostok. Thus, I had boarded the train at Waterloo unaware I'd be paying to see somebody who shouldn't have been in the league for at least another year after battering Pedro Mendes. How depressing. What a chore, being a fan. You're just trying to get away and have a good day, and you have to pay money to see somebody who did something depressingly creepy. Many times you have to cheer him, as would Charlton fans that day.

Ah, yes, here came the old cheering-the-indefensible routine. I'd witnessed it in volumes. My thoughts turned to University of Nebraska fans, from the heartland, anointed the American breadbasket of law and order and decency. The awesome 1995 Nebraska team, possibly the best ever, won all twelve of its games and annihilated previously unbeaten Florida 62–24 for the national championship.

That team also saw six of its one-hundred-odd players receive special attention from the police, most prominently a gifted running back who got mad at his girlfriend and dragged her down a stairwell by her hair. It remains the textbook case of fan bewilderment because of its tough-on-crime conservative fans who yet believe deeply in the liberal rehabilitation potential of misguided young men so long as these men can gain one hundred yards on a Saturday and help us beat those bastards from Oklahoma or Colorado or Missouri.

So when the university first dismissed the player, Lawrence Phillips, then reinstated him in the subsequent month, many Nebraska fans felt uncomfortable, but the overall misgivings decreased as the victory total increased. The applause reached din level at the championship game, in which the player excelled. Nebraska's God-fearing, conservative, revered coach, Tom Osborne, handled things abominably, then got elected to Congress in a landslide. There's a chance they elected him because they noticed his impropriety and deemed Congress the best place for him, but that chance is probably remote.

As I rode toward Fratton Park for the privilege of paying £35 to watch a thug, I sensed the match's aftermath might bring an added wretchedness. If England were anything like the United States, the aftermath might subject us to a manager moaning on about what his player had "been through," or if not moaning, then expressing some sort of quasi-manly respect for how the player had "handled" his adverse situation.

There's a word for that: ugh.

Now, if you ask a reasonable human, which means not a coach or manager, most would agree there's a justice in a player getting grief for having, just for example, gratuitously attacked a player on the opposing team. Most would agree the grief rate doubly justified if the offender happened to receive, say, a paltry penalty. Further, a great many would agree that fans put up with enough crud without having to listen to some craven manager moan about the player enduring "adversity" when the "adversity" would fall under the heading of "self-created."

Still, I dared to read on, risking untold grimness, which magically did arrive.

The Guardian reported that Lomana LuaLua, my first favorite Portsmouth player, had spent the previous Thursday night in the Port Solent police station near Portsmouth after his arrest on suspicion of causing bodily harm, and that it marked his second arrest emanating from apparent disputes with his fiancée, the first having come in October and having remained unknown to my clueless self.

Yes, the road from objectivity back to fandom lies pockmarked with many a garish sight. You might adopt a favorite player. You might like his biography, his will, his gymnastic capability, his recovery from malaria even if the malaria resulted from forgetting medication. Then you might see that the police detained him once, but you might invoke the old American saw "innocent until proven guilty." Then you might see that the police have detained him for a second time, whereupon it becomes possible to grow squeamish and feel conflicted, when feeling conflicted is not fun and fun would seem high among the reasons to follow this stuff, even if we'd have no idea what else to do with our time otherwise.

That's a lot to digest on a Saturday at one-thirty in the afternoon.

Still, I dared to read on more, risking still more untold grimness, which magically did arrive.

On the surreal details of three days prior at a B&Q store (think Home Depot), every newspaper had reported, and really now, who wouldn't? It seemed that on the previous Wednesday at the B&Q in Dartford, near Portsmouth, Glen Johnson, my new favorite Portsmouth player, had conspired with friend Ben May, who played for Millwall in the third division, in a foiled attempt to steal a toilet seat. Awash in cleverness, they had taken an upscale—even posh—toilet seat, stashed it into the box of a cheaper brand and proceeded to checkout, where they received a fine of eighty pounds (about $155 at the time).

Seeing this astonishment first in *The Guardian,* I went flinging into my other newspapers, because you just can't know enough about a rich dim bulb trying to steal a toilet seat. I wondered as to Johnson's weekly salary. Reports had it at £30,000. I wondered whether the Dartford B&Q possessed CCTV equipment, which could deepen the profundity of the stupidity. It did possess CCTV equipment. I wondered how the store discovered this toilet-seat thievery by a guy making £30,000 per week. An employee told reporters, "We all recognised Johnson. No one could quite believe that a bloke like him, with all that money, would be moronic enough to nick a toilet seat. They were spotted by one of our security guards, a chap of 74, and cops arrived as they were trying to leave." The employee indicated that the two nitwits grinned and giggled when questioned by authorities.

In one swoop, I'd read that my first favorite player might've endangered his partner, and I'd read that my second favorite player had attempted to steal a toilet seat by placing it in the box of a cheaper toilet seat. I'd realized I rode a train on a perfectly good Saturday to see a thug (Thatcher), a toilet-seat thief (Johnson), and an alleged fiancée-abuser (LuaLua), and I gave thanks that the alleged fiancée-abuser apparently would not play because of injury. The last residue of my old anti-fan snobbery turned to dust and yielded to a fresh respect for this durable subspecies, the fanatic, who persists despite being put upon and overcharged and made aware that often he has placed his fervent and heartfelt hopes in the hands of a bunch of lunkheads (or worse).

It's not an easy plight, and it doesn't seem to get any easier over time . . . but I figure you must try to recover from these things. I decided it could prove mildly fascinating to watch somebody play after getting caught trying to steal a toilet seat. I inaccurately thought him too marginal to incur heckling from opposing fans, but I thought it might affect his play just to know that people knew he had gotten caught trying to steal a toilet seat.

That, and I had to fumble around for a new favorite Portsmouth player. I thought straightaway about goalkeeper David James, who opined with amazing thoughtfulness in his *Observer* columns, and even though we Americans have our share of keen athletes who know about more than themselves, I doubt we have his equal. Still, I sort of wanted a non-goalkeeper, even while having nothing against the goalkeeping profession, which does beat, for example, congressman. I settled quickly upon Sol Campbell. I decided that this fearsome giant provides an important public service. When some opposing offense tries to depress the Pompey public with some sort of bid at a goal, Campbell often cleans it up by himself. His public role entails warding off misery or defusing worry. It's important in the life of a village.

The only potential caveat I knew about Sol Campbell was that as an Arsenal player he once, flustered, drove away from the stadium at halftime after a subpar performance. I decided that qualified as one of those things a fan could strain to forgive, especially if there's a smidgen of honor in his disgust with himself, or if by leaving early he beat heavy traffic and left a smaller carbon footprint upon the earth.

20

"HAVE WE JUST . . ."

Mildly woozy, I turned up in the Fratton End at about 2:58 PM, ready to cheer my squad against Charlton but feeling embryonic as a fanatic. Having spent decades in objective and moralistic press boxes, I had not cultivated the hard shell of rationalization that adorns many fanatics and helps them through such fanatic crises.

Many fans could rationalize that of the eleven Portsmouth players on the pitch that day (lacking the injured LuaLua), fully ten had refrained from acts vile or base during the preceding week, with fully ten neither threatening a fiancée (vile, if true) nor attempting to stash a more-expensive toilet seat in the box of a less-expensive toilet seat (base, and true). Other fans would re-act otherwise. The wise, grizzled, weather-worn fans of the ancient nation of England, long since inured to the lunacy of the world, might read about LuaLua and Johnson and roll their eyes or sigh. The green, hopeful, starry-eyed sorts from the young nation of the United States, trailing by centuries in the development of a clue, might disbelieve the LuaLua part—he's an avowed Christian, he'd never do that—while writing off the Johnson bit using the oily PR sentence, "He made a mistake." Still other fans, like many I'd seen in my homeland, might think Johnson entitled to the odd larceny so long as he abetted victory.

I, meanwhile, still took the time to cringe, my inexperience a naive and glaring deterrent to my enjoyment.

I sort of winced through the Portsmouth-Charlton first half, listening for creative taunts directed at Thatcher while watching for scientific evidence regarding Johnson: does a failed attempt to pilfer a high-end toilet seat on a Wednesday detract from the capacity to play high-end defense on the following Saturday?

The Thatcher taunts proved durable yet insufficient. They included both eloquence and beautiful ineloquence. The eloquence came from a sole burly man about five rows down from myself, who kept yelling, with simple elegance, "You're a disgrace, Thatcher!" This I found oddly civilized and inarguable of content. The ineloquence came from all around and specialized in the kind of language you might call contemporary Tony Soprano. Yes, I occupied the rowdy Fratton End, the stand I'd chosen after months of sampling, but I occupied the less rowdy edge of the rowdy Fratton End, on the left looking out, halfway up, behind the goal but off to the left of the goalkeeper's left shoulder, rather than the middle, all the way up and directly behind the goal, which teemed with hard-boots who had endured a second-tier year or twenty and who thought up all the best stuff. I could decipher their words only seldom. I did make out "bastard" one time. Around myself, the "f——'s-sake"-o-meter reached seven, unprecedented in my lifetime. I often heard that word almost unused in American dialect: "rubbish."

At one point midway through the first half, Thatcher himself suddenly alighted in the corner of the field twenty rows down from myself, and I do know I felt a hot flash of contempt I did not know I had in me. Otherwise, I wished him no ill save for a ceremonial removal from the premises plus a suspension of roughly two seasons.

Meanwhile, I monitored the essential performance-related question of the afternoon. I had to surmise that attempted toilet-seat thievery indeed does detract from performance, for I detected from Johnson (shirt number 4 on the Pompey side) an unusual assortment of botched possessions, useless passes, and feckless defense. Whether Johnson actually committed more botches and uselessness and fecklessness than usual, or whether I simply noticed all of the above out of micro-studying or perhaps even mild resentment, would remain the last, lingering scientific question of the misspent afternoon.

The first half transpired without a scintilla of intrigue, with sixth-place Portsmouth (thirty-seven points) and troubled nineteenth-place Charlton (sixteen points) combining for zero goals and seemingly half-empty effort. Just then, the public-address announcer reminded us that if we all looked down the pitch at the giant video screen, we could rewatch the "highlights" of the first half, and even as a know-nothing, I wondered whether some wise guy had infiltrated the public-address area, perhaps armed and holding hostages, in order to make wisecracks about such "highlights." They showed the highlights, which contained no highlights. Still, with Charlton already having suffered through fifteen losses and one managerial change and this only January in an August-to-May season, and with Charlton sitting 0–1–10 on the road—or, in American parlance, 0–10–1 away: zero wins, ten losses, one draw—I still reckoned three points imminent.

Then the second half insisted on transpiring, and that proved a merciless insistence, as the match droned on goal-less and I began to think the sure three points might morph into the dreaded one point. Eventually we all reached the seventy-ninth minute, when suddenly, at the other end, far from my view, a ball seemed to loop into the net that James had fought gamely to defend. Charlton players seemed to run over into the corner and carry on some rare exultance together. Charlton fans, just behind the Charlton players, seemed to jump up and down. A boy two rows in front of me, listening on radio, turned around and smirked and explained to his father that Amdy Faye had scored the goal for Charlton. I wondered what the boy might have against Faye and learned only later that the boy meant only disappointment in that Faye once had played for Portsmouth, plus bewilderment in that Faye didn't tend to score goals and that in fact Faye had *never* scored a goal in England. This goal sort of caromed off his shin, and Uncle Harry would sneer, "They fluked a goal through Faye."

And what enabled this fluky shin goal? The answer would be a misdirected defensive header from one Glen Johnson, who after this mistake would have to go home to some second-rate toilet seat.

The final fourteen minutes of the match, then, featured one excellent Portsmouth chance in front of our end—Charlton goalkeeper Scott Carson hauled himself leftward to save Andy Cole's promising strike—and the sight of Charlton, stalling. At any chance, any stoppage in play, Charlton's players would stall for, by my estimation, stints of anywhere between five minutes and a day and a half. As we awaited one throw-in, I felt certain I had missed my next birthday. I began to develop completely irrational contempt for the hapless bald linesman. Thatcher remained on the pitch, offending all known human sensibilities, and the agony waned into added time and then clunked with the final whistle, whereupon Charlton's red patch of away fans jumped up and down with delight.

In just that moment, I felt a middling envy of those people over there on that other side. Because I had fallen for my club the previous spring as it sailed the wacky seas of relegation avoidance, I knew ever so slightly the seafaring thrill of relegation avoidance. Their club, a model of small-club viability given seven straight seasons in the top tier, thirteenth place in 2005–2006, had wallowed through a perilous half season in the drop zone, while my club, on the top shelf for only four seasons, seventeenth place in 2005–2006, had turned out to be this titanic European Champions League powerhouse—slight cough— for which losing to the likes of Charlton felt particularly stinging and unwelcome. These Charlton fans had just gone along, riding trains or buses or cars, and kept track of their team hoping to squeeze at least a modicum of glee out of the process. They had come to Portsmouth expecting little, and they had come out of it with a 1–0 win that instilled hope. I had gone to Portsmouth expecting three points, and I had come out of it with a chilling loss, the wretched memory of watching Ben Lucifer for a day, plus the realization that my favorite two players included an alleged fiancée-abuser and a bona-fide toilet-seat thief who even lacked the essential toilet-seat-thief skills, such as common sense.

"Have we just lost to Charlton?" said the man who sat three seats to my left for that day and for the rest of the season.

It seemed that "we" had, and it seemed the 19,567 of us had witnessed Charlton's first away win in fourteen months and twenty-five days, the previous one also at Fratton Park.

Uncle Harry chimed in with "This was our worst performance of the season."

This, all told, would be one of the things you forget when you're a sportswriter: that the people in the seats among you, or outside the press-box windows, have paid money, and they have cared, if even lightly, and they have used up one of only fifty-two Saturdays granted per year, and for all that risk, they still might undergo a visual abomination. At least when a sportswriter witnesses an abomination, he or she has received a salary, however insufficient to our towering societal importance that places us in the same stratum with heart surgeons and Nelson Mandela.

The thing you never forget as a sportswriter, however, would be the capacity of managers to utter inanities they actually deem plausible. So here it came, later that night, in my ill-advised light reading on the match, an assortment of comments from the popular and nice Alan Pardew, new manager, Charlton.

"We do silly things in our lives that we regret, and Ben wants to forget that one."

(Yes, from time to time we all brazenly knock other people unconscious during sporting events.)

"He has apologized for it, and today he was brilliant."

(Oh, when does the Ben Thatcher honorary parade start?)

"I just whispered in his ear . . ."

(Anyone have an airsickness bag?)

". . . that with what he had to endure he gave a thoroughly professional performance."

(Yeah, let's drag out the violins for the woeful duress one

must face after one causes somebody a seizure and oxygen treatment and a night in the hospital on a drip.)

As lame manager pronouncements of faux valor go, these, I guess, count among the moderately lame. They're lame, but I've heard lamer. Managers, in the end, must unify their clubs, so they can't go around saying such truisms as "Well, of course he was taunted, deservedly, after he disgraced the game and damaged a player from the home roster." Further, managers often must uphold some sort of male credo, wherein we all reserve the right to attempt to crash stupidly into somebody and then to turn around and cry victim, having our bravery extolled after those really mean people yelled at us for attempting to maul the pure living hell out of somebody else just five months prior. In a sociological sense, all of this might even help to explain why, of the two known genders, one has caused the world immeasurably greater destruction.

21

OLD TRAFFORD

On a dismally dreary and cold Saturday, January 27, in Manchester, some 71,137 people swept from the city train line toward a gigantic stadium that is home to fabled Manchester United, for the fourth round of the FA Cup. We passed lampposts with LOVE UNITED HATE GLAZER, restating the contempt for inaccessible and poorly shaven American ownership. We crossed over a bridge. We passed various vendors selling either clothing items or the kind of food that heightens the earnings potential of cardiologists.

In these throngs of northwest England striding to see this global colossus of a soccer club, surely I became the only one who noted the American-style largeness of it all and began thinking of Tennessee's 104,000 at Neyland Stadium or Michigan's 107,000 at the Big House or Penn State's 107,000 at Beaver Stadium or Ohio State's 101,000 at the Horseshoe, where in combing through the detritus behind the end zone after an on-field celebration that followed a win over Michigan in 2002, I once found caps, buttons, pompoms, game programs, and *a pair of pants.* As 71,000 or so strangers and I streamed toward one of the most famous stadiums on earth (capacity: 76,212, plus lucky paramedics), surely only I thought of Southeastern Conference football stadium throngs and the frothing contempt for rivals felt by hordes of churchgoers, and of how England had given up the church part of that weird equation.

And then, with the curse of sportswriterdom in life, surely, too, I might've been alone that day in pondering parity as we approached a Manchester United–Portsmouth FA Cup match with a 95 percent certain outcome. We Americans long since have commended the NFL for its parity and derided baseball for its lack thereof, but then baseball tweaked itself a bit and watched ten different franchises grab the twelve World Series slots between 2002 and 2007. Yet even at its most numbingly predictable, as with the American League East and the abysmally tedious Yankees payrolls, baseball drubs the Premier League in life's parity sweepstakes. In the twelve seasons from 1995–96 to 2006–2007, of the twenty-four major domestic championships (twelve league titles, twelve FA Cups), all twenty-four went to the four most lavish clubs: Manchester United, Chelsea, Arsenal, Liverpool. The puzzle for myself: how can the presence of extravagant advantage over sixteen of your nineteen rivals *not* detract from the satisfaction of a title?

Denial, I reckon.

Yet in England you hear few wails about this from the English media wilderness. Yes, you hear ample worry about skyrocketing ticket prices shooing the masses, but little shouting about implementing any NFL-style salary cap for the clubs. As I walked to Manchester United's sure win over Portsmouth in the fourth round of the FA Cup, I wondered whether people sometimes don't warm to a *lack of parity* because it's not confusing. The idea that your NFL team might clamber from 4–12 to the Super Bowl within two seasons (or, heck, one) certainly appeals to fans, but if the kingpins keep changing, maybe it also diminishes the joy over beating one of the kingpins.

During periods of NFL parity, we sometimes decide that parity is formless and boring, which would mean that imbalance is boring, and parity is boring, and life is absurd.

Like several thousand Portsmouth brethren, I traveled to Manchester knowing Portsmouth would not defeat Manchester

United. I walked up to the stadium wearing my spiffy new Pompey ski cap knowing Portsmouth would not defeat Manchester United, and I entered the quarantined away zone like a lab rat and walked up the quarantined red stairwell knowing Portsmouth would not defeat Manchester United. As I noted that the Old Trafford away zone seemed plusher and cleaner than other away zones, and as I yecched that the away concession area sold Budweiser, which I don't mind but did not move all the way to England to rediscover, I never once thought Portsmouth would defeat Manchester United.

Still, I went, we all went, we all support the systems that uphold the tedium, possibly because we prefer the tedium at the stadium to the tedium at home. Besides, I could always check off life's list that I'd been to a match at Old Trafford and cease having to tell people I'd been there only for a Friday-morning tour with a Hungarian father and son incensing the tour guide by trying to walk out onto the field.

Out we went into the seating area in the upper deck of Old Trafford, where the seats proved comfortable and the surroundings proved roofed and so protected from any elements that I actually felt as if indoors. Then again, each seat lacked the one feature each seat probably needed, that being a telescope. The match began at 5:15 PM, the fourth round of the FA Cup, everybody present, from the number-one BBC team in the luxury-box studio to the new manager of England's national team, Steve McClaren, and our Pompey ants began trying to fend off the advances from the Manchester United ants. The people supporting their ants didn't seem so loud, possibly because we sat so far away from them, but also possibly because they'd experienced roughly eight Premiership titles in the last fourteen seasons and waited to be impressed rather than trying to inspire their players into achieving the impressive. A mocking chant about the home fans' silence rustled up from the Portsmouth section, the one up near the moon:

You're supposed to
You're supposed to

You're supposed to be at home
You're supposed to be at home

I sang along with this chant even while figuring that they could not hear us from our post up there in Iceland. I learned later that they chanted, "Town full of seamen," at us, and I wished I'd been able to hear them to accept the honor.

Even from yonder up there, I could see that Portsmouth played gamely and admirably, even yanking an actual goal right out of the mouth before the referee could see it had been a goal. At twelve minutes, Manchester United's Nemanja Vidić sent a header trickling just over the line, but the glorious Pedro Mendes rooted it out of there and back to safety, while the knighted Manchester United manager Sir Alex Ferguson raised a ruckus. Oddly, I learned one day later, Sir Alex Ferguson had not protested in January 2005 when Mendes himself scored for Tottenham into that very same goal, even though Manchester United goalkeeper Roy Carroll had cleared it out similarly, unbeknownst to the referee. If in the NFL, Sir Alex would've possessed—in a pocket, maybe—a pretty blood-red flag, which he could've thrown down dramatically to the ground in that situation, whereupon a referee would have halted the game and gone over to a video player inside a TV camera and stuck his head inside a bizarre little draping that covered only his head and neck so as to avoid glare while he checked the accuracy of the earlier judgment. While he had his head stuck in there, the whole stadium would've waited, giving some fans a chance to go to the loo and others a chance to order another beer at their seat.

Not that we're weird or anything.

On this young evening at Old Trafford, the referee certainly would've emerged, announced that a goal had scored, and become the most popular guy in the stadium for about two minutes, but English soccer persistently resists such a system.

We reached halftime all goal-less, and we Pompey fans felt lucky, but I had not kidded myself. I knew Manchester's manager, Sir Alex, had not fielded his best possible squad—in the hopes of resting some guys for future games, like the upcoming league match with mighty Watford (sitting twentieth place), or maybe for recovery from the 2–1 loss in an Arsenal thriller down in London the previous Sunday. I had been around long enough to know there existed these advanced nations of humanity that had long since proved capable of playing for more than one trophy at a time. I saw no Portuguese marvel Cristiano Ronaldo on the pitch, and no Liverpool-raised hellion Wayne Rooney. Of course, the thought that Sir Alex could simply bring in Ronaldo or Rooney hovered in goblin mode over the entire match, much like lines of Rudy Giuliani's police cars glowered outside New York nightclubs during the 1990s.

The silent majority below in fact did seem to receive a blood transfusion from the appearance of a single twenty-one-year-old not all that far removed from that Liverpool childhood of Everton support. When Ferguson beckoned Rooney at sixty minutes, the Manchester United offense went from threatening to doubtless, and all of David James's excellence through the match—big stops on Michael Carrick, on Paul Scholes—would amount to a loss. Rooney tapped in a Ryan Giggs cross at 77, and the masses below chanted, "Rooney! Rooney!" so that even we could hear them.

Those chants mushroomed utterly six minutes later when Rooney treated everyone to the game's lasting memory, a twenty-yard chip that drew gasps of awe even from the Portsmouth supporters, many seemingly glad they'd witnessed such a treat. As if imbued with a GPS device, this ball left Rooney's foot and fluttered up over James and then down into the gap between his tall head and the crossbar, freezing the goalkeeper and doubling the lead. This ball sang, it did, and it quelled whatever doubt or ennui still lingered in the home supporters. Manchester United would advance to the fifth round of the FA Cup, and Portsmouth would call it a good FA Cup at four rounds and resume concentration on that UEFA Cup spot.

We all knew that, but at eighty-seven minutes, the lad next to me suddenly decided we shared a bond or perhaps even a family tree. Throughout the match, I'd sat on the end of the row next to the stairs while this guy and his two friends, all about twenty-five years old, hopped and roared next to me. The ushers kept telling them to sit down so the people behind them could see—a new and lamented development in once-bawdy English soccer—and I kept feeling sorry for the ushers, having to do such things, and I marveled that the twenty-year rehabilitation of the English soccer image had evolved to where the fans we Americans deem fearsome had to sit down so other people could see. These lads never looked my way nor spoke to me.

Yet when Mendes managed to bounce a shot off Kanu's leg at eighty-seven minutes, and when that thing fooled Manchester United's goalkeeper, Tomasz Kuszczak, and rolled into the net, just below us, close enough that we could see it like you see the Grand Canyon out of an airplane window, this guy just grabbed me and squeezed me and began lifting me up and down. Again, there went the stunning resiliency of the English soccer fan, down 2–1, hopeless, witness to a Rooney masterpiece just four minutes prior, yet exultant because our favorite club just scored a goal at Old Trafford.

He hugged me again on the way out, after the 2–1 loss, just as James came over our way, down on the pitch, and looked up while we chanted to him, "England's number one, England's, England's number one," a routine hymn whose American translation means the fans think he's the top goalkeeper in England. We serenaded him as if to say, "Don't worry, we understand, we know you just got frozen solid in front of 71,000 people, but it literally could've happened to anyone, and besides, those other great saves." I actually found this about as enlightened as anything I'd ever seen in the grand annals of fandom.

On my way out, in my Pompey ski cap, as I peeled through the masses in the cold, one Manchester United fan hissed at me, and another grunted. The old image of English soccer fans may linger in uninformed circles, but all I ever got was one hiss and one grunt.

22

"WE WERE MENTAL"

Portsmouth had not won since Boxing Day at West Ham, and did not win against Middlesbrough on January 30 even though it had managed to win at Middlesbrough by 4–0 only five months earlier. The 0–0 draw on January 30 prevented both a leap to fifth place and the establishment of some distance between Portsmouth and the howling, trailing pests just below, such as Everton and Reading. It kept Portsmouth below 40 points at 38, and as a person who had not endured the 1990s, which Portsmouth spent entirely in the second division, I grimaced at the 38, ignorant of its bountiful exceptionality. I'd foreseen January matches with Sheffield United, Charlton, and Middlesbrough, and I'd imagined nine points but gotten two. As a fanatic, I learned that I wanted more, see, more! And more! And more!

The game accounts from Middlesbrough's visit to Portsmouth would say that Sol Campbell had played wonderfully, and I saw nothing to discredit that even though I cannot rate defensemen or, for that matter, strikers, midfielders, goalkeepers, trainers, or water personnel. After the match, Uncle Harry said, "It's amazing when you get up there in the table and expectations rise," and likewise, it's amazing when you drop into a new country with zero knowledge of legacies and find it irksome that your club has drawn 0–0 at home with Middlesbrough five months after blasting same by 4–0. That also happened to be the first night I spotted the wall of honors for deceased Portsmouth fans, appealing in its simplicity, even barrenness, just an arrangement of plaques, including one about a late fan named Thelma York (1935–2003), and how if you'd listen to the wind, you can hear her singing "Play Up, Pompey," the Portsmouth fight song that uses the tune of standard church chimes. She withstood decades of slumps, and here I'd lamented one. She'd been to the fourth division in the 1970s and back, and she'd spent ample time in the third and second divisions through her lifetime, while I'd spent the entirety of my Pompey fandom in single-digit Premiership positions, like a spoiled American or something.

Well, on a dismally dreary afternoon way back up in northwest England (okay, about four hours by train), I alighted at Wigan for a second time in a single lifetime, setting a record for Americans. No one greeted me at the train station with a plaque or a trophy on Saturday, February 3, 2007, but I let it slide and marched around the appealing downtown, then out to the strip malls and the stadium. Eighteen months prior, I'd turned up in Wigan in a black sweater hunting the first clue, and now I turned up in Wigan in a dark blue Pompey jacket hunting three points and heartened by the line in the newspaper describing Wigan's results from the previous six matches: LLLLLL. Had that form line run to the last eight matches rather than the customary six, it would've looked like this: LLLLLLLL. It had been hard for Pompey to score lately—two fluky goals in four league matches in 2007—but it had been harder for anybody in the Premiership to lose to Wigan.

Clearly, losing to Wigan would take some doing.

With twenty-two points, Wigan sat seventeenth, two points above the drop zone that at that moment included Watford, Charlton, and West Ham. Wigan fans responded in kind, filling JJB Stadium to only 15,093 out of a possible 25,138. Gloom ruled. Clouds menaced. I sat in the away upper deck among Pompey faithful near some Pompey children who'd turned up with their Pompey parents, and it felt warm to join my people at a place so far away from Fratton Park. Weirdly, I felt that feeling one gets when one travels to a foreign place but sees someone one knows, the caveat being that I didn't know anyone.

Well, Wigan's offense went Lazarus on us and began peppering the Pompey goal with serial threats. Campbell and James and the ever-honorable Linvoy Primus cleared out trouble here and there and over there, but the whole Pompey exercise felt unmistakably uphill, and against Wigan no less. The match remained goal-less by halftime. We did croon the greatest hits of Pompey cheers, including one that had become my favorite for its poetic simplicity and sheer unlikelihood among soccer brutes:

> *We love you, Portsmouth, we do*
> *We love you, Portsmouth, we do*
> *We love you, Portsmouth, we do*
> *Yahhhhh, Portsmouth, we love you . . .*

Still, our crowd was somewhat sparse, and our songs steadily waned. Somebody tried to dredge up the "Yellow Submarine" European tour song, but it just sagged, because even though Portsmouth held down a radiant sixth place in the Premiership, Portsmouth could not score anymore, and it couldn't pretend to threaten to hint at a score against the newly impenetrable Wigan defense. I wondered if the lyrics could change to say, "We might be going on a European tour," and I began to resent hearing the other version anymore for its prematurity, never mind that you should always sing about a European tour whenever you can sing about a European tour upon this wretched planet. For years I'd witnessed teams in slumps from press boxes and even cringed trying to think up questions to ask the players when the answers would seem so obvious. So here was a slump from a fan's view, all piddling little three weeks of it, exasperating because you couldn't do anything about it and because the team just couldn't score and because there was that fear of plummeting through the table into somewhere like thirteenth place, which in Johnny-come-lately absurdity I found alien and unacceptable.

Then, just after halftime, I swear, somebody began piping fog into the stadium through the gap in the stands to our left. It seemed to stream in with such abandon that I briefly wondered if the Wigan club had bought some sort of fog machine and produced the fog in hopes it would help muster a draw, even as it played a club that had forged its own offensive fog. The fog accrued so thickly that it called to mind January in the NFL, the greatest annual month in American sports, even if some would argue for October in baseball or March in college basketball. I began to think about the Philadelphia-Chicago Fog Bowl of December 31, 1988, back before the NFL playoffs shifted entirely to January, and that made me think of the 1982 San Diego–Cincinnati AFC Championship at minus-fifty-nine degrees, which made me think of the Dallas–Green Bay 1967 Ice Bowl and the 2002 Oakland–New England snowfall, but mostly Philadelphia-Chicago. That day fog descended—or whatever fog does—next to Lake Michigan, then had a fog convention, Chicago being a known convention town, and soon the broadcasters strained to call a game they could not see and used puckish lines like "Gain of five, I think," although not enough of them.

After halftime at Wigan, as Wigan came to resemble Chicago, I began to realize fog can be a blessing. Fog can prevent you from having any inkling of how, at the other end of the pitch, Wigan's David Unsworth crossed, and his teammate Lee McCulloch turned up on the edge of the box, and the ball broke to McCulloch, and McCulloch struck for a 1–0 lead, a reward for Wigan's match-long superiority. I could see their celebration, but murkily.

Now, here was one dreary day. That 1–0 lead would prove every bit as insurmountable as it looked, and Wigan's new form line would read LLLLLW. Woo, boy, a loss to Wigan, to garnish the loss to Charlton. As we began to file out, the Pompey drum played and about fourteen Pompey supporters danced, and I found these people rather Herculean. As I ambled back toward town in the fog and the gathering darkness, I passed through one of several adjacent ugly-American strip malls, and off in the distance I could see yet another of our contributions to global health, Burger King. Only the lights had gone out on some of its letters, so in the mist it said only RGER NG. So these can be English soccer days: you're in the gloom of winter at a lofty latitude, you're walking through a strip mall, you've just witnessed Wigan's first victory in nine matches, it came at the expense of the club you came to see, and you're looking at a sign marked RGER NG.

I did feel profoundly depressed, doubtless from light deprivation and Lee McCulloch, then tried to count it as an important component in the suffering aspect of my Pompey development. I had a pint in one of Wigan's handsome downtown pubs, then boarded the train and sat down.

I once viewed trains as metallic vessels that transported people and luggage, but during the course of my Premiership wandering, I came to view trains as living, respirating agents of the soccer experience, almost as important as strikers or referees who cannot spot obvious handballs. To ride a train through England on a Saturday or Sunday can be to drink in a soccer day in the entire country, even while often drinking in other properties as well. On trains, you can hear people giving scores from other matches, discussing the events of other matches, stating their relegation fears and maybe even arguing. I began to make it a habit to eavesdrop on trains. I began to love eavesdropping on trains. I began to completely forget my etiquette training about eavesdropping on trains that I had received in my small Virginia hometown.

Actually, we never rode any trains, so I never got any such training.

As the season progressed, I heard people discuss their disbelief that David Beckham married *her*. On the Tuesday night of January 30, 2007, I heard a guy tell his two friends he'd follow his girlfriend to Sydney come summer, and I began to notice that the residents of Sydney soon would hear one of the most extraordinary, rollicking laughs on record. Other times, you'd have no choice but to hear other people's voices, because some ten-year-old boy would blare his lovely song to the "London Bridge" tune:

Gary Neville, he's a Red
He's a Red
He's a Red

Gary Neville, he's a Red
He hates Scousers.

(Points of information: Gary Neville would be a Manchester United player since 1992, "Scousers" would be people from Liverpool, and parents who encourage such bellowing because they find it cute would be derelict.)

As this train rolled, I began to eavesdrop on a remarkable conversation between two eighteen-year-olds just across the aisle. It grew clear that they supported Brentford, and that they had spent the day way, way up at Blackpool on the west coast of England near the Irish Sea, at a stadium called Bloomfield Road. I guessed Brentford occupied either the "Championship," or League One, and as for Blackpool, I'd visited only during the 2001 British Open golf at Lytham and had found it quite unbelievable, mostly because my own country lacks the ripeness to boast a resort in which everyday tourists revel and guffaw at drag queen shows.

Chris and Jak—I'd soon learn their names—went on about Blackpool versus Brentford with such exuberance and with such endurance that I began to believe they deserved their own *Match of the Day* show. They analyzed every single aspect of the match their minds could recollect. They dredged detailed memories for discussion. Had that train continued on through London under the Channel, they'd have reached Paris without exhausting their topics. They epitomized the appeal of the postmatch rehash.

Why?

Well, you want a slump? Now, they knew a slump. I didn't know any frigging slump. I knew three matches in which Portsmouth couldn't score and seemed to have left the knowledge of how in a dresser drawer somewhere. I knew a lull that threatened to swell into a slump. They'd gone twenty-four league matches with one win. They'd gone four months without an away win.

They had gone *eleven away league matches without a goal.*

As Chris and Jak effused over there, I opened a newspaper and checked all three lower tables, just to see where this Brentford club would turn up. I found it twenty-fourth out of the twenty-four clubs in League One, which is the third division, with twenty-three points, five behind Bournemouth and six behind Cheltenham, a sure bet to plummet to League Two, the fourth division. I did not see—but soon would look up—that Brentford's season had begun brilliantly with three wins and four draws in the first seven matches. Then it had careened. A goal in a 1–1 draw at Millwall on September 26 would serve as the last away goal until—well, until February 3. In league play on the road, Brentford had lost by 2–0 at Rotherham, 3–0 at Oldham, 2–0 at Nottingham Forest, 2–0 at Cheltenham, 1–0 at Port Vale, 2–0 at Carlisle, 2–0 at Swansea City, 1–0 at Bournemouth, and 1–0 at Yeovil Town. Home losses included 4–0 to Doncaster, 4–0 to Crewe, and 4–1 to Millwall.

Yet Chris and Jak had gone to all the home games and most of the road, and here they'd gone on February 3, all the way up to Blackpool, four hours on the train, to stand among the attendance that day, as listed adorably in the Brentford Bees match report as "6,086 (202 Bees fans)."

Suddenly, in all their travels and travails, they'd come upon a jewel, with a Brentford goal just twelve minutes in from Andrew Frampton, but wait, with another Brentford goal at twenty-nine minutes from Jo Kuffour, but hold on here just a minute, another Brentford goal at thirty minutes, again from Kuffour, only ninety seconds after the previous goal.

Three!

"We were mental," they said, a line I will not forget.

Indeed, they described themselves jumping literally all over the stand, feverish in their unforeseen mirth. Against a Blackpool club with hopes of promotion to the second tier, last-place Brentford won the match 3–1, and the Brentford match report would read, "Brentford finally broke their away hoodoo," reminding me of the glorious word "hoodoo." But first, there would come what was, in my opinion, the best *Match of the Day* in the whole land, that on the Virgin train from Preston to London, starring Chris and Jak, my new icons of the intractable, blood-borne English loyalty to soccer clubs.

"You support Portsmouth?" one of them said to me suddenly, having noticed my jacket.

"Yeah," I said with my American accent, providing my short-version explanation of how I'd come to do so.

They'd heard the Wigan score, but I noticed they just didn't consider it all that arresting. Unlike myself, they had lived repeatedly through the long slog of the English soccer season, and they knew the vagaries, especially in a sport more capricious than most. Besides, they hadn't seen an away goal since September, and really, what's a loss at Wigan with an RGER NG in the fog?

For hours we talked. We disembarked at London Euston and walked down Tottenham Court Road to a pub and talked more. I asked their opinions of all things soccer, and from them I gained another layer of understanding of how English soccer fans attach to their clubs no matter the circumstance. Jak said something that would take up residence in my brain for the remainder of the year. He said that if Brentford did suffer relegation from League One (third division) to League Two (fourth division) after the season—as, ultimately, it would—he would feel sorry, yes, but as a consolation, he also would look forward to the League Two season.

It would give him a chance to experience some of the League Two stadiums.

That statement gave me my latest epitome of fandom, plus a glorious mental picture of two devotees, come September, turning up in the away stand at, say, Bury.

23

CHIMES AND MAMMALS

On a pleasant February Saturday in London with patches of blue visible in the sky, I crossed the bridge toward Waterloo station employing one of my favorite little tricks of life. When walking through a metropolis that has become old-hat to myself, I often attempt to picture it as I saw it for the first time, back when it seemed so mysterious and rife with possibility, long before I returned and brought along all my credit card bills and middling worries. In London's case, that would be 1986, when two friends and I danced like rubes at the Hippodrome and slept on the sidewalk and absurdly saw Sarah Ferguson go by in a bridal gown and horse-drawn carriage. Just as I'd transported myself back to how vast and haunting London had seemed back then, Big Ben played its chimes and whooshed me to the present.

That's because, when I heard those standard chimes, my brain immediately and without provocation heard the Portsmouth fight song that carries the same tune, "Play up Pompey, Pompey play up!"

Once, I had seen Big Ben in one of those surreal there-it-is moments when you realize something you've seen in a thousand photographs actually does exist and, in fact, towers right over there before your eyes. Now, twenty years and change later, the chimes of Big Ben forged a cranial chemical reaction that immediately transported my mind to the Fratton End of a stadium near the English Channel. Hearing "Play Up, Pompey" about eight or ten times per match had imprinted the lyrics somewhere within my skull.

I counted this as either progress or dementia and headed for the southbound train. That day, slumping Portsmouth would welcome to Fratton Park the same opponent that had backlit the phoenix routine eleven months prior. That would be Manchester City, mercifully sans Ben Thatcher and languishing fifteenth in the table, albeit with only eight points fewer (thirty) than seventh-place Portsmouth (thirty-eight). To Americans who follow this stuff, Manchester City has a distinct parallel, the Los Angeles Clippers of the NBA. The Clippers, like Manchester City, share a town with a cultural icon (Manchester United, the Los Angeles Lakers). The Clippers, like Manchester City, remain anonymous to foreigners who follow the game only casually, such that said foreigners can hear there's another club in the same city and respond with outright bewilderment. The Clippers, like Manchester City, plod along without titles while the in-town titan hoards them (in the Lakers' case, nine).

The Clippers, unlike Manchester City, share an actual building with their in-town giant, so that instead of a "derby" pronounced "darby," they play a "hallway rivalry," their locker rooms only a hallway apart when they play each other. The Clippers, unlike Manchester City, have never actually won anything, what with Manchester City winning a League Cup as lately as 1976 and an FA Cup as lately as 1969. The Clippers, unlike Manchester City, have never been relegated, but they have deserved it on many, many occasions.

The Clippers, in fact, have done worse than Manchester City for years and years and years, eliciting a favorite joke from the erstwhile talk-show host Arsenio Hall, who said Los Angeles has everything because, "if you like basketball, we've got the Lakers, and if you don't, we've got the Clippers." The Clippers, in fact, have been so woeful that even though their former coach, Larry Brown, remains the only coach to win both NBA and NCAA men's basketball championships, I consider his feat of coaxing the Clippers twice to the playoffs tantamount to the accomplishments of Galileo, Aristotle, or Bill Gates.

So as I was thinking briefly of the Clippers—someone has to—as I rode toward the match with Manchester City, suddenly, on the train, no kidding, I heard that laugh. You know, that laugh from the train of January 30. The laugh that's moving to Sydney. From about eight rows away. I could not believe it. Could . . . not . . . believe . . . it. My ears did the ear double-take. Craning my neck, I also recognized his friend with the Saharan wit, who kept instigating the laugh. I marveled again at the laugh, but also thought of this bizarre case in the United States in which a woman's body had adverse physical reactions to hearing through her television the voice of *Entertainment Tonight* host Mary Hart. The afflicted woman's ears could not go anywhere near that voice or, if we're to believe the reports, her body would crumple with some sort of seizure. As I wondered whether this remarkable laugh from the Middlesbrough and Manchester City trains might produce such reactions in some people, the guy with the laugh stood up and walked out of the train car toward the loo, but carrying his backpack, which sort of got stuck in the closing sliding glass doors before he yanked it on through. I figured he planned to move to another car, meet up with someone.

The conductor happened by, and I asked him how many cars the train utilized that day, and he said five, and I couldn't believe that with a 20 percent chance on the train itself, and trains running all morning from Waterloo to Fratton and Portsmouth, I once again had turned up on the same train, in the same car, as this laugh.

We rode on a bit.

Just then, that sliding glass door at the end of the train car reopened and . . .

Well . . .

Oh . . .

You have to be kidding . . .

The guy with the laugh came back into the car dressed as a five-foot-eleven, furry, electric-blue bear, but with a yellow-crescent Pompey insignia on the front. I looked over and saw two teenage boys chatting and saw them stop and saw them grin and heard one say to the other, "That's brilliant." I was in such a state of disbelief that only as the day wore on did I notice that the bear had blue paws, the bear had a bear head but with a hole open for the human face, and the bear had blue bear ears.

This type of situation, of course, immediately raises a whole phalanx of questions.

Is it not possible to wear the bear suit right from home without getting leers from neighbors or having some old woman with poor vision call the police or being corralled by an overzealous zookeeper? (I guessed not.) Must this guy plot to don the bear suit only when safely within the greater Portsmouth fan zone area? (Perhaps.) Doesn't that thing get hot during games in, say, May? (Surely.)

What kind of soul does it take to go to soccer matches dressed as a blue bear? (A singular one, I reckoned.)

As the train rolled on toward the inevitable rail replacement, I could see that bear head bobbing and tilting during conversation, eight rows away. I could not hear the laugh very often, which made me wonder whether the blue bear fur actually muffled the sound of a laugh. Four guys nearby blithely ignored the blue bear and played cards loudly on a table and seemed to believe that everybody on the train held a vital interest in the outcomes of their hands.

Then came rail replacement, and we all disembarked at Havant. Rather than sixty or so humans lining up to board a double-decker bus, we were fifty-nine or so humans and one blue bear. The blue bear lined up with his friend and the rest of us, and by the time we boarded, the first deck proved full, so we hiked up the stairs to the equally crowded second deck. The gaudy mammal sat on the right side by a window, while I sat on the left by a window. I did not hear the laugh and reckoned the blue bear might've been just as miffed as myself once the bus became stalled in stadium traffic and once it seemed we might not make the kickoff.

In light of such duress, I believe it's a moral imperative that rail replacement include an open bar.

During the anxiety, though, I did notice that as the bus windows repeatedly fogged up, I had to use the left sleeve of my new blue Pompey jacket to clear the glass so that I could see outside when we passed such sights as the muddy sound with the moored boats near the stadium or the cemetery with the Pompey flag sticking up from one of the gravesites. Meanwhile, the blue bear, I noticed, would clear the glass with his right blue paw, and so, for just one moment, I wished that I too had a blue paw, preferably a left one.

We disembarked just in time in front of Fratton Park, and I walked right behind the blue bear and his friend, essentially following them into No Sumo Wrestlers Alley, where, of course, we had to walk single file. A fat bear couldn't have made it through. I listened as the blue bear absolutely guffawed at something the friend had said. Oh, what the heck. I'd decided to be a fan and not a sportswriter for this season, but I simply could not quash the twenty-year habit of asking people for interviews when a blue bear stood right before me. I introduced myself, and we shook hand and paw, and he gave his name. "Charlie." I said that I was sort of a Charlie too and asked him if I could interview him sometime and gave him a (yuck) business card, whereupon he handed the card to his friend because of course he had no pockets.

How stupid to hand a business card to a mammal I knew had no pockets, a mammal I knew full well to be not a kangaroo.

Within five minutes after kickoff, off a Matt Taylor corner, Portsmouth's Pedro Miguel da Silva Mendes (that's his full and glorious name) sent a heat-seeking blast from twenty yards, and that thing literally jolted the roof of the goal net, and the goal drought had ended, and I hopped up and down alone among my people, and Fratton Park felt a twinge of a searing, gorgeous memory from March 11, 2006. The game proceeded apace, Portsmouth looking fresh and sparkly, until late in the first half when suddenly Mendes went down again in a heap. Manchester City had struck again.

This time the ruffian Manchester City player Joey Barton had gotten ticked at something and wound up trying to crush Mendes's heel. Mendes left the match on a stretcher. The Fratton

End had its justified topic du jour, and the "stick" once directed at Thatcher went full-on at Barton. I heard mighty and majestic songs I never knew existed.

Loosely to the tune of "She'll Be Coming Around the Mountain" there came:

> *If Barton plays for England, so can I.*
> *If Barton plays for England, so can I.*
> *If Barton plays for England,*
> *Barton plays for England,*
> *Barton plays for England,*
> *So can I.*

I figured that song was old, but I adored it nonetheless.

There came a chant about "dirty northern bastards," the kind of thing that still, after all these months, startled me, because in the United States we frown upon unvarnished profanity in the presence of children. Then I remembered that Jak and Chris had told me about a man they knew who set unyielding rules for his children about language appropriate for soccer grounds versus language appropriate for the house. Then I thought about the philosopher Bertrand Russell's line, "All sin is geographical."

I heard a mysterious song, crooned to Barton, to the "Guantánamera" tune:

> *Down with your brother,*
> *You're going down with your brother,*
> *Down with your brohhhh-ther,*
> *You're going down with your brohhhh-ther . . .*

I didn't ask anyone, because I'm from Virginia, but I jotted down the lyrics and wondered about Barton's brother. Did he play in the second division or, more likely, the third division or the fourth division? And for whom?

Songs continued to flow from the heart of the Fratton End, a heart that did include, I noticed for the first time, a blue bear, as it's easy to spot a blue bear upward and rightward in the distance. Suddenly Manchester City equalized at sixty-two minutes. Bernardo Corradi headed in a Darius Vassell cross, one of only three goals he'd score all season, and once more Portsmouth versus Man City seemed trammeled at 1–1. The minutes wore on. Uncle Harry inserted Kanu for offense.

Just then, at eighty-one minutes, a certain soul named Glen Johnson made a defiant run and a clever reverse ball just below me in the corner to the left of the Man City goal. He got the ball to Kanu, and Kanu toe-poked an eight-yard goal into the right side of the net, and the team hugged in a blob below me, and I actually felt welling tears of a dubious nature. Oh, I'd weathered most of the long, hard, goal-less January and had come upon a moment when the offense flowered again, a mere hour of gloom next to the Brentford brand.

My tears came viscerally, because the goal and the group hug seemed so frenetically emotional. They did not come on behalf of Glen Johnson, although I did get my answer as to the recovery time from failed toilet-seat larceny to public recovery (twenty-one days). And they certainly did not come for Barton, who received jeers all the way off the pitch after Portsmouth's quenching 2–1 win.

I did, however, do some Internet research on Barton's brother and learned that he played in neither the third division nor the fourth division, or even the volumes of leagues below the fourth division, but sat in prison for murder. Such a song would seldom fly in the United States, where we're more cautious with humor, but then, all sin is geographical.

24

LONELY WALKS HE
WHO WALKS TO PLAINMOOR

If granted three guesses, most Americans can surmise that the French Riviera must be somewhere in France. Some of us have heard of the Italian Riviera, and a percentage can link the Italian Riviera to Italy. Almost none of us know about the English Riviera, so it gave me a *huh* to read that I would go there to watch some soccer on February 17.

While the FA Cup moved on with its fifth round and Portsmouth spent the Saturday idle, and while some grating kid somewhere went to see Manchester United while singing on a train that Gary Neville hates Scousers, I sated a long-held curiosity. Ever since alighting in England, I'd cast my eye now and then to the bottom of the League Two (fourth-division) table, and I'd wondered how it must be on a Saturday at the ground of the club standing ninety-second in the ninety-two team, four-division Football League, before the whole thing falls off into the vast network of tiny clubs embedded in something generally called "conference." Which club sat ninety-second, doomed to drop off into "conference"? As a lifelong fan of extremes, as somebody who once reveled in writing about a Kentucky high school that had lost forty-six football games in a row—I lauded them for not quitting, which is chirpy, I know—I scanned down the mid-February tables until I found it, there at the bottom . . .

Torquay.

Technically, that'd be Torquay United, reposing down there with twenty-five points, five points adrift of Wrexham and Macclesfield Town, and ninety-one spots and three leagues adrift of Manchester United. Once an American has identified the word "Torquay," the second act is to learn the location of this mystical Torquay, and that's when I began to do some studious studying. I learned that Torquay graces the English Riviera portion of Devon, that strand of southwest England that juts out into the sea, and that's when I learned there's such a thing in the world as the English Riviera.

The English Riviera turns out to be utterly lovely, even if February does not necessarily count among the prime times to visit the English Riviera. When you walk through central Torquay down to the mall and behold the Tor Bay, you have come upon one of the most beautiful sights in England, in my opinion.

When you walk up an elongated hill from town toward Plainmoor to see Torquay United play soccer, though, well, lonely walks he who walks through Torquay, in the rain, on a dismally dreary February afternoon, straining to see twenty-fourth place Torquay United (twenty-five points) play third-place Hartlepool (sixty-one points) in a League Two, fourth-tier tussle.

Lonely walks he while the rain starts angling in sideways and he begins to soak and to question just where he went so awry in life.

Normally, you can find a stadium you've never seen by following the traffic line, but no apparent traffic pattern materialized for Plainmoor, so I just continued upward, into the little village there, then turned right per directions, looped around a curve, and voilà.

Plainmoor, as it happens, has an outdated edifice and outdated old light stanchions and looks like a slightly more beleaguered Fratton Park, and so, at once, I felt charmed. The charm intensified when, happening into the club lobby, approaching the apparent ticket window, and inquiring about a ticket, I found out that you don't necessarily buy tickets per se, you just pay £15 at the gate as you would to enter a county fair or such. For still more charm, the wall of honors in the Torquay lobby included a framed certificate that read as follows: "This is to certify that Torquay United won the Barclays League Fourth Division play-offs 1990–91." Other frames included notice of the club's monetary donations for an air ambulance, a lifeboats group, and a hospice (£510.62).

I had hoped that the bottom of the fourth division would look something like this.

If there's an American likeness to Plainmoor, it's probably one of any number of high school football fields. That's not a slight, of course. High school football engulfs American towns, especially in Tennessee or Florida or Georgia or Alabama or most especially Texas, where stadiums can expand once one community decides it wants to keep up with that snooty community over there. Just a few Texas high school capacity figures: Pizza Hut Park in Frisco, 21,000; Mesquite High School in Mesquite, 20,000; Ratliff Stadium in Odessa, 19,300. I love the Friday night lights of stadiums in Tennessee mountains or in Alabama hills or on California boulevards, because those lights make me wonder what vivid lore and seething resentment lurk below. In Gold Beach, Oregon, there's a high school football field right up next to the Pacific Ocean where, no kidding, osprey have dropped eels on the team's practices and deer have taken the field during games and run so fast that coaches have tried to get their parents to relocate into the school district. Torquay itself has animal lore, I learned, in the form of the famed police dog named Bryn, who, during the last match of the year in 1987, while the whole place trembled over a potential relegation, suddenly jumped out and bit the thigh of one of the players, Jim McNichol. Seeing as how McNichol had scored earlier to halve visiting Crewe Alexandra's lead to 2–1, it seemed that Bryn must've been a dog with secretive away leanings. Paul Dobson scored famously in the bulging four minutes of injury time granted because of the delay wrought by Bryn, and Torquay United drew with Crewe and stayed up, as it had entirely since joining the Football League in 1927, always in lower divisions, until spring 2007, when finally it plummeted to "conference."

As the crowd of 2,194 filed in—far shorter men's room lines in League Two—I remained unaware (as usual) that referee Andy Penn twice had emerged to check the condition of the pitch and might have come close to ruling it unsuitable. This would've been quite a downer after two changes of trains, four hours of train rides, and one train malfunction that led to the boarding of another bus, and without even a single blue bear to lighten the ride. Luckily, Mr. Penn decided the match could carry on, so that not only did I get to see Torquay United play, but I could behold a match in the wondrously muddy conditions suggestive of the NFL playoffs.

I took the kind of folding yellow wooden seat that proves that people had tougher gluteus maximi back in the day when men were men and they built stadiums like Plainmoor. I sat near the press area, observing eight beleaguered reporters hunched together outdoors—outdoors!—and suspiciously devoid of access to a free buffet. Ludicrously, I sat near a man wearing a cap with an insignia of the Anaheim Ducks. I saw a church jutting up from behind the corner of the stadium in the gray grayness. I heard the public-address announce that Kevin Hill, presumably a Torquay player on their roster, had proposed to his girlfriend Laura on Valentine's Day, and that Laura had accepted, and I yearned for a day when I might hear a similar announcement noting that the woman actually declined, just for variety.

Other than shivering, I relished the day at Torquay.

As the match began with Hartlepool, the Torquay players took the pitch, and I stood and applauded with the Torquay supporters mostly because I'll always applaud someone who'll play for our entertainment in a downpour. One player, Hill, turned around and applauded the fans. I noticed that Torquay United wore the appealing colors yellow and blue, again suggestive of Portsmouth. The one hundred or so Hartlepool away fans began singing that Hartlepool was the greatest city "the world has ever seen," and I made the inane realization that many people sing that claim, not just Pompey supporters plus scattered others in the Premiership. They also chanted to their "Blue Army," and I got a greater sense of the universality of blueness. They also cheered a goal at six minutes when their Eifion Williams, who once played for Torquay United, found himself alone in front of the goal and supplied a 1–0 lead.

I saw and heard some excellent things at Plainmoor. Not only does the stadium remain so small that you often can hear the thud of a foot striking the ball, but many of the players' passes simply had no chance to reach their targets. You'd hear the thud, and then the ball would roll along, and then it would hit a little puddle of water or a pit of mud, and it would just stop there, all bogged down and ornery, while players had to turn around and give chase. This added another dimension to the sport. In a sport gone glamorous, Torquay had one player who looked just a little bit like some California biker dude, and I loved that. Torquay's goalkeeper looked a little chunkier than David James or any Premiership goalkeeper, and I loved that too. Hartlepool's manager wore a suit, which I found noble on a day when I felt an urge lingering from childhood to wear only a pair of shorts and go out sliding around in the mud. The mud began to cake and then cover the kits of some of the players, which I adored thoroughly out of an innate American affinity for those memorable sporting events that complicate the laundry.

The match slogged on, mildly eventful in the mud, and highlighted when one Torquay player who shall remain nameless sent a long, looping back pass toward his goalkeeper and almost scored the most incredible own goal I'd ever seen. Torquay pelted the Hartlepool goal without scoring, the 1–0 Hartlepool victory seemed somehow imminent, and come 4:35 PM, maybe fifteen minutes from time, I heard the fans of the ninety-second-best of the ninety-two Football League teams begin to sing:

Torquay till I die
I'm Torquay till I die
I know I am, I'm sure I am
I'm Torquay till I die

Thereby did I hear the most touching "till I die" I'd heard yet. Hartlepool finished off its victory and pointed toward eventual promotion to League One, the third tier, while Torquay's players got an ovation from their crowd—from us—for their game effort in the muck. I decided to have a beer in the pub that's attached to Plainmoor at one end—nice touch—and I received a flyer about some sort of action the fans' group might undertake. Before I did that, though, I decided to make a circular tour, and as I did about ten or fifteen of those "Torquay till I die" supporters marched through the exits and out into the street, chanting. I couldn't quite translate their chants, but they seemed to be peeved at some guy named Roberts, and indeed, when I checked later, a guy named Roberts ran the club and would cease running the club on the ensuing Wednesday.

With a couple of police officers looking on to forestall any shenanigans, the Torquay-till-I-die-ers continued their chants out into the street until the chants died off and everybody went home or into the pub affixed to the stadium. I thought about the world, and how even when you go to the ninety-second-place club in England, or a college in Montana, or a high school in Kentucky, or a cricket ground in India or Pakistan, there's almost always somebody who's mad at the chairman or the coach or the general manager or the athletic director. I thought about this as I found my way to the waterfront of the English Riviera, and I thought about this on the long train ride home while some guy engaged in an endless series of cell-phone calls, his voice blaring throughout the train car. His beloved Derby County club had lost 2–0 to Plymouth Argyle in the FA Cup, and had incurred two—two!—penalties in the match, whereupon the match ended and some police officer misconstrued something this guy's father said, so they had to go to the police station, where the father probably would have to spend the night.

I heard this story roughly five times.

By contrast, Torquay had been a dream.

25

A BLACKBURN FIASCO

I had first seen but not noticed Portsmouth on Saturday, February 25, 2006, at Chelsea. I witnessed the full, unforgettable glory of Portsmouth on Sunday, February 25, 2007, at Blackburn, up the middle of England, beyond Manchester. I saw this on a sunny but gruesome day when I traveled cluelessly and the club played hideously.

That's right. It took a lousy day to find the real Portsmouth.

Now, it can baffle a greenhorn American to hear English away fans lauded as the "truest" of fans. Sure, away fans have gotten up and gotten out of the house and refrained from sedentary afternoons spent bitching through a TV screen because the referee just missed a handball obvious from here to Glasgow. Sure, away fans make the effort so that they can ruin their afternoons bitching in person about the obvious handball. Away fans make the drive or ride the train or ride a bus that has no bar or no loo. Away fans risk urinary tract infections.

It's just that it can take time to appreciate the grit of away fans when you hail from a gigantic country wherein college kids make ten-hour drives to football games, then drive home all through the night taking turns napping while risking their grade point averages, their lives, and the lives of others. In the United States, some people make three-hour round-trips just to meet somebody else for breakfast, even if such people do reside in the

164 · BLOODY CONFUSED!

Los Angeles area. In England, no trip would exceed about five hours.

The sacrifice can pale.

I have learned, however, that careful study hones the appreciation for these people, the away fans.

Let's say that, just for example, you have an imbecile from the United States. Now, let's say the imbecile books a £40 (about $75) pair of single train tickets three weeks ahead of time in order to travel to Blackburn and back. Let's say the imbecile manages to coordinate that feat with the booking of a £25 (about $48) away ticket for Ewood Park, with Blackburn having famously shaved ticket prices during the 2006–2007 season. Let's say the imbecile congratulates himself on his excellent preparation skills and how he's really learning this game of fanhood.

Okay.

Let's say, then, that the imbecile has failed to account for the fact that Blackburn still breathes in the UEFA Cup and that European competition, which invites English clubs that finish fifth through seventh the previous year, might have an impact on the schedule of Blackburn versus Portsmouth on Saturday, February 24. So the Premiership might just eyeball an upcoming Blackburn UEFA Cup date on February 21 and, out of common decency, shift Blackburn's match to Sunday, February 25. Then the imbecile will have to telephone the train company and seek to change the ticket.

Now, it would take some kind of frigging imbecile to call up a train company seeking to change two single tickets when anyone with remote seasoning in England would know that after some time on hold to hear that the call may be recorded the answer will come back that it would be wiser for the imbecile to go ahead and buy a whole new return ticket, using the original tickets as coffee coasters or as fireplace kindling.

Even still, the forfeiture of another £63.90 (about $120) would not ensure that the imbecile wouldn't just go step on the wrong train, the 10:05 to Wolverhampton, rather than the 10:01 to Lancaster across the platform, if trying to reach Blackburn. If the average American can't find Texas on a map with two mulligans, even somebody who has been to all fifty states can have trouble getting to Blackburn from London. That's even given the knowledge that Blackburn lies somewhere up there just above Manchester, which at least rules out accidentally going to Torquay. So it's still possible to buy two different tickets to get to Blackburn and still wind up sitting for an hour and six minutes in the station at Rugby, waiting for the train one should've boarded an hour ago. And after that, it's still possible to ride that train experiencing one of the wretched turns of twenty-first-century life, the overhearing of others' cell-phone conversations. That alone exalts away fans. And then, that train—or any train—always reserves the right to stop just shy of any given station for ten precious minutes—it's 1:45, 1:46, tick-tock, tick-tock, kickoff at 3:00—because some dunderhead up ahead apparently kept his local train on that track for too long.

So the away fan, especially if an imbecile, might wind up in Preston at 2:34, with the next train for Blackburn not actually a train but a bus arriving at 3:45, so another £30 ($57) might go into a taxi for the twelve miles to Blackburn, and more than £30 ($57) if you count the possible overdraft fee from extracting the £30 ($57) with only £9.79 ($17) lingering in the account. The American away fan deals with absurd costs, yes, but the English away fan often deals with two costs so widely lamented as to become national issues—the cost of soccer tickets and the cost of trains—plus the occasional cost of taxis in the event of runaway stupidity.

Either that, or he/she rides a bus for eight aggregate hours.

And still, after all this strain, the away fan, if imbecilic enough, runs the risk of arriving in the twenty-third minute, feeling excitement because three points would make Portsmouth leapfrog from eighth to sixth in the table, plopping down at Ewood Park, checking the big video screen over to the right, and finding his club down 1–nil already (that secured in the very first minute via a rare Sol Campbell blunder I could muster relief at having missed). Whereupon the imbecile might proceed to absorb the most abominably pulseless performance humanly possible from the away club—a 3–0 loss that resembles 6–0. The home club, Blackburn, might've played miserably just four days prior, drawing 0–0 with Germany's eighth-place Bayer Leverkusen to exit the UEFA Cup meekly, while the away club might've played nada for fourteen days, yet the away fan still risks that those two factors will appear reversed during a turgid display of feckless soccer from the away fan's club.

That and, lest we forget, the away fan takes a chance his father might end up spending the night in jail in Plymouth.

If after ninety minutes on Sunday, February 25, the public-address had announced there would be a minimum twenty-four hours of added time, Portsmouth still would not have scored or much threatened Brad Friedel, the American goalkeeper from Ohio and UCLA. A good chance in the seventy-fourth minute found Andy Cole in front of goal fashioning a promising header, which he promptly headed into about the third row of the stands, some feat itself. At some point a Pompey fan near me angrily reminded our squad, "You've got to shoot to score!"—and if only they had heard him, they might've caught on. It grew so bad that possession seemed a disadvantage to the visiting squad. Possession seemed to entail an automatic transfer to Blackburn possession.

Watching this rubble of Pompey, the bubble of thought floating above my head suddenly contained that fan at Birmingham. That brilliant, brilliant fan. Okay, so it's a tired old trick in England, but to an American that fan who ran onto the pitch during the 2006 FA Cup quarterfinal 7–0 loss to Liverpool and tore up his ticket in front of manager Steve Bruce—that nonviolent trespasser qualifies as novel. He became the first guy of my experience to shred a ticket before a manager just before the cops hauled him off, and long shall he turn up in my accounts of the Premiership to curious fellow Americans. Long shall he occupy a beacon's spot in my cranium, even while I could never do such a thing to Uncle Harry.

Blackburn, meanwhile, having managed to refrain from scoring for an hour and a half against mighty Bayer Leverkusen, somehow bombarded our net with three goals and repeated threats while generally resembling all Arsenal. They made sublime crosses. They grimaced at their point-blank misses. They didn't even care when they flubbed a fifty-eighth-minute penalty granted them by our wacky, tackling goalkeeper, so nattily coiffed for such a mindless ruffian. By that point, they inhabited the happy realm of toying. And they did all this despite the thick, dispiriting swatches of empty blue home seats that exhibited how Premiership prices might've reached their realistic crux.

Yet through this afternoon desolation, something floored me again. Through several minutes in the sixties, the drums and throats in the top visitors' rows carried on an impressively durable and upbeat chant of "Blue Army."

In the seventy-ninth minute:

We love you, Portsmouth, we do,
We love you, Portsmouth, we do,
We love you, Portsmouth, we do,
Yahhhh, Portsmouth, we love you.

We do?

Yes, we do, because in the eighty-fourth minute there again went that hapless horn, that respiratory rogue of a bugle, that same Pompey fan playing on again, giving the distinct aura of encroaching death yet playing on, hitting every third note or so, skipping entire notes in a way that gave a mental picture of punctured lungs. Resiliency of the fan species had found new definition—in my book, anyway—in this soul gasping air into an obstinate instrument in the eighty-fourth minute of a debacle.

Then, suddenly, in the late-eighties minute:

We are staying up,
We are staying up!

And when the match did end—an occurrence some might interpret as proof of the existence of a higher power—which group of fans would forge the last human noise of the day at Ewood Park?

Their club had just played hopelessly. The European tour of

which they'd sung for months had slid firmly into doubt. They had traveled afar and risked, in certain circumstances, the prospect of spending an hour in Rugby despising themselves. They had paid outrageous ticket prices. They had paid outrageous train prices or outrageous fuel prices—or ridden a bus for four hours. The smattering of home fans had mocked them and then filed out. Their goalkeeper had committed a penalty in the box, then lorded his ensuing save of the penalty kick over the home fans even though his team trailed by a score organically close to 10–0. The home fans had mocked this visiting goalkeeper. With justification.

Yet there they lined the upper rows, my heroes, roughly twenty-five in number. One held a stuffed Portsmouth elephant. One held a stuffed Portsmouth bear (brown, not blue). Two guys who couldn't have been older than twenty-three had gone shirtless even though they'd yet to age enough to develop the fat that helps fend off the cold. One twirled his shirt, round and round, as if in the sixty-second minute of some wrenching melodrama of a match. All chanted and sang. Drums played. Moments later, out in the streets, amid the quietly sated Blackburn fans, about six Portsmouth types marched through singing about a European tour.

If you can take a dismal 3–nil day and transform it into an early evening spent marching down the street and singing that you're going to Europe, you have an indomitableness simply lacking in the 99 percent majority of the 300 million Americans. You do. You simply do. That's what I learned about myself at that moment: having emerged from a U.S. birth canal, I'm simply not conditioned to celebrate eighth place, especially after a chance to vault to sixth fails to lend my side even the slightest apparent inspiration. What's that old poll result about American children who'd finish, say, tenth in the world on a math test but when asked where they suspected their country would finish, always answered, "First"? I had come along in that. We emerge from the womb with a pancreas, a spleen, and a built-in arrogance. We simply don't handle eighth all that well, which might help explain why we don't live as long as do Britons.

For us, it can take a blue bear to supply perspective. I'd be-gun e-mailing with the blue bear, and he explained that for sea-sons, Pompey fans have wished and strained and added up potential points just aching to conjure the forty that figure to clear relegation. This season, forty came ludicrously early, on February 10, against Manchester City, when Pompey hit forty-one and the slots literally gushed coins. Maybe nobody knows quite what to do, the wise creature explained.

Nobody—save for twenty-five crooners, two drummers, and a breathless bugler.

26

NEVER MISS A CHANCE
TO HANG OUT IN A PUB WITH
A BLUE BEAR

Those e-mails from a blue bear had become the first ursine e-mails I'd ever received. I confessed that I'd sort of stalked him inadvertently, and that I knew already that he'd follow his girl-friend to Australia in the summer of 2007, and that he'd cleared his bus window with his removable right blue paw, and that at that moment I'd wished that I too possessed a removable blue paw. He somehow refrained from freaking out and invited me to the Shepherd's Crook pub just a David James punt from Fratton Park before the home match with regal Chelsea. The match with Chelsea would begin at 5:15 PM rather than 3:00 PM, a source of frustration to long-term fans but perfectly ordinary to a Premiership interloper like myself.

My soccer guru Tom, who can tell you the Liverpool score from most any important juncture in his life, has lamented that in the preferable days of yore, a Saturday in England would've brought ten games, all starting at 3:00, simple as that, none of this 12:45 or this 5:15 or this Sunday at 12:45 or this Sunday at 4:00 or whatnot. This lament reminded me that NFL games once started at only 1:00 and 4:00 on Sundays save for one game on

Monday night at 9:00, and how that brought routine and familiarity to my childhood, and how I never could wait for my parents to drive us home from the drudgery of church so I could shed the wretched forty-pound church shoes and strangling tie, plop down for the pregame show at 12:30, and watch until 7:00. Now, with games strewn all over the clock, even two on Sunday nights, a child conceivably could miss church altogether, start watching the NFL pregame shows at 11:00, then watch games from 1:00 PM until midnight, leaving even less time for homework and further contributing to the decline of a superpower.

England's rescheduling for the real god of TV, meanwhile, has posed challenges even more fundamental. It has tested the awe-inspiring English digestive tract and forced it to prove again its uncommon sturdiness. Where once pub-goers could schedule their beer reasonably from, say, 12:30 to 2:45 for a reliable 3:00 PM kickoff, now they have these 12:45s and these 5:15s, which distort everything. For the 12:45, the drinker must shove down the amount of beer requisite for viewing pleasure by about 12:30, thereby interfering with a recent breakfast or threatening the organism as a whole if there has been no breakfast. The 5:15 might be even more perilous, for that subjects the consumer to beer's cunning sneak attack over extended periods lasting several hours. As life on earth has shown, judgment about whether to have a fourth pint can blur after a third, and judgment about whether to have a fifth pint can vanish altogether after a fourth.

And then, if you have a 5:15 on the same day you have a Liverpool–Manchester United enticement at 12:45, so that everybody wants to get to the pub by soon after 12:45 to watch that match, let me just tell you that I experienced this on March 3, 2007, and your vision can get sort of furry.

By about 4:51, you might be having the fourth pint while conversing in the Shepherd's Crook with a blue bear and his friend dressed as a regular human, Dan, whom you recognized straightaway from the Middlesbrough train. At some point between 2:00 and 4:30, their other friend from Woking and the Middlesbrough train and the No Sumo Wrestlers Alley might've walked in, and they might call him Hopkins, one name only, like

Madonna or Ronaldinho. The bear might've rushed across the pub to actually bear-hug Hopkins, the bartenders might've poured more beers, one of the world's better laughs might've rattled off about twenty times, and you might've chatted with two or three other Pompey fans. You might see the blue bear sweat in his suit and wonder new things, such as whether the dry cleaners handles such outfits and whether there's even a place for them on the little dry-cleaning form somewhere near "shirts" and "trousers" and "jackets." You might not ask, though, if you're from Virginia.

Pretty soon, everybody might end up having to scurry over to Fratton Park at the last minute to see José Mourinho, Didier Drogba, Frank Lampard, and the like, the icons of Chelsea, as if just remembering why we all came to town in the first place. Breathless at your seat, play already under way, you might find in your pocket two wallets, the second belonging to Charlie, because you had to hold it hours ago, because one of the problems with being a bear is having no place to put a wallet. Then you might watch Chelsea's 2–0 win over Portsmouth, and you might think it perfunctory, with the amazing Drogba's twenty-ninth goal of the season at thirty-three minutes plus Salomon Kalou's at eighty-two. You might not recollect too many of the details.

True, Andy Cole's header at seventy-seven minutes almost tied the match, and that can ring sort of memorable, and Chelsea goalkeeper Petr Cech's save rose to the level of world-class according to Uncle Harry, and, true, Cech contorted himself so improbably for that save that I could've sworn there were two of him.

Yet my vision of Chelsea's gritty win seemed unclear even by my clueless standards. I did not join in the early-game rendition of "Where's Your Title Gone?" (to the tune of "Where's Your Momma Gone?"), which noted how second-place Chelsea trailed Manchester United in the standings. I did not notice anything particularly noticeable. All blame, of course, goes to the 5:15 kickoff, which also explains why I crib here from Glenn Moore's eloquent report in the *Independent*.

The report, like all that day, had little to do with Portsmouth, and not because the Blackburn eyesore had dropped Pompey to eighth behind the big four plus Bolton, Everton, and Reading. This match figured in the title race between Manchester United and Chelsea. When the day began, the twice-defending champion Chelsea trailed by nine points, but then Manchester United (playing the same day at Liverpool) scored what Britons call a "shock goal"—we'd call it "shocking"—in added time to win 1–0, and Sir Alex Ferguson bounced in joy like he'd suddenly lost half his age, even as I tried to explain to a blue bear how I hadn't understood that Joey Barton song. Manchester United therefore led the table by twelve as Chelsea took the pitch under pressure to get it back to nine in the rugged Pompey den. As Moore wrote of Fratton Park after the match, "The location of Mourinho's press conference, by the gentlemen's toilets in a draughty concourse under the ancient main stand, illustrates its uniqueness in the sanitised modern game."

As added backdrop, the wondrous but chatty Chelsea manager, Mourinho, and Sir Alex Ferguson had some little back-and-forth snit-fit going, a reminder that at the helm of great teams stand unmitigated divas, their diva-ness contributing inescapably to their success. I tune out this stuff very rapidly these days, but Mourinho evidently had complained about the refereeing in Manchester United matches, possibly because of the fact that the staggeringly talented pinup Cristiano Ronaldo, age only twenty-one, tended to "dive," or sprawl to the ground in an attempt to cajole penalty calls from the referee. Even a lost novice could see that Ronaldo had spent the year bolstering Portugal's hopes in the Olympic diving competition for both Beijing 2008 and London 2012, in both platform and springboard. In turn, Ferguson had responded to reporters that Mourinho should "button his lip." In Fratton Park after the win, Mourinho had responded to Moore and other reporters, "Why should I shut up? He was allowed to talk about referees for the last twenty years of his career. What's the difference between me and him?" In life, high school actually never ends, even though they hand you a paper and tell you farewell. The prom kings and prom queens continue to snipe at each other for the duration of existence.

So much meaning and undercurrent in the match, but to myself it seemed just to ooze on by. Much like the 2–0 Chelsea win in 2006 when first I saw Portsmouth, this seemed the depressing foregone conclusion against one of the big four. I might've even wondered why I bothered, had I bothered to wonder. Even the-only-bear-named-Charlie-I'd-ever-met said he'd spent a good portion of the early evening obsessed with the red moon. He removed his paws and called me up frantically after the match, wondering if I had his wallet. We met up again at the Shepherd's Crook because we definitely needed another beer. Dan and I discussed the eternally mysterious story of the ineffectualness of England's national team, and he theorized that the English media freights the whole operation with spiteful pressure that renders the players afraid of erring. I chimed in with my American tales of teams that adore media doubters so that they can "prove the experts wrong" and then say, "Nobody respected us." The United States literally crawls with such athletes who have made a cliché of alleged disrespect. They can find the one denigration amid one thousand compliments, even if it came from a fishing columnist in Nome, Alaska. They're desperate for somebody to say they're hopeless so they can locate some motivation.

It had long since grown tiresome.

Sometime after I finished subjecting these unsuspecting souls to my diatribe on that particular cultural difference, we began to make our halting way home. We stopped at the little Tesco convenience store near the stadium to amass supplies, which included some abominable snack sausages and some heavenly little éclairs. This seemed a ritual for the three. Dan and Hopkins had met at university in Portsmouth, and Hopkins met Charlie, who hails from a lineage of Pompey allegiance, in the Fratton End. All three were twenty-seven, i.e., newborn. They became the first Portsmouth fans I knew personally, and this would mark an upgrade in my development as a fan. Once you know some Other People who follow the club, your fanhood intensifies. You begin to watch the club while wondering what they might be thinking while they watch the club, even if they're just thinking about a red moon, as would any worthy mammal.

If knowing Other People means walking the streets and train platforms with a blue bear, then I heartily endorse this approach, for a blue bear just makes life better in ways you don't expect. For one thing, people tend to greet you in pubs, and children might wave at you out car windows.

On the glum side, our ride home somehow included a rail replacement bus. We all sat on a back row, one row behind the only other apparent passenger. We offered him some sort of food, which he accepted, and he continued living. The blue bear fell asleep during that ride, then woke and asked for an éclair, only to hear Hopkins utter a deathless line, "Éclairs are dead to you now." Eventually, we did get to ride a train, on which a young male-female couple boarded with the male dressed as a Southampton fan. He immediately saw the blue Pompey bear and, proving that it's fearsome to see a blue bear on a train, promptly disclaimed any Southampton fandom. He said he and his date were headed for a costume party.

As we rolled toward Waterloo, a singular blue bear repeatedly stated his loyalty to Portsmouth with what I came to regard as haiku:

Any manager.
Any players.
Training on the moon.
Fratton Park as it is.
Pompey till I die.

Over and over he said it, and I must tell you that you haven't really lived until you've ridden home on a train with a blue bear vowing support for his club given any manager, any players, and with Fratton Park as it is, no renovations or new stadiums necessary. Just the same, none of us could discern the meaning of the inscrutable passage "training on the moon." Hopkins asked for an explanation of this peculiar "training on the moon," and none came.

At Woking, which forever sits between Portsmouth and London, Hopkins would disembark, but as a blue bear wished the party to continue, he tried to prevent Hopkins's departure. Hopkins managed to escape and exit and then, with the train waiting for five minutes and the doors still open, turned around and taunted the blue bear as if to say, *Come and get me*. Repeatedly the blue bear sprinted off the train toward Hopkins, only to hurry back for fear the doors would close. Repeatedly Hopkins tried to lure the blue bear once more. Repeatedly Dan and I doubled over on the train, and while it doesn't sound funny in the least, everyone really should see a blue bear chase somebody on a train platform late on a Saturday night at least once.

27

BETRAYING A KIND
READING FAN

Even when an American has lived three-quarters of a full Premiership season, some part of his underdeveloped brain retains a vague big-bad-wolf fear of the English soccer fan. It's irrational, but then, I'm from Virginia, and I come by irrational fear honestly. My mother once became the only person in global history to buy that flight insurance in the airport, and my beloved maternal grandmother, of course, envisioned the concept of carjacking way back in the 1970s before it ever became fashionable in Miami.

That's the only way I can explain my ludicrous behavior of March 17, when I spent a whole game declining to come out of the closet as a Portsmouth fan to a Reading fan, despite the Reading fan being clearly one of the most decent people extant—so decent, in fact, that he relinquished a corporate job to work at the Royal Society for the Prevention of Cruelty to Animals. People who work for less money to protect animals generally tend to refrain from berating or slugging other people, even opposing fans, but you never know.

I came to sit beside Mark in the Reading section via my usual ineptitude. To begin, Reading versus Portsmouth did not shout from the schedule when the Premier League drew up the

2006–2007 schedule, but it had sprouted as a little March colossus plump with European implications. Reading, having never graced the top flight previously in its 135-year history, had debuted with aplomb and picturesque soccer. Portsmouth, having just poked its head from the abyss of relegation eleven months prior, flirted with its best top-flight season in fifty years.

By the sun-splashed morning of Saturday, March 17, a chunk of the table looked thusly:

6.	Everton	43 points
7.	Reading	42 points
8.	Tottenham Hotspur	42 points
9.	Portsmouth	41 points
10.	Blackburn	40 points

Understandably, all the home tickets sold for number 7 Reading versus number 9 Portsmouth, and with Reading only forty-four miles from Portsmouth, we away sorts had to enter an away-ticket lottery. I had no idea how to enter an away-ticket lottery, because being a sportswriter for twenty years thoroughly debilitates the portion of the brain that deduces how to enter away-ticket lotteries. That's how I wound up standing on the sidewalk near the away entrance of Madejski Stadium, watching my people pass by, hoping someone might commit a crime and sell me an unused ticket. That's right, as police informed me one day at Fratton Park: it's a crime to sell a ticket to a stranger.

Well, tick-tock, tick-tock, tick-tock, and I began to wonder where I'd spend the match. Madejski Stadium sits outside of town, suburban and all, very much like many an American stadium. It's next door to a B&Q, which must've made it either haunting or enticing for Glen Johnson. It's a lovely, spiffy stadium, but its anti-neighborhood doesn't exactly teem with pubs in which I could watch a little colossus of a match. Maybe one day they'll put pubs in that field on the other side of the parking lot, but on March 17 there was no way they could complete them by kickoff.

At last, before conceding and boarding a bus back into town,

I decided to circumnavigate the stadium. At the door of the home ticket office, I played ditzy American tourist—one might call it typecasting—and I asked one guy if this match happened to be a sellout when already I knew the answer. He replied that he thought so but that his father had not been able to attend and that he sought somebody to buy that ticket for £30 (about $57). I volunteered eagerly, but I knew it might worry him if he knew he'd bring in a Portsmouth fan who, for all he knew, might start taunting Reading fans, creating a gigantic brawl replete with hurled projectiles and getting him banned from Madejski for life. I decided to remain quiet.

So with kickoff nigh, Mark and I hurried toward the gate together, and we marched right on up the steps to his family's seats in the top row, which in cozy, 24,200-seat Madejski Stadium actually afforded a grand view. We sat almost straight up behind the goal David James defended during the first half, all the way across the stadium from my people, so as to render my people inaudible. I dug into my pocket and excavated the £30. The match had begun. I figured Reading would win by probably 2–0, and I could not dislike Reading, as I'd visited practice on a newspaper assignment one day, found it a jovial place, and interviewed its American goalkeeper, Marcus Hahnemann, who said his two sons had lived in England for a large-enough percentage of their lives that they chided him about his unacceptable American pronunciation of the English words "Harry Potter."

That's appealing and all, but I wanted Portsmouth to win some kind of badly, especially because I'd begun to fear Blackburn getting bumptious down there in tenth, as I'm that rare Pompey fan who'd spent my entire fan experience exclusively at single-digit Premiership positions, fearing the spiraling darkness of double-digits. In a testament to my prosperity of timing, I'd only just learned that, until 2005–2006, Portsmouth had not played in a division higher than Southampton since 1960. Here I worried about Blackburn and Reading, not to mention Everton and Tottenham, while for forty-five years (forty . . . five . . . years . . .) Pompey fans often seethed about a rival seventeen miles away. I'd never even really seen a Southampton uniform except on a train, and that one evidently was bound for a costume party.

In my scant experience, Southampton seemed dead as éclairs.

Well, Reading menaced our David James fortress early on, and I started to feel both nervousness and the wish to contain it, which I typically achieve by practicing perspective and thinking about calamities such as typhoons, poverty, or Tom Cruise. For the match's early stages, Reading kept making ambitious bids, and Sol Campbell and the ever-admirable Linvoy Primus kept thwarting them, and I kept suppressing the urge to stand up and salute quietly, and I kept feeling guilty I had not told Mark the truth.

Moreover, Mark and I began to chat.

One of the first things I noticed about English soccer was that people don't chat during matches. You never hear anybody talking about how they've bought a new sport utility vehicle, or how they're having trouble with the middle son who recently egged somebody's house in the adjacent neighborhood, or how the workmen adding the deck to the back of the house have taken far too long so it might've been better to have hired Mexican illegals. In general, we Americans do chat during games. There might not be so much chatting at NFL games, because many NFL fans only grunt, but we chat a bit at basketball during routs and time-outs, and many of us chat profusely at baseball, where the slowness lends itself to chatting. On the right side of the ocean, I've never heard English fans speak much more than brief comments to an adjacent person about a certain play or the subterranean IQ of the referee or linesman. It's never about, say, their wife's annoying new poodle.

That's why I felt self-conscious just sitting there chatting even as I chatted with a profoundly cool individual. Mark talked about how his job change (working to prevent cruelty to animals) had left him driving home from work feeling his workday had boosted the world ever so slightly. He talked about how British politicians all espouse pretty much the same ideas and American politics seem to display more contrasts. He talked about Hillary Clinton. He talked about how he'd never been to the

United States but saw England win the rugby World Cup in Australia. I talked too. I talked about how I still couldn't believe rugby's the game played by gentlemen while soccer's supposedly the one played by ruffians. I talked about how David Beckham exudes a certain decency, as I'd just seen him on the previous Wednesday at Old Trafford thanking Manchester United fans at halftime of an exhibition. I talked about Iraq. I talked about how Senator John McCain refused to appease the religious right wing when it had clout during the 2000 presidential campaign, thus costing him, and how now he plans to appease the religious right wing for the 2008 presidential campaign just as its clout has diminished, thus costing him. I talked about the huge American college football stadiums and plush dressing rooms vis-à-vis Manchester United. I talked about Reading's unpretentious practice facility and how players have to walk outside from their showers back to their dressing area wearing nothing but a towel, and along the way they sometimes kid the forty-ish female locker-room attendant—"You want some of this?"—whereupon she rolls her eyes.

Mercy, did we talk, and of course, I talked more than he did, and even though I tried to keep the tone relatively hushed, I felt certain I saw this blumpy guy in front of us tire of overhearing the chatting and glare at me through the corner of his left eye.

On the field, Reading's assaults on our goal made a Reading score seem inevitable, and I still did not tell Mark of my dread. A header by Reading's Steve Sidwell darted somehow wide, and I still did not tell Mark of my relief. Portsmouth's Campbell the giant defused a Dave Kitson chance, and I still did not tell Mark of my ga-ga pleasure at that defusing. Some fans around me sang the Pompey Chimes, only with "F—— up, Pompey," and I still did not tell Mark that his brethren lacked creativity.

No, I just sat there gabbing but not telling, and I learned that the longer you wait to tell somebody you're posing as neutral while feeling very partial, the harder it gets to tell somebody you're posing as neutral while feeling very partial. I let on that I'd been to Fratton Park many times, but also that I'd been to Madejski Stadium twice and to Aston Villa's Villa Park in Birmingham and Newcastle's St. James' Park and Bolton's Reebok Stadium and Wigan's JJB Stadium (twice!). I felt lamer than lame, unable to divulge my true self to this gentle soul, while the match played on and I definitely wanted my club to rip the pure living stuffing out of his club.

Then the energy reversed after halftime, and Portsmouth began conducting the show, and Benjani Mwaruwari banged a great shot that Hahnemann saved. As time dragged by, I began to think Pompey might get out of there with a point, even if the melodramatically troubled West Ham couldn't possibly win to keep Blackburn at bay. I also began rationalizing that my secrecy made perfect sense. Any rational person would wait until the end of the game to tell this Reading fan he'd harbored an infiltrator.

Suddenly, boom, at eighty-one minutes, a Portsmouth player I'd seldom noticed, Richard Hughes, struck one from thirty yards out just below us. It beat everybody, including Hahnemann, and for a fleeting second I thought about sixth place. Then it banged off the right upright and straight back out of danger, and I smothered an intensely guttural groan. I could not express to anyone how desperately I wanted that shot to glance off that upright and into the goal, or to miss the upright altogether and depress my fellow American in goal down there. I don't know why. I certainly felt no disdain for Reading. Something had bit me, and after a lifetime of viewing standings bookishly, objectively, I wanted sixth place so much more than tenth.

When the match ended, nobody had scored, whereupon we walked out, still talking, and I decided I'd loathe myself even more than usual if I did not tell Mark that all along I had been supporting Pompey with undetectable twitches and phantom fist pumps. Before he made off I thanked him for everything and I confessed, even telling him how that Hughes post-banger had left me in a mild state of anguish. "I am sorry for betraying you," I said.

Well, he seemed so very peaceful as to make my game-long misgivings seem toweringly ludicrous. He even told me that either the best man in his wedding had been a Portsmouth fan or that he had served as the best man in the wedding of a Portsmouth fan, I can't remember which, because I felt too consumed with my own absurdity. But at least Portsmouth got a point to reach forty-two, and somehow, apparently with a referee's help, struggling West Ham won 2–1 at Blackburn. The day had been lucky, if preposterous.

28

JUST DISGUSTING

The March portion of the Premiership season contains these gaping breaks so that England's national team, which draws talent from Premiership teams, can flourish on certain weekends without distraction. On Saturday, March 24, England played at Israel in a qualifier for the Euro 2008 tournament, and I walked all over Central London seeking a pub with enough room to stand and watch. It was a challenge. I finally found one near the British Museum, where I could only squeeze inside the door and watch from a crummy angle in the foyer. This qualifies as irony, for the dismalness we watched—on a big screen, so we could observe it more closely—gained its best summation from Rod Liddle in the *Sunday Times*. Having suggested that the TV rights for England's national games should go for "£8.50, a used Oyster card and maybe a couple of bags of Walkers crisps," he then wrote: "By pure chance I was in Tel Aviv last Saturday and could have gone to the game. My options were: watch England play Israel, or go to the West Bank and get bricked or maybe beheaded by angry and oppressed Palestinians. No question: 'Shalom! Take me to Hebron!' I shouted to the nearest taxi driver."

This ceaseless national melodrama with the England team counts as choice entertainment for Americans, seeing as how we're probably too spacious to have our own similar bonding-and-griping experience. When we lose at a game we invented—

example: basketball, 2004 Athens Olympics, semifinal, to Argentina—we often just opt for some excuse (didn't bring our best players) and get on with it. Or if we lose at a game of privilege we ought to dominate—example: Ryder Cup, repeatedly—we just turn our attention to something else, usually the NFL, where we'll never lose, mostly because almost nobody else actually plays the game.

We're sunnier sorts in general. It's probably the weather or the newness as a nation.

But after marveling at another cycle of English national team angst—at least, media angst—it can seem the Premiership season got discontinued long ago and that, oh, it's time for that again, and good. I'd never been to Fulham's Craven Cottage, a stadium somewhere in London, never heard much about Craven Cottage, and never knew if Craven Cottage really had any lore. I had to dig into my London A-to-Z map book to find the location of Craven Cottage, and I made my way on the Tube on March 31, a luminous Saturday. Amazingly, the Pompey troika had continued to e-mail me, and we'd made loose plans to convene so I could even meet "Ms. Pompeybear" before she led her mammal off to Sydney. In our third and fourth cases of running across each other by accident, I found myself standing next to Dan on the platform at the Notting Hill Gate Tube station, and after we boarded we found ourselves by chance in the same Tube car with Charlie, furless in civilian clothing, and with Ms. Caroline Pompeybear, an outright gem from the get-go.

At some point in that ride on the District Line to Putney Bridge, or out of the station through Bishops Park along the Thames, we discussed one of my favorite new subjects of my Premiership tutelage. As Dan had explained on Chelsea day at the Shepherd's Crook, there's a sign in Craven Cottage just as you enter the away end. This sign has an arrow. It gives directions to the uninitiated.

It reads: AWAY AND NEUTRAL FANS.

That "neutral fans" bit just really galled Dan, to my great amusement as a native of a country of stadiums rich in neutral fans such as business travelers, weary parents, or those people who drive around on clichéd baseball pilgrimages, collecting stadiums and wasting petroleum. Where I would've never given it a thought, Dan found "neutral fans" borderline-appalling. How could a person even be a "neutral fan," and why would a "neutral fan" even bother? That, in turn, made me eager to witness this sign for myself, here in this country of devout soccer partisanship and partisan soccer din. I mentioned my excitement that we'd see the "neutral fans" sign—he rolled his eyes—and my theory that perhaps the neutral-fans zone of the stadium could serve as some sort of temporary holding place. Maybe somebody would arrive as a neutral fan, but then during a given match might take a shine to a player or a club or a club's colors, whereupon that person could proceed to another section or go to a newly formed subsection of the neutral-fan zone. (The post-neutral-fan zone, possibly.) Or maybe a home or away fan might become so aghast at his own club's malfeasance or a manager's ineptitude that he might forfeit his own zone to access the neutral zone, seeking a respite from the unbearable emotional investment.

Well, a few things about Craven Cottage: It's gorgeous. Its away (and neutral) section offers a grand view of the Thames, of even the current on the Thames, of even the crews rowing along on said current of said Thames. It's expensive in ticket prices and concessions, perhaps gouging people for that view of the Thames and the rowers. It's not really all that loud, befitting a club owned by the owner of a chichi department store. And it does have one of the craziest signs of the Premiership, the one that kindly offers directions to those potentially lost neutral fans.

Portsmouth remained in ninth place with forty-two points, three behind seventh-place Tottenham but with an advantage in "goal differential," as I dumbly called it before Hopkins corrected me to the proper "goal difference." Fulham had fourteenth place, with thirty-four points. We'd bought tickets separately, so while my three new friends went to their section, I went to mine, plopping down about thirty rows behind one of the goals and just to the right of a man named Chris, who said he'd been a Pompey fan for fifty years and had lived his entire life on the Isle of Wight. I said I'd been a Pompey fan for one year and might've said that during my teen years my school in Virginia had a fierce basketball rivalry with Isle of Wight Academy, which sat just up the highway. I did not say we had a chant about the Isle of Wight Chargers that might just illustrate our national deficiencies in singing and chanting, for it went like this:

Chargers are what? Rednecks!
Chargers are what? Rednecks!
Spell it!
R-E-D-N-E-X, rednecks, rednecks, rednecks!

Then again, I don't tell this to many people.

Chris had traveled alone and seemed so gentle and amused by some of the inventions that would emerge from our end, particularly the "Scummer, Scummer, Scummer" derivations, directed all game long at Antti Niemi, the Fulham goalkeeper. Eventually, at moments when Niemi seemed alone while everybody else played the other end, I began to figure out that, of all the Fulham players, it was Niemi they taunted, and not because of any bias against Finland. He probably once played for Southampton.

Early on, though, there came a jolt, one I still love to call up on YouTube. As the videotape begins, you can still hear one group of fans and not the other, and guess which. Yes, the outnumbered. It's one of my favorite songs, sung to the "Volare" tune:

Benjani, whoaaaaa-oh,
Benjani, whoaaaaa-oh,
He comes from Zimbabwe,
He's gonna score today,
Benjani, whoaaaaa-oh.

At the other end of the pitch, only four minutes in, it might've been Portsmouth's Benjani who played the ball into the middle to Kanu, who headed it out to our left to young Niko Kranjcar, Croatian, age twenty-two. Kranjcar edged to his right and let fly around the defense a ball that from our angle seemed headed well wide-right of the goal, for a useless skitter into the corner.

In the next instant, however, that thing crashed into the net.

We went absolutely berserk.

I'd dare to say that we were mental.

That ball had headed right and curled around leftward and left Niemi frozen while it helped itself to the top right corner of the goal. The away side of Craven Cottage began to shudder utterly, which freaked me out slightly and prompted two disparate thoughts. It made me think of the 6.1 earthquake I'd felt in Los Angeles on October 1, 1987, and how my friends' swimming pool out back had little ripple waves, but how their golden retriever lay there unmoved and unimpressed, as if saying, *I heard this coming before you did.* And it made me think of old Mile High Stadium in Denver, before it yielded to a new stadium across the way. Occupying the Mountain Time Zone, the least populous of the American mainland's four time zones, the fans of the NFL Denver Broncos don't get a ton of national credit for their passion, but passion they possess, as one of the few professional-fan groups with passion to match England's. Normally, for anything to rival English zeal, one must visit a college stadium or coliseum, even as a neutral fan. The old Mile High Stadium in Denver, though, remains the only American stadium to cause wavelets in my press-box coffee, and when I think of Denver set against the stunning Rocky Mountains, I think of those wavelets.

When the east end of Craven Cottage stopped shaking and I resumed normal respiration, I foresaw forty-five points and maybe even sixth place. That led me toward a terrible bit of education, the terrible strain felt when you care about a match and you hold a one-goal lead through almost its entirety. In all of sport, there might not be another routine scenario so nerve-shredding.

Neighboring Pompey supporters bitched at the team's performance for the second half of the first half. They railed that Uncle Harry couldn't get them to sustain anything. David James made a dazzling save at forty-two minutes as he neared the all-time

Premiership record of 142 of what we'd call "shutouts" but the Brits call "clean sheets." The second half crawled by. I felt almost ill and pleaded for time to hurry. I kept my cell phone in my right hand and eyed it repeatedly. Portsmouth's Svetoslav Todorov, whom I did not recognize, barely missed one good chance and one golden chance for 2–0, but I thought we still might make it. We made it to seventy minutes, to seventy-five, to eighty, to eighty-five, eighty-seven, eighty-eight.

We even made it to ninety minutes, and through a good bit of the four minutes of added time. Added time had begun at 4:51 PM, but I couldn't be sure how many seconds had passed within that minute, so I felt confused. Play continued mercilessly. I reached that point where you think just one or two more solid defensive plays might finish off matters.

Then, in a crowded sequence I couldn't see clearly, Fulham's Ian Pearce struck a prayer. James shifted in the prayer's direction. The prayer caromed off Linvoy Primus's leg. It hurried back toward the right portion of the goal that James had departed. It wrong-footed James. It dribbled sickly into the goal for Pearce, who had spent five minutes of the match on the sideline with the physio, then hobbled through the next ten. I felt an imcomparable thud. I wished they'd equalized at twelve minutes rather than ninety-two. James took the ball and disgustedly punted it over the roof and maybe into the Thames, maybe even whacking some unsuspecting rowers and influencing the outcome of some sanguine crew event. I had my first genuine, galling, what-if defeat, even in a draw. Yes, this supplanted Charlton, even with that a loss as opposed to this 1–1 draw. Uncle Harry would call it "a real opportunity lost." Sol Campbell and James would walk off looking crestfallen.

I believe that signaled that I'd signed on to caring archly, and I thought a bit about Bostonians and Chicagoans, the United States' most accomplished connoisseurs of last-second pratfalls. The Red Sox's tenth-inning capitulation in game 6 of the 1986 World Series always struck most people for Mookie Wilson's bubbling little trifle of a ground ball that slipped through the legs of first baseman Bill Buckner, but I always felt even more dumbstruck by the preceding sequence of looping singles that wandered into unmanned spaces. People always focused on the Chicago Cubs fan who interfered with the fly ball down the left-field line in Game 6 of the 2003 National League Championship Series, but I never could get over the way the Cubs' doom seemed so obvious even with a 3–0 lead. That they would crater from there seemed obvious—and to them.

People in my job always chronicle the fan masses beholding these fateful disasters, but we often don't quite comprehend the feelings. I felt I knew just a little inkling of it when that ball redirected itself past James. Carried to its ultimate definition, it's powerlessness, right? Whatever powerlessness I felt, my more veteran Portsmouth brethren felt it exponentially. The entire stand seemed powerless. What could it do?

As the tepid Fulham fans made their little roar, Pompey decided to lash out in the only direction possible and in the only vein available—toward the home fans, and with an assessment:

Your support is,
Your support is,
Your support is f——ing s——!
Your support is f——ing s——!

I felt astonished, while gutted.

29

RATHER HOPELESS

A visit from Manchester United on a sunny first Saturday in April probably should resuscitate a fan to the brink of foaming at the mouth, but I felt only glum and peeved. The Fulham bit had really taken some starch out of me, to a surprising degree given my twenty years as a detached chronicler who had allowed himself only fleeting bouts of rooting for this side or that side, often only because their opponent practiced obnoxiousness. After Fulham, I even wondered why we bother placing such psychological emphasis on something that can hinge on a prayer ricocheting off the leg of a commendable defender.

As the Pompey fans walked out of Craven Cottage in a barely budging blob, the foremost buzz concerned Southampton's concurrent 6–0 win over Wolves, and that illustrated the difference between the seasoned crowd and myself. Where the idea of a tying goal in the very last moments of a game, thereby robbing your club of two points, deeply rankled me, it rankled them less, some having ventured to the fourth division and back during their lifetimes. And while I thought of Southampton as pretty much just another second-division club trying to elbow toward promotion, they knew it as Satan.

One must always keep an eye on Satan, but I had no Satan, with the possible exception of Ben Thatcher, so I reeled. First, we proceeded to a London pub near Earl's Court, an idea I wel-

comed because repeated scientific studies show that beer pos-
sesses an elixir component that shoos from the cranium that horrid what-if feeling after a prayer has ricocheted off a leg. That
component is widely believed to be alcohol.

For the next Saturday, April 7, I plied another time-honored
defense mechanism in the fanatic's repertoire—the downplaying
of the next game or match, the grand pooh-poohing, the careful
practice of low expectations. The brain suffers greatly from fluke
goals ricocheting off legs during injury time, or from ninth-
inning home runs that wipe out leads, or from fumbles at the
two-yard line on the brink of the Super Bowl. My brain carried
it to an extreme in which I not only expected nothing from
Portsmouth versus Manchester United but began to resent that I
had spent time and concern on seeing Portsmouth versus Manchester United or on any of this crud in the United States or its
mother, the United Kingdom.

As I walked toward Fratton Park, I pretty much mumbled
grumbles. I railed within my own brain against the system that
subjected us to such predictability. I counted myself as part of a
manipulated public and loathed the dishonor. I did spend a millisecond wondering about the wisdom of Sir Alex Ferguson's
comment that he could almost taste the Premiership title, but I
figured he'd honed a keenness on such matters and knew predictability when he saw it. I just knew the Manchester United
match would bear a rote resemblance to the Chelsea match, what
with Manchester United in dire need, only three points ahead of
Chelsea (seventy-eight to seventy-five) by kickoff.

Really, I just about up and questioned an entire life of following games, and I felt contempt for the tiered Premiership system
in which you could have a big four hogging the last twenty major domestic titles. The money athletes make, I'd never once resented. I'd always figured it made marketplace sense. If the public
wants to resent the salaries, then the public can stop funding the
salaries. Besides, better to have the largesse in the hands of, say,
twenty-five athletes and one club owner than in the hands of one
club owner. If you spread the money around more, maybe it will

trickle down more, as when the athletes give it to, say, needy lap dancers.

Yet the system that allows four or five clubs to outspend the others, then pretend they've achieved something when they finish in the top four . . . I decided I hated that as I ambled up Goldsmith Avenue. Money, always, always money. I always loved sports, not money. Salary negotiations make me yawn. Contract details, even the lavish accoutrements of athletes, bore me to beige. The NFL and the NBA and English rugby have their salary caps, and most everyone agrees that's wise, but if you start to get into salary-cap details, I start to tune out and mull more compelling things, which include just about anything else on earth. I love to read a good sports section and can't make it through three paragraphs of a good business section. Yet as long-term members of American sports sections, my cronies and I had become business writers ever more until one day in 2005 when I found myself refuting the business logic of George Steinbrenner, shipping magnate and Yankees owner. The absurdity! And yet, I was right, and Steinbrenner wrong! The double absurdity! Steinbrenner had argued against NFL-style revenue sharing among baseball clubs by noting that Wal-Mart doesn't share revenues with the Target up the boulevard. That argument is, of course, fallacious, and maybe even devious, because he'd misidentified his product, and surely he knows product. The Wal-Mart and Target brands are Wal-Mart and Target, while the New York Yankees' product is baseball, and if you don't believe it, let the Yankees play alone every night and see how well that draws after a short period of people turning up for intra-squad exhibitions.

Around and around and around we go, we sports people, paying attention to sports and paying for sports and even writing about sports, thus generating money, then reeling from that dulling sense that comes from the proliferation of . . . money.

Sigh.

As I entered the antiquated brick gate at Fratton Park, the powerlessness had grabbed me again, I suppose. Still, once inside, I had to admit the occasion seemed boosted by the presence of star-shine from Wayne Rooney and Cristiano Ronaldo, soon to be the Premiership player of the year. It just made things seem heavier, more pertinent, with the red of Manchester United fuller and redder than normal red. And on a sunny spring afternoon on the south coast of England, Fratton Park seemed unusually plugged-in, even for itself, doubtless because of the presence of Manchester United as opposed to say, Wigan. Many of these souls probably bore Fratton Park witness to Portsmouth's wins over Manchester United in 2004 and 2005.

So here came Manchester United. Ronaldo's progresses up the pitch could take your breath away and dredge a gasp had you any concern for the preservation of the home goal. Rooney's very presence instilled dread. Ferguson had just finished playing a European Champions League quarterfinal leg at Roma on Wednesday night, so he rested the stalwart Ryan Giggs for the first half, but his team hadn't lost in the Premiership in seven matches, or since the Sunday before playing Portsmouth in that FA Cup fourth-rounder on the dismally dreary January 27. At ten minutes, Kanu headed one into the arms of Manchester United keeper Edwin van der Sar. I had that foreboding feeling that even such half-opportunities would prove scarce.

Ronaldo began treating us to a recital of his catalog of dives. He dived often enough that I began to wonder if he missed opportunities that would've come moments after the dive had he merely stayed up and not dived. Other teams like Tottenham and Middlesbrough had complained about his diving, and Ferguson and Ronaldo more or less had accused other teams of envy, when in reality other teams had complained about his diving for a completely different reason: because he had been diving. As he dove at Fratton Park and the Fratton Park faithful along the north end barked their gripes, the referees acknowledged some of the dives with free kicks. Ronaldo sent a thirty-five-yard free kick wide-left at twelve minutes, another into a two-man wall at twenty-four minutes (those times according to football.co.uk). In other scary sequences, Ronaldo blew by both Dejan Stefanovic and Linvoy Primus, but sent a shot wide-right, and Rooney fell at the behest of Primus's sliding tackle, and the referee managed to rule it a fair challenge.

The Fratton End got involved.

To the tune of "If You're Happy and You Know It," there came a charming version we never sang in grade school back in the Colonies. It went:

> *If you really f——ing hate 'em, clap your hands,*
> *If you really f——ing hate 'em, clap your hands,*
> *If you really f——ing hate 'em,*
> *Really f——ing hate 'em,*
> *Really f——ing hate 'em, clap your hands.*

I marveled at how my American schoolteachers shielded us, often not teaching us the real lyrics to songs.

As a special gift to Rooney, the Fratton End sang "Guantánamera":

> *Fat, ugly Scouser,*
> *You're just a fat, ugly Scouser,*
> *Fat, ugly Scouuuuu-ser,*
> *You're just a fat, ugly Scouuuuu-ser.*

That one just struck me as sort of unkind.

At twenty-five minutes, Manchester United's Kieran Richardson missed a reasonable chance from a Ronaldo free kick, high and wide, and we mocked him, and the match had settled in. It seemed plausible, even with scant knowledge of strategy, that Pompey had opted to challenge Manchester United rather than sticking its proverbial tail betwixt its proverbial legs in proverbial hope of a proverbial 0–0 draw. Pompey did forge a few more chances than I'd expected in my apprenticeship and my misery. After all, in the league matchup at Old Trafford in November, Manchester United had won 3–0, then the 2–1 in the FA Cup, and across the winter, Pompey's offense had withered further. But even with that, Pompey's chances did seem spotty, while Manchester United's chances suggested the beach, as you could set the waves by your watch. In one of those spotty moments at thirty minutes, Benjani Mwaruwari shot one from, oh, I don't know, maybe thirty yards, and van der Sar saved it, but did not quite corral it, at the goal just below the Fratton End and just off to my right.

Just then, Matt Taylor slid into my line of sight, where veteran observers probably noticed him all along. He beat Rio Ferdinand to the ball and flicked it right back into the net, just like that. It happened so suddenly that it seemed untrue. I waited for a signal that somebody had gone offside or committed some arcane infraction wholly unfamiliar to myself. Pompey led 1–0. There seemed a vacant split-second there until the Fratton End heaved in mass mirth. I jumped up and down a bit but felt just as much amazement as joy, plus that twinge of caution because we're at only thirty minutes and the other side still goes by the name Manchester United.

A 1–0 lead against Manchester United presents the terrible specter of hope, so the brain must counterbalance that by anticipating a sure equalizer. The equalizer's coming, you know. It's coming. When? It's coming, you know. At the distant end, that souped-up red offense believed likewise. Michael Carrick quickly had a chance but sent it wide. A stray ball found Rooney at thirty-five minutes—the worst thing a stray ball can do—but he missed a long shot wide. Carrick then pried open the defense, giving Fletcher a point-blank shot, but James saved it with his considerable legs. Lauren got a yellow card for fouling Ronaldo.

Pompey had a few mild chances.

Then the whole thing slid into halftime, Portsmouth ahead by that 1–0. Here again came soccer's peerless precariousness, but in an outsized version. For it's one thing to suffer through a second half with a 1–0 lead at Fulham, wishing time would accelerate, but to do the same against Manchester United, there's a temptation just to refrain from looking—you know, just go ahead and leave the premises.

I didn't leave, of course, just sat there for more spite from the sport beast—what else would I do with my time?—while Pompey and Manchester United emerged to go on with an ominous second half. With every extraction of my pen and little pieces of paper for jotting down notes, I'd find my hands quivering increasingly, until the writing got all wavy and illegible. With every futile extraction of my cell phone, fixing to extend the grand tradition of text-messaging friends from soccer stands, I'd find my thumbs too atwitter to text efficiently. They'd blight the phone screen with an errant letter or numeral, and I'd just stop before I committed a semicolon. In this twenty-first century, a great match means one during which your hands cannot text.

At the mouth of the goal just down below, during the fifty-something minutes, Manchester United left James so festooned with shots that I just went ahead and conceded the goal. Counted it. Regarded the score as 1–1. Began adjusting to what had not transpired. As Primus cleaned up a through ball destined eerily for Rooney in the fifty-third minute, I remembered with trademark ineptitude that Portsmouth didn't have the unfit Sol Campbell that day, and that I'd been so tremulous that I'd completely blanked out on the absence of a giant. The biggest peril came in the fifty-eighth minute, when it pretty much turned into Times Square down there in the Portsmouth goal mouth. Seemingly half the population of Manchester took shots at the home goal. James made at least one astounding save that I believe might've been the one-handed Spiderman prevention of a Ronaldo try from a corner from Giggs, a Ferguson halftime insertion. The thirty-six-year-old keeper once dubbed "Calamity James" had upheld a stadium's spirits for just that much longer.

Ole Gunnar Solskjaer followed that save, and Lauren cleared that rebound.

Pitiless, this match.

Fifty-nine minutes, and Giggs loosed a screaming hazard that forced a fingertip save from the taller, dark-haired Spiderman in goal. Sixty-three minutes, and Rooney and Giggs set up Carrick, who shot wide. Sixty-nine minutes, and dread fear, Rooney, on the loose, corralling a Giggs pass, ready to gut the whole of us, then, suddenly, down went Rooney, courtesy Primus, in the box, and pleading for a penalty I suspected he'd get. Yet it did not come. Primus, once considered insufficiently gifted for the top flight, once more had foiled a twenty-one-year-old star deemed extravagantly gifted since his single-digit years.

So the 20,223 of us lurched into the seventieth minute, officially entering the concentric circles of horror. An equalizer in the 70–75 range would smart; an equalizer in the 75–80 range would sting a bit; an equalizer in the 80–85 range would sting for real; and an equalizer in the 85–93 range could make you wonder why you continue to put yourself through this kind of thing. Seventy-one minutes, seventy-two, seventy-three. With every time Portsmouth pushed the ball into the Manchester United end, I'd lop off another thirty seconds that we'd no longer have to suffer. I pictured us all clambering to various plateaus—the seventy-five-minute plateau, the seventy-seven-minute, the eighty-minute.

It was almost unbearable. Nobody chatted, because nobody ever does, but nobody even made a sound sometimes, as every eye in our section remained fixated upon the field. Maybe this represents the positive health effects of sport, the fact that you're so diverted from everyday worries, but I just didn't feel all that positively healthy. I'd begun quaking, not so much unlike the time at age ten when I thought I heard a burglar in my grandmother's house in Suffolk, Virginia.

Ronaldo crossed to Giggs. Giggs sent a header just wide. Benign torture persisted.

The referee booked James for taking too long for a goal kick at seventy-seven minutes, and it barely registered with me, and my lack of concern reiterated the duplicity of fandom just ten weeks after Charlton's stalling had vexed me utterly. Eighty minutes. We made eighty. I don't know how. Almost eighty-one, but here came Ronaldo, dashing as if on a horse, getting inside the box but shooting wide. Eighty-one. Help. Please. Help.

This had begun to take the shape of something epic, something that would always stand out from my first Pompey year. Even though I'd spoken personally to nobody around me, and even though none of us had hugged any strangers from what I could tell, I felt us all together in the wretched art of hope. I looked over to my left at the North End and felt kindred with those strangers as well. Ronaldo tried something from afar in the eighty-fifth minute, and James saved it easily.

Eighty-five, eighty-six, eighty-seven, and hyperventilation, and the woozy effects of hyperventilation, and please, put a stop to this. The Fulham debacle remained entrenched in mind, and if I'd thought of it, I could've grimaced at a different Fulham debacle, the one Ronaldo pulled out at the end at Craven Cottage for Manchester United back in February, or maybe Manchester United's added-time win at Liverpool when I first hit a pub with the blue bear. But I believe my brain blotted out those memories to prevent a dread overflow.

Eighty-eight, and at moments Fratton Park seemed oddly subdued, probably fretting, even with two recent-years wins over Manchester United stashed in these other fans' memories. Those squads, however, lacked the fully formed Ronaldo, and the fully formed Ronaldo added a dose of fear even if he looked sort of, you know, pretty. No one knew where this thing might head, until it headed in exactly the last direction anybody on the Premiership planet would've guessed.

In that eighty-ninth minute, the ball rattled around midfield a bit. If you look on tape, you can see it trickle to Matt Taylor, but I could not see that clearly from my end and in my state. You can see Taylor then try to send it to Lomana LuaLua as the latter darts toward the goal, but too many players scurried between myself and the fray for any clear vision of that. Then you can see the decorated Manchester United and England national defender Rio Ferdinand materialize to outrun LuaLua and clean it up, and then to back-pass the ball to van der Sar and to safety.

Again, from the other end of the park, this all looked muddled.

Then we could see the ball, having left Ferdinand's foot, begin rolling.

It kept rolling.

And it kept rolling.

It seemed to roll for a few minutes even though it didn't, and it seemed to roll right into indelible memory.

I suppose a roll so slow could qualify as sickly were that ball rolling into your team's goal. It probably turns up sometime in a nightmare similar to one I'd have as a child in which I'd hit a baseball to the fence but continually trip on the way to first base until they threw me out. Maybe the rolling ball turned up in van der Sar's REM stages soon thereafter, and maybe he could even see himself probably too far out from the goal, moving left to fend off LuaLua's possible charge, then wrong-footed, then seeing the ball slip back to his right, not really so far from his hand as he leaned opposite. Maybe in the nightmare it went through his fingers. Maybe he could revisit the sight of his feet, which looked so frozen in his alarm that it's possible he might've tried to move them but couldn't. On tape, it appears he might've caught up to that ball had he wheeled and sprinted.

Suppose, though, that the trickling ball turns out to be absolutely one of the most gorgeous things you've seen in a lifetime of sport-viewing. It would never seem nightmarish, but first it would seem . . .

Weird. Seemed just weird. It seemed a whistle must've blown, and play must've stopped, because only in odd circumstances could a ball roll in that leisurely a way for that long without some fast sort intervening. So only in instant recollection did that ball join my list of the greatest things ever. Only in rethinking did it seem to smile on its way into the Manchester United goal, maybe even giggle. Only in rehash did it come to rival a line-backer tackling a receiver on the one-yard line on the last play of a Super Bowl ending so riveting I couldn't breathe, or the sight of Tiger Woods set against the waters of Pebble Beach winning the 2000 U.S. Open by fifteen shots, or the ninth son of Wyoming dairy farmers winning a Greco-Roman gold medal at Sydney against a god who used to train by pretty much running around Siberia carrying refrigerators.

Right up there with them goes one plucky little ball rolling across the terrain of Hampshire, southern England, rolling away from myself and toward the Milton End and the away support-ers, rolling into the "wrong" goal, indelibly.

So as Fratton Park palpably went from this moment of vague

confusion to this moment of grand realization, and as the realization seemed to spend a lagging second creeping up the rows and across the sections and into the top corners and the wigs and the drummers and the buglers and at least one blue bear, and as I began to absorb the truth probably another second after everybody else, something happened to me that I would not confess to just anybody.

I cried.

The dubiousness.

But I cried.

Oh, come on, I was new.

Twenty years of proud and relative objectivity, then one year of fandom, and here, near the end, tears streaming down because some ball just inadvertently trickled into some mastodon club's goal. Nobody hugged me, and I didn't hug anybody, and it's clear I happened upon a section of nonhuggers in a country full of huggers, but it didn't matter, because I hopped and hopped in disbelief, and the tears rolled. Even in a cramped old rodeo ground, there seemed ample room for hopping, because everybody hopped, and the whole Fratton End of the stadium seemed to come unglued and convulse with relief and exhilaration. Then I scanned as much of the stadium as I could and found the whole long North End convulsing similarly.

The moment soared, Pompey led 2–0, and Pompey would get all three points from Manchester United after getting only one at Fulham. This was one of the greatest things I'd seen, and something about the blundering nature of the goal added to its appeal. The best team in the league had gotten confused; the ruthless order of the standings had been upturned. Bizarrely, it could not have been any better had that noblest of Portsmouth noblemen, maybe Primus, headed in one à la West Ham. The gaffe fed the charm. Injury time, which would be so much easier than anticipated, began. And then, at the outset of injury time, Solskjaer shot, and James deflected, and John O'Shea gobbled up the rebound and banged it in, scoring the perfunctory Manchester United goal I'd expected all along. Now it stood 2–1, with still more horrid injury time remaining, but with my central nervous system almost incapable of reactivating steep worry. Manchester United held another goal-mouth convention of keen passers below us; Alan Smith wreaked a dangerous shot; James stopped that. The convention reconvened; Solskjaer fired; that one whizzed over the bar.

James gathered it and punted, and as that ball went up, the whistle sang its long-awaited aria.

A roar filled the ground.

Then, most patrons turned to depart. American fans might behold an upset and stay, making more roars. English fans, I suppose, have seen it all already. As the left edge of the Fratton End began bunching up and leaving, I stayed put, standing there looking out over the pitch, trying to comprehend the exhilaration. I fielded some texts cleanly and confessed to some that I had blubbered after that ball finished dribbling into the goal.

But it's strange. It really doesn't make much sense. It's not like Portsmouth's 2–1 win decided the title, helped decide the title, or clinched anybody's spot in Europe. It's not like it proved all that much of a downer to Manchester United, which spent the ensuing Wednesday doubling as the Old Trafford symphony in a 7–1 win over Roma in the European Champions League quarterfinals.

It's only that I'm certain that for the remainder of my days I'll be able to recount the feverish eighty-ninth minute of April 7, when the best own goal I'll ever see went trundling into the net on the other end of the pitch like some little trickle of charm.

30

YOU HAVE
TO BE KIDDING ME

If roaming a town aglow after a landmark win, I highly recommend tagging along with a blue bear, if at all possible. I realize the option may not exist for many people and, in fact, may not exist for 99.9999994 percent of the global population, given the world's appalling shortage of blue bears. Still, without boasting or anything, I must say that a blue bear simply improves a festive evening in ways you'd never foresee. Indeed, it's possible to forge something approaching a good cry because most people go through their entire lives without ever walking around with a blue bear.

It's not just that children beam and wave from car windows, even though it's pretty damned great that children beam and wave from car windows. It's more the look on people's faces when the pub doors open and a blue bear walks in. You can just tell that in a world of hardship, strife, divorce, famine, drought, debts, and Floyd Landis, it lifts people a mite when one of the organisms coming through the door happens to be a blue bear. Even if they already knew a blue bear lived and breathed and bought season tickets in their midst, their expressions still take on a smile or a hint of wonderment that tells you the daily drudgery just subsided for a moment.

What's more, once inside, Charlie's an ursine Pied Piper. He makes everybody feel welcome, a part of things, whether he knows them well or knows them only through a Pompey chat room or doesn't really know them at all. He so obviously improves the spirit of a room.

On the night of April 7, we lacked Dan (Mum's birthday), but had Hopkins plus Dave, an Aston Villa fan I could treat to my tedious account of almost having chosen Aston Villa. We swept through several pubs in the Fratton area, plus one convenience store, and the whole thing seemed some sort of zenith of fun, partly because the memory bank had just annexed that ball trickling across the soil into the Manchester United goal. We reached a pub I'd never visited and would have trouble finding again. We met more Pompey fans, who increasingly to myself had begun to develop specific faces and names and existences. We checked departing-train schedules on cell-phone screens and repeatedly missed those same departing trains by ordering fresh rounds. We completed the whole merry trek in the pub across the street from the train station, where some wry sort saw the blue bear with Pompey insignia and said, "Man United fan?" And then somebody else from management asked that we leave, because occasionally there's somebody who can't share billing with a blue bear, who feels insecure within the caste system of the animal kingdom. We see this all the time on Discovery Channel.

Whatever lurks in human tissues and makes us crave victory and makes us grin for days over the thought of an own goal rolling in, that thing grabbed me through the rest of the weekend. On the walk home that Saturday night from Waterloo through London, near midnight, I beamed preposterously and yearned to tell people I had been there at Fratton Park, but I refrained because they stood in lines for dance clubs and seemed for all the world as if they absolutely would not care. With the Sunday newspapers, I did what fans do. I read the accounts not to plumb my own copy for glaring and career-threatening errors, but to relive the match.

I found the whole thing refreshing, but I didn't have much mirth time. Only forty-two hours after David James punted and the referee whistled, the Premier League started up another match involving Portsmouth, at 1:00 p.m, on the banking holiday the day after Easter. In a world of oddities, there's an official holiday adjacent to Easter in the United Kingdom, a secular country in which it's socially acceptable to be an atheist, while there's no such holiday in the United States, a religious country in which "atheist" finishes last in those "Would you vote for . . ." polls, well behind "grump." Thus, on to Vicarage Road in Watford, just northwest of London.

Pompey, sitting newly eighth with forty-six points, just two behind Tottenham's forty-eight, would make the relatively short trip to Watford, which sat twentieth. With just another break here or there, such as a certain penalty call at Fratton Park, we might've found Watford embroiled in a compelling scrap to avoid the relegation scrap heap, but with its twenty points fully nine behind nineteenth-place West Ham, Watford had all but booked the drop. Walking to London Euston train station, I wondered if it was humanly possible to defeat the number-one club in the Premiership and lose to the number-twenty within forty-four hours.

On the half-hour train ride to Watford, I sat across from a Pompey family, a mother and father with a daughter and younger son. They were still reading about Saturday's glories in the Monday *Guardian,* and I could see, across the train car, on a page, a photograph of that ball rolling into that net, and I decided I might like one framed for future walls. The daughter, maybe eight, and son, maybe six, were completely decked out in Pompey regalia, which in the daughter's case included red Pompey knee socks. When I saw those red Pompey knee socks, I thought about how much of life hinges on where we emerge from the birth canal. If that girl had started life in my Virginia hometown, then instead of the red socks she might've worn some sort of regalia of the Washington Redskins. She might've worn shirts or hats or socks with a likeness of a Native American head, and the people in her hometown would've found this completely normal, but other people elsewhere would've found it thoughtlessly racist, whereupon other people would've defended the logo as an homage to the battlefield valor of Native Americans, whereupon critics would've lambasted these people as rubes, whereupon any people who did not follow sports would've found all of us completely insane.

As the train rolled barely northwest, London seemed vacant and forlorn and depressed, as it does on many a holiday, as if it would rather just go to work. I disembarked and walked through a network of pleasant roads to reach Vicarage Road, and the stadium looked wonderful, tucked into the city near a hospital, which would make it convenient in case one Ben Thatcher wannabe gratuitously tried to maul another. The corner gate for bubonic-plagued away fans came up right away, and I took my seat around many empty seats. Seemed the Pompey fans—including my favorite three—had beheld this tilt and decided to save money. On a sunny spring day just northwest of London, with fine foothills just off in the distance, we taunted Ben Foster as he readied himself in the Watford goal:

> *England's number two,*
> *England's, England's number two . . .*

Foster turned to us and grinned with this expression that said, *Oh, those Portsmouth fans,* and I cannot tell you how much I loved that. The match began. Nine days prior, Watford had carried Chelsea into added time drawn 0–0 before succumbing 1–0. Two days prior, Watford had looked haggard in losing 4–1 at Middlesbrough. I saw the prevalent yellow of the Vicarage Road seats and thought about how somebody from the Canary Islands had just told me of yellow's bad-luck status in his culture, but no matter.

No matter, because Watford's defense bungled a possession that, thank goodness, didn't involve Jay DeMerit, leaving my cheer undiluted as Matt Taylor curled one into the goal at sixteen minutes. Pompey led 1–0 and looked to build upon the incredible momentum of forty-two hours and sixteen minutes or so prior. I turned to the young man of about twenty-five to my left, and he turned to me, and we suddenly hugged each other while hopping, even though we barely uttered a diphthong to each other the rest of the match.

We hugged partly because we had no idea that we had come to witness the unleashing of the mighty Watford offense. I had no clue I'd come to wish Pompey would just go ahead and sign the Algerian national Hameur Bouazza—preferably right after the match—as he ran rings around our complacent squad. He banged a penalty past James at twenty-eight minutes, then assisted with a world-class, curving mega-goal from Gavin Mahon at forty-five minutes, Mahon's first in the Premiership.

No, I really didn't imagine reaching the Vicarage Road urinals at halftime and hearing Pompey fans bemoan a "disgrace" to reinforce the place of men's room urinals as bastions of insight. And I really had not imagined the Watford offense, flying free by the second half, wreaking a beautiful display of fundamental soccer on our hapless defense for Tamas Priskin's first Premiership goal at fifty-one minutes, nor Bouazza scoring again at seventy-three minutes for a 4–1—4–1!—lead.

If you dare to look it up, as I did afterward, you would've seen what you already suspected: Watford had scored four goals only once all fall-winter-spring, and that in a 4–1 FA Cup win over fourth-division Stockport. Watford, in fact, had scored three goals only once, back in October, in a draw with Fulham. Having achieved a watershed victory over Manchester United, Portsmouth had managed the added feat of loosing the potent Watford attack, a feat no other Premiership club had accomplished.

Then again, we always admire those clubs that play hard when they're playing for nothing. Another of the greatest things I've ever seen happened in downtown Detroit on the last Saturday night of September 2003. My bosses had sent me there because the 2003 baseball Detroit Tigers began their four closing games with an imponderable 40–118 record, a rapacious threat to the New York Mets' legendary record of 120 losses in 1962, the season that launched a legendary American line from the legendary manager Casey Stengel: "Can't anybody here play this game?" On Thursday night, September 27, Detroit won the first game of four against Minnesota to reach 41–118, then lost the second on September 28 to access 41–119. Before the third game, that Saturday, a wee batch of reporters interviewed Alan Trammell, the former great Detroit player and current Detroit manager, and as an incompetent interloper, I asked what he'd pondered driving to the stadium. He replied testily that he walked. I asked what he'd pondered as he walked. He cut off everybody's interview. I apologized to everybody. He put his arm around me a few minutes later and said he understood. Hours later, Detroit trailed in the fifth inning by the insuperable, moribund score of 8–0. The 1962 Mets, long alone in the dungeon, could see company coming up the dungeon hallway.

Just then, for no apparent earthly reason, the Tigers rallied and won 9–8. You can go years watching baseball daily without seeing anybody turn 8–0 against into 9–8 for, and the comeback had intoxicating qualities. I felt as if I'd witnessed something phenomenal even as technically I'd witnessed something trivial. I saw Trammell in the hallway beside the dressing room, and he looked at me, an outright stranger, and I said, "That was really something," and he said, "Thank you." On Sunday, Detroit beat Minnesota again to reach 43–119 and leave the 1962 Mets alone in the dungeon. Having seen Detroit four times the whole season and having seen them win thrice, I decided they'd actually been a very good team, just misunderstood.

Likewise, I decided Watford must've been very good but misunderstood. A late Portsmouth goal wrought a glorious chant indicating that we were going to win 5–4, but it ended at 4–2, and I felt baffled and texted a blue bear, who replied that he'd figured. You know those veteran viewers. And I texted my soccer guru Tom, who wrote back, "Oh, the predictable perversity of this game. These 48 hours exemplify the beauty—and pain—of football, surely"—an exhibition of why he's my soccer guru.

Slightly miffed (but more just perplexed), I decided to buy a newspaper and eat lunch. I walked into a W. H. Smith newsstand, and I overheard a little boy and his father meet up with the boy's mother after the match.

"Watford won 4–2!" the little boy exclaimed.

"No!" the mother said.

The son and father persisted with their report.
The mother still thought they kidded her.
The son and father persisted.
The mother finally believed them.
Maybe.

31

NOT-TAKEN ROADS

On a pleasant spring Saturday on the south coast of England, April 14, 2007, five matches to season's end, at kickoff we crooned the old standard to Benjani (tune: "Volare"):

Benjani, whoa-ohhh,
Benjani, whoa-ohhh,
He comes from Zimbabwe
He's gonna score today . . .

My love for this I could not overstate. To me, this song almost justified following the bilge of sport on a regular basis. Here I was, an American, joining part of England in expressing our love for an African. Here we were in Hampshire, a crowd of mostly white people who had been to Zimbabwe an aggregate next-to-nil in all our 20,165 lives, some of whom knew it only from media coverage as having a lousy president, yet we serenaded a Zimbabwean. It reminded me of 1990s surveys the queried white Americans and black Americans for their ten favorite prime-time television shows and only one show appeared on both lists: *Monday Night Football*. Only sport seems to construct such bridges.

After sensing—but not getting—victory at Fulham, then assuming—but not getting—defeat against Manchester United, then figuring on—but not getting—victory at Watford, I decided

I'd just stop sensing, assuming, or figuring. Then, just seven minutes in at Fratton Park, Benjani Mwaruwari muscled Steven Taylor off the ball, wheeled, and blasted one in from twelve yards, perhaps my favorite goal of the season scored by an actual Portsmouth player rather than Manchester United's Rio Ferdinand. He'd come from Zimbabwe; he had just scored today. Pompey led Newcastle, 1–0, and the same offense that went hopeless in the winter suddenly went Brazil on us, with help from Newcastle's indifferent defense. I do love a nice, indifferent defense, for it makes sports so much more entertaining. When Kobe Bryant scored eighty-one points for the Lakers on that night in January 2006, the second-most in NBA history, we all went wow but gave far too little credit to the visiting Toronto Raptors and their invaluable contribution of indifferent defense. In an era in which clubs study each other so intently and learn each other's tendencies so thoroughly, the games have dulled, a point made seminal when noted by the iconic ice hockey coach Scotty Bowman. Defense impedes pleasure. Defense hampers life.

But Newcastle's defense on April 14? That one was kind, even cuddly, and much appreciated. It abetted the most entertainingly carefree half of the year. The same Pompey employees who had no chance of scoring at, say, Wigan, sprayed the Newcastle goal with so many chances that it could've been 4–0 by halftime. It suggested a spring thaw. Kanu won the unofficial prize for most agonizing when his strike caromed off the bottom of the crossbar and downward, barely outside the line. Newcastle manager Glenn Roeder made a defensive replacement at thirty minutes.

It had been 365 days since I first saw Fratton Park and saw Pompey trip Middlesbrough 1–0 in the rush toward survival. I held my own little observance in the stands by marveling at how I'd learned so much that I felt almost certain that the goalkeeper could not touch the ball with his hands outside that second, larger box there. Now, with April 14 upon us, all of England would start divvying up the trips to Europe and doling out the relegations during the last five weekends leading to the May 13 finales. The standings at breakfast, April 14, found Manchester United still three points ahead of Chelsea at the top, then Tottenham in seventh with forty-eight, Portsmouth in eighth with forty-six, Reading in ninth at forty-five, and Newcastle in tenth with the usual civic melodrama (and impending managerial change) and with forty-one. The dungeon looked like this:

16. Wigan ....34 points
17. Charlton ....32 points
18. Sheffield United ....31 points
19. West Ham ....29 points
20 Watford ....23 points

And in those days, with exceptional irony, Fratton Park occasionally would break into a chant: "We are staying up! We are staying up!" It cropped up against Newcastle, and it reminded me of the uncommon brightness of the season into which I'd plopped unawares. Then I saw the faithful all the way down the length of the pitch, in Newcastle black-and-white, thickly packed into the Fratton Park away section. But for a subliminal fear of long train rides, but more so my weariness with talk of "curses" in the beleaguered baseball cities of Boston (eighty-six-year title drought, 1918 to 2004) and Chicago (eighty-eight-year title drought for one club, the White Sox, 1917 to 2005, and astonishing title drought for one club, the Cubs, 1908 to the present), I could've stood in that visiting crowd, bemoaning the lack of defense. Sitting tenth after finishing seventh in 2005–2006, with all-the-rage employee Michael Owen still healing from his 2006 World Cup knee agony, Newcastle had lapsed into horrific form since February. Sure, the previous winter it had won only its second cup—and second trivial cup—in fifty-two years, but the Intertoto Cup, while a fine and hard-won cup, somehow lacks the resonance of other cups. In the UEFA Cup, which supposedly you can enter by winning the Intertoto Cup—although I don't really know, and certainly don't comprehend—Newcastle crashed out to AZ Alkmaar of the Netherlands. What fans, though. Many of the young and middle-aged ones had spent their lives on a crusade for that moment of rapture. Unlike Portsmouth or Southampton or even Torquay, their club had spent every year since 1993–94 in the Premiership, so their expectations tilted toward swelling. Many of these same away fans at Fratton Park, I reckoned, had lived minute to minute through 1995–96, when Newcastle's twelve-point lead in the table over Manchester United disintegrated very much like a sinkhole. Some of them might've even participated in the early-season fan protest that followed a galling 1–0 home loss to Sheffield United. Looking across at them, I believed I could see them trudging across the veritable desert, mirages of water in bubbles above their heads. If you can hate fans while they traverse the veritable desert, maybe even revel in their horrendous thirst, then you might just qualify as a sadist.

Newcastle's defense improved not much early in the second half and proved ripe for another Matt Taylor long ball. This one, from thirty yards on the left, at fifty-nine minutes, hurried diagonally to the right, all the way to the right corner of the goal, into which it absolutely screamed. And then, so did we (scream). Pompey led, 2–0. To the wondrous season, the club continued to add these little bonuses. It lacked the capability, though, to deliver us from worry, and so at sixty-nine minutes, our own Dejan Stefanovic either nudged or savaged Newcastle's James Milner in the box, and Newcastle's hammer-footed Belozoglu Emre scored the penalty, and we had to spend the last twenty-four minutes suffering from the sweat glands.

Take that anxiety and double it at eighty-two minutes, when David James had to make a heavenly save on Obafemi Martins, but finally, still three more points came, and Portsmouth had risen to forty-nine, eleven more than in the entirety of 2005–2006, with four matches remaining.

Minus the bear, whose vacation would mark a temporary increase in Portugal's ursine population, Dan and Hopkins and I overcame our shouting lack of fur and had a festive beer outdoors at the Shepherd's Crook. There, by the picnic tables, I saw Newcastle fans—"Magpies"—in their stripes mingling with Pompey fans in their blue. In the United States, we love this sort of thing because it informs us that we can have a conversation even with the vile enemy. We often refer to it proudly because it suggests a reasonable tinge to our frothing contempt. In England, I've heard more people lament the presence of away fans at a pub, as if it dilutes the colors.

I noticed two particular Newcastle fans at the pub, two guys, then noticed them again at London Waterloo, then noticed them again boarding the Tube, then noticed they sat across from myself. I decided to strike up a conversation, in which I told them of their brethren in Boston and Chicago whose support did not deteriorate despite long-held frustration. I had no idea they'd won the Intertoto Cup, mostly because I had no idea of the existence of an Intertoto Cup, and they did not bring up their Intertoto Cup or try to shove their Intertoto Cup in my Intertoto Cup–less face. They seemed excellent company, and we'd just gotten into good conversation when I had to step off at Tottenham Court Road to return to my overpriced shoebox. At the end, though, I believe I breached etiquette when I mentioned like a dope that I'd almost chosen Newcastle as my club.

We shook hands as I disembarked, and then as I moved along the platform one of the guys leaned out the open Tube doors and exclaimed:

"It's not a choice!"

I felt that old pang of guilt as the interloper who'd wandered into someone else's country and treated his profound emotional attachment like some quiz question. I thought about how he'd emerged from the birth canal ever so mildly accursed, destined to follow Newcastle through the cupless years unless he'd ignored soccer and decided to follow, say, opera, whose endings, come to think of it, often bear striking resemblance to Newcastle's. I thought he should be more understanding of people from distant birth canals. But it didn't matter what I thought, because the Tube doors had shut and the Northern Line had rolled off toward Goodge Street.

Besides, nobody should belittle choices. Choices are tough. The problem I've noticed with choices is that when you choose one thing, then you don't get to have the others. Eight days after looking down the Fratton Park pitch to find Newcastle fans I might've joined, I looked down the Villa Park pitch at the Holte

End I'd once inhabited for as goose-bumpy a day as I'd ever known, Aston Villa versus Birmingham, April 16, 2006, that day of such great and durable noise.

Only April 22, 2007, lacked similar fervor. Aston Villa would play Portsmouth in a match involving two fan bases that had never had reason to despise one another. This brings such a downer in sport, this complete lack of scorn, hatred, or even appalling condescension. As a result, Villa Park approximated the din of a golf tournament's faraway fourteenth hole on Thursday, when you might hear mild clapping from next of kin, recent one-night stands of the players, or people who've happened by while walking to the hamburger tent. Such a hush ruled the day that at one point a Portsmouth fan shouted at Villa's Gabriel Agbonlahor, "Diver!" and the criticism resonated such that Agbonlahor looked up at the fan. No one enjoys being accused of taking penalty-drawing dives, but normally players cannot actually *hear* such single-voiced commentary.

This blurt came from the away end of Villa Park, behind the goal opposite the Holte End. With no Birmingham on the premises, I'd walked right up and bought a ticket without giving any identification. I had decided to go early so I could have a beer and watch Chelsea's crucial bout with Newcastle. Well, they have no televisions in the away end, nor do they serve any beer, although they do have the far less healthy option of sodas. I figured the away fans of today probably pay for the sins of the away fans of yore, and this felt something like traveling the world with a Colombian passport, always a suspect because of others' transgressions.

So I did the only thing there was to do: I leaned against a wall.

A Pompey fan leaning next to me asked what I expected for the match, but I couldn't understand his question because of his accent.

He asked again, and I couldn't understand his question.

He asked again, and I couldn't understand his question.

It reminded me of that Ultimate Fighting Championship reality show where the American producers used subtitles for the guy from Liverpool. Finally this guy from Hampshire stammered out the question, and I hemmed and hawed and said I expected very little, and we began a conversation in which he said it might be a bad move for Portsmouth to qualify for the UEFA Cup. The whole operation just wouldn't be ready, he said. The squad just didn't seem deep enough for playing in four competitions rather than three. There would be the issue of Fratton Park's fitness as a ground for European play, he said. I had never once mulled these things while singing blithely about a European tour. Seemingly a nice guy—after all, he'd repeated his question four times—he then made a quick trip through the roster and noted which guys had proved "useless," and I nodded as if I had the first clue. He said we definitely needed a new left back, and I couldn't have agreed more even if I could have named the current left back.

Seated in a section lean on people, next to a section almost completely empty, I looked across at the Holte End and wondered how my life might've felt different had I stood over there with the Villa fans after all these days and all these games doubling as melodramas. (For one thing, I'd know one fewer bear.) I might've been singing that catchy Aston Villa theme song. I might've told people I followed Aston Villa because it's the club with the loveliest club name on earth. I could've routinely witnessed my host for the Birmingham match over there, leaning over furtively to smoke during the match.

But as Aston Villa and Portsmouth played to a goal-less draw, I suffered Villa's scary bombardment of our goal, and when David James became the Premier League's all-time leader in what they call these clean sheets, I applauded as loudly as I could, as a fan of his club, his play, and his weekly newspaper column that showed astuteness well beyond that of most athletes.

32

ADOPTED

Alan Ball's Blue Army
Alan Ball's Blue Army
Alan Ball's Blue Army . . .

The chant echoed through Fratton Park on Saturday, April 28, as Portsmouth took on Liverpool.

Alan Ball's Blue Army
Alan Ball's Blue Army
Alan Ball's Blue Army . . .

It reverberated at kickoff, and in added time, and every so often in between.

Alan Ball's Blue Army
Alan Ball's Blue Army
Alan Ball's Blue Army . . .

The cheer never became maudlin or overwrought. I found it both understated and intensely emotional, the latter partly because of the former. It just carried on through the afternoon. Sometimes it would overrun itself, so that one group of people would be on "Army" while another would be starting up with another "Alan."

In dealing with the ultimate subject, death, Americans often feel impressed by the English, who, as an older culture, treat the subject more as part of life and less as cause for apoplexy. On the Tuesday midnight of April 24–25, Alan Ball, sixty-one, died of a heart attack at his home while trying to contain a ravenous backyard fire. Every English soccer person and most every English nonsoccer person knew Ball, the youngest member of the England team that won the 1966 World Cup, as if he were a cousin. Portsmouth fans also knew him well as the manager of Portsmouth from 1984 to 1989 and then again in 1998 for a great escape from relegation into the third division. I thought of him in another vein, for a reason fully trivial. He had hired the top division's first American player.

In January 1987, John Kerr, an American born in Canada to Scottish parents, turned up in London shortly after graduating from Duke. Through connections, he wound up getting a tryout at Harrow Borough in suburban northwest London, where for training the club could use only one set of lights or the neighbors complained. Harrow Borough started winning and getting some attention, which catapulted Kerr toward a spot in a reserve-team match in March between Portsmouth and Crystal Palace, which led a certain flat-capped Portsmouth manager, Alan Ball, to the dressing room after said match.

"John, I want to sign you," Ball said to the staggered American. "I want you to play here next year." That happened to coincide with Portsmouth's first promotion to the top flight in twenty-eight years, and so, in a 4–2 loss at Oxford United on August 15, 1987, Kerr debuted, after which Ball congratulated him in postmatch remarks to the team. Kerr would play four games before joining the reserve team and leading that league in scoring.

As someone who spent my first four decades on earth knowing nothing about Alan Ball, and who lacked the emotion we attach to sports figures we've known for decades, I joined in the chants until my throat hurt on April 28. And whenever I'd refer to the current Portsmouth squad as "Alan Ball's Blue Army" in honor of the erstwhile manager, I'd add some oomph because he'd given that chance to a starry-eyed American, whose dream of playing English soccer would've counted as bizarre had it not actually transpired. By so chanting, I felt as if I were just an itty-bitty part of England, just as I gained a second indoctrination that came from Portsmouth versus Liverpool. I experienced my first match in which a manager, Liverpool's Rafael Benitez, purposely gutted his team in anticipation of a different competition. For an American, it's a bit like learning some Sanskrit.

On a blistering English day—seventy-two degrees!—on the southern coast, Benitez did not bring Steven Gerrard. He did not bring Jamie Carragher. He brought neither Peter Crouch nor Javier Mascherano, nor John Arne Riise, nor Daniel Agger, nor Pepe Reina. In the United States, where teams play for one title per year, we occasionally have managers who show up so bereft of stars, but only because of injuries. We feel for them. We write sonnets to them and laud their willingness to carry on in spite of fate's nastiness. We even lend them adjectives we probably ought to reserve for soldiers.

Benitez had not brought his bright lights because Liverpool would play Chelsea three nights later in the second leg of their European Champions League semifinal. This would be my first experience with a match that would conclude with a manager saying something like, "It's clear the European Champions League is the priority." So it was a bit weird. You know you're pulling for your club to defeat one of the big four, yet you don't know whether it's really one of the big four, and you don't know enough to know whether what's left of Liverpool would still inhabit the big four. Maybe it would. I did know of one player present at Fratton Park, Craig Bellamy. Any tourist even just changing planes at Heathrow might know of Bellamy because he turned up in news reports detailing how, on a team training mission in Portugal, he got irked at a teammate who refused to sing karaoke and threatened the teammate with a golf club. It wouldn't take a soccer savant to know of the central figure in a case so puzzling in that it's hard to know which aspect of the story was more preposterous, the weapon or the motive. I also knew, as a seasoned observer, that Bellamy tried to blame the reports about the golf club and the karaoke on the reporters and lamented that he'd encouraged the media by apparently threatening a teammate with a golf club in a dispute that began when the teammate wouldn't sing karaoke.

In most groups of males, however idiotic, golf-club threats would stem from insistence upon karaoke rather than from refusal.

With the one point earned for the tie at Villa Park, eighth-place Portsmouth had a whopping fifty points, pining for seventh (or at least I was, for that UEFA Cup slot); Tottenham sat at ninth but had played one fewer match. Reading sat seventh at fifty-one. My worry about an underlings' revolt from tenth had dissipated as Blackburn sat stuck on forty-four, with Newcastle in eleventh at forty-two. Liverpool sat third with sixty-seven points and figured to remain there unless overtaken by Arsenal, in which case Liverpool still would sit fourth. There seemed no reason not to take three points from Liverpool and make it a commendable eight points out of a possible twenty-one thus far against the big four.

There really seemed no reason after we sang about Zimbabwe and then Benjani Mwaruwari scored in the twenty-seventh minute with a bold header in a crowd for a 1–0 lead, with help from a miscalculation by goalkeeper Jerzy Dudek. There really, really seemed no reason after the young Croatian Niko Kranjcar chested a long ball in the thirty-second minute and finished for a 2–0 lead, somewhat fluky but perfectly welcome. The best Portsmouth season in fifty years just went bouncing along, with Manchester United and Liverpool defeated at Fratton Park within the same month.

Of course, Liverpool had not yet been defeated, what with Sami Hyppia's header off a Robbie Fowler corner at fifty-nine minutes, after which the Fratton End showed again something that mystifies me by tying its own world record—0:01—for time between adversity on the pitch and cheer in the stands. To earlier cheers of "We are staying up" and "We love you, Portsmouth, we do," there came the traditional "na-na-na-ing" of "Vindaloo." The rest of the match would bring the singular agony in which soccer specializes.

Reading back over my jittery notes afterward, I found this: "OK, made 70." That means we made seventy minutes. "OK, made 75." "OK, made 77." "I'm a wreck." Liverpool took all the élan left in its roster—which amounted to plenty, by my estimation—and seemed to unfurl it toward the Portsmouth goal. Fans chanted Alan Ball's name. Some had brought along the flat caps as homage to Ball. In the eighty-eighth minute, at the goal distant from myself, Fowler looked certain to score, but James saved somehow. What a cruel concept is this soccer. Then, just when you might exhale, there's added time, the slowest time in life, far slower than even the five minutes before the cinema lights dim, far slower than the unbearable time it takes to unload all the rows in front of you on an airplane, far slower than church, even while clearly its own form of church.

This added time, though, carried added purpose. Through all the hours in the three minutes of added time, you could hear . . . "Alan Ball's Blue Army . . . Alan Ball's Blue Army . . . Alan Ball's Blue Army." Nobody I saw cried, although I did notice one burly guy with tattoos repeatedly chanting just the name "Alan Ball! Alan Ball! Alan Ball!" Finally, one of life's kindest acts occurred: the whistle tweeted, and Portsmouth had a 2–1 win over Liverpool to go with the 2–1 win over Newcastle, the 2–1 win over Manchester United, the 2–1 win over Manchester City, the 2–1 win over Wigan in the FA Cup, and the 2–1 win over West Ham, the only wins since Boxing Day, to go with five draws. This jacked the total to fifty-three points and hiked the place to seventh, one behind sixth-place Everton and two behind fifth-place Bolton, as the club headed to that very Everton the next Saturday.

In order to do as the Romans do while in England, I would have stuck with Portsmouth even through a relegation, as the Brentford sages Jak and Chris did teach with their fourth-division aplomb. Yet I'd alighted on the best topflight Portsmouth season, points-wise, in fifty-seven years, and the best topflight season, placement-wise, in fifty-two years. Without any knowledge of history earlier than Pedro Mendes against Manchester City or maybe a desolate pitch at Stamford Bridge, I'd happened upon a club that went down to the second division in 1959 for two seasons, then to the third for one, then to the second for fourteen, then to the third for two, then to the fourth for two, then to the third for three, the second for four, the first for one, the second for fifteen, and the first for four, with finishes of thirteenth, sixteenth, seventeenth, and pending.

A win at Everton might all but secure a UEFA Cup spot. Does an unwitting gate-crasher still count as a gate-crasher?

So, burrowing into the village past the easy readiness of the Shepherd's Crook pub, Charlie and Hopkins and I persisted toward the Devonshire Arms, the place I'd happened upon ages ago, back on November 4 when Portsmouth played at Old Trafford in Manchester, when I'd felt like a preposterous impostor. Now, six months and one eternity later, in the same pub, I got to assist when a Pompey bear asked me, "Could you unzip me a bit?" in the back, so he could contort out of his suit without tearing his fur. This ever so slight contribution to the well-being of my club gave me a sense of belonging. It resembled childhood memories of when my mother used to come home from work and ask us to unzip the back of her nurse's uniform, but it did not resemble those memories precisely as, for one thing, my mother made us dinner as opposed to buying us a round of beer.

In between greeting people left and right, Charlie told me that a Pompey friend had told him, "I'm glad to see you've adopted an American." It's a unique and welcome experience for an American to feel ancillary after so many years of inflating ourselves with so much preposterous pertinence. This, after joining Fratton Park and stadiums all over England in appreciation of Alan Ball. That had been some day, and we stayed in the Devonshire way too long. I finally galumphed out and went to Brighton for that night, waking sometime after arrival to find myself alone on the arrived, motionless train. Hopkins and Charlie left the Devonshire even later than I did. They made the last possible train. Hopkins left at Woking, and at Waterloo a guy cleaning up the train came upon a sleeping blue bear, which simply had to brighten his grueling work shift.

33

IT'S REALLY THE HEART
OF ENGLAND

First Saturdays in May resonate in my American cranium because of the Kentucky Derby, the oldest annual sporting event in the United States, for which 100,000 chums convene in the underrated river city of Louisville for a poignant bacchanal of wagering and binge-drinking. It all leads to a two-minute cavalry charge at 6:00 PM that can define the legacies of participants and make the heart beat outside the chest for observers, even those like myself who find wagering almost as tedious as listening to people rehash their wagering.

Two first Saturdays in May ago, in 2005, I covered the Kentucky Derby and could not have told you the location of the Everton Football Club if I'd needed the answer to avoid purgatory or a life sentence of residence in Texas. Now, two Saturdays in May later, on a hot spring day in Merseyside (the side of the river Mersey), I rode the last long train of the season eavesdropping on four people, three men and one woman, all Everton fans. With two matches left in the exhausted season, we all headed for Everton for the potential momentousness of sixth-place Everton versus eighth-place Portsmouth.

As the conversation bubbled along, the woman and one of the men wrangled over whether they followed Everton for the pursuit of cups or for the love of the club. Shockingly, the man preferred the former, the woman the latter, a point she later bolstered by telling me she'd relinquish her cherished season ticket if Everton dared sign that creepy Joey Barton, who had just finished sucker-punching and beating up a teammate during practice before a group of visiting schoolchildren in a sign of Manchester City cohesion. Finally, she agreed to disagree with her friend, and he fell asleep, and as she seemed so keen on soccer that I began to imagine little soccer balls coursing through her bloodstream, I consulted her.

I explained my tragic childhood deprivation of relegation and promotion and wondered which match I should attend on Sunday on the final day of the "Championship," the second division. With two promotions assured by then—Birmingham and Sunderland, coming right back up after one year down—and one promotion to go, and with the eventual third- to sixth-place finishers to play off for that, should I go to third-place Derby County, at home against the utterly fascinating soccer train wreck of Leeds, with its impending second relegation within four seasons? Maybe I should go to still-contending Preston North End for Birmingham's visit? What about Southampton, sitting sixth, with Southend inbound? She ran down the list of pros and cons for the half dozen pertinent matches. I pined away slightly for the bourbon fumes in the Louisville air, yes, but I also thought I'd found the sports heart of another country, a weekend of Liverpool plus promotion/relegation fever. Seeking knowledge, I quizzed the four Everton sorts on one of my favorite newfound topics, the idea that Everton and Liverpool might indulge in milder loathing than some rivals, and that many families might contain fans of both yet still fight no more than other families, which means just about all the time. I asked if they'd rooted for Liverpool or Chelsea the previous Tuesday night in the European Champions League semifinal won by Liverpool on penalties. They'd all pulled for Chelsea.

The train arrived at Liverpool Lime Street, and off we went— they to their usual pub, and I to Everton's Goodison Park, which

I loved straightaway. The away section had a wooden charm and great sight lines, save for a support post here or there that might block your view at times, but for some eccentric reason I always love craning my neck around old support posts in old stadiums, perhaps because it affords me a hint of suffering. Goodison has this excellent verticality, seeming to rise straight up beside the pitch, ideal for absorbing pivotal proceedings such as Portsmouth (fifty-three points) trying to vault over Everton (fifty-four) and maybe even Reading (fifty-four) and maybe even sputtering Bolton (fifty-five) and into fifth place. With rookie denseness, I'd forgotten that ninth-place Tottenham (fifty-three) had three matches remaining to everybody else's two.

I walked in past somebody in a T-shirt reading PORTSMOUTH IS MY RELIGION/FRATTON PARK IS MY CHURCH and sat down behind a burly guy who would spend his day in the sun complaining about Pompey's play and the refereeing. I myself moaned about the refereeing during the first half when the referee achieved an unquestionable feat of incompetence and gave a yellow card to Portsmouth's Noé Pamarot. I counted this absolute and impenetrable accuracy as progress in my tutelage.

Being in Goodison Park, in the city of Liverpool, I felt stationed at the aorta of English soccer, what with two huge and heaving fan bases right across a park from each other. We have some arrangements like the mere 10.27 miles between Yankee Stadium in the Bronx and Shea Stadium in Queens, but that's nothing like the Liverpool situation. For one thing, I once walked that Yankee-Shea path just to amuse myself and to write a column about it, and I learned that when crossing New York's Triborough Bridge, it's wiser to take a bus or a taxi. For another, the pleasant greenery of Stanley Park in Liverpool stands in contrast to the concrete of Queens, as well as to the Queens couple having a loud spat as I passed them on the sidewalk.

In the Everton prematch, we observed silence for an Everton fan and soldier killed in Iraq, Alan Jones (1986–2007), and his photograph appeared on the video screen, and it grabbed me as much as has any such story since the war began, something about the confluence of something so vibrant (Premiership soccer) with something so catastrophic. The Pompey players trotted out, and I realized that even while I don't know Gary O'Neil and sometimes got mad at him for coughing up a perfectly good possession, I'd miss him plus the rest once this trail ended eight days hence. The public-address read the squads and my Pompey brethren again showed a MENSA-level grasp of all past Southampton squads by jeering James Beattie.

As the 39,619 of us got under way at Goodison, our thickly packed away section mockingly crooned Liverpool's staple "You'll Never Walk Alone" to the home fans, many of whom responded with popped blood vessels in bald foreheads as they screamed back chants and songs I found so unintelligible they could not possibly hurt my feelings. I began to think of the two rotten lost points at Fulham, and how "we" should have had fifty-five points and not fifty-three and how I'd received permission to use the word "we" from a blue bear, about as authoritative a figure as exists in the animal kingdom. I marveled at the astonishing presence of a song called "Is This the Way to Amarillo," an American-penned song I'd never once heard until moving to England, where it became a hit in both 1971 and 2005, a song sung heartily by English soccer fans who wouldn't know Amarillo from Lubbock.

I also found it impossible to detest Everton and did not join in the chorus of the semipopular old hit "You're the S—— of Merseyside."

Halftime found us all goal-less, but it didn't feel quite right, as our squad posed scant threat, what with Matt Taylor injured and unable to send a forty-five-yard symphony over Tim Howard's thinning hair. Sure enough, things soon careened into the ditch. The wondrous young Evertonian James Vaughan got loose in the box in the fifty-ninth minute, and Glen Johnson attempted to do something to him, perhaps shove him as one would a toilet seat into a cheaper box. Mikel Arteta converted the penalty, and I wondered without griping if I'd ever see David James stop a penalty. Joseph Yobo scored three minutes after that, off a

Manuel Fernandes corner, and Everton cemented its European tour, as well as becoming insuperable to us with fifty-seven points to our fifty-three with one match remaining. Any trip to Europe for us would hinge on the match eight days later against Arsenal.

Still, it says something about the astounding buoyancy of Portsmouth fans that the away section chanted "Scummer" at Beattie during the eighty-ninth minute, when many an American fan would've exited to sit in the car listening to the radio or to go home to the couch to assume a state of intractable inertia. Four minutes later, the hosts had an added-time goal, they had 3–0, and they had their home season's end. The players left the pitch, then returned and paraded around the stadium to some of the greatest noise ever steered toward my ears, which had hailed from a country where fifth place seldom draws ovations. Most of my fellow visitors filed out, but I stayed in the empty section for the whole clamorous celebration, listening to their catchy theme song, even discerning one of the lyrics (ellipses indicate lyrics I didn't decipher):

Everton, Everton . . . Everton . . .
Everton . . . Everton . . . Everton . . .
Everton, Everton . . . Everton . . .

I felt actually lifted, even at 0–3, even as the woman from the train text-messaged me with "Take that," proving she might follow Everton also for the cups. Still, my pilgrimage persisted. As an American accustomed to suburban stadiums in vast parking lots, it's terribly refreshing to visit a stadium that's tucked into a real neighborhood with row houses and corner stores and children playing on sidewalks. I'd also decided it's a must when visiting Liverpool's stadium, Anfield, to walk across Stanley Park to look at Everton's Goodison and, when visiting Goodison, to walk across Stanley Park to look at Anfield, especially the memorial for the ninety-six victims of Hillsborough.

Covering sport, you wind up chronicling death more than you'd think. You'd never expect to see rugged men sob into their meaty hands at Daytona Beach, but then Dale Earnhardt had just rammed into the wall and died. Probably no event ever teemed with life more than the 1992 Olympic opening ceremonies at Barcelona, but days later a batch of American reporters heard the devastated voice of an American swimmer, Ron Karnaugh, whose father had died of a heart attack that night in that stadium. You'd never think of sport as the backdrop for one of the grandest human gestures you've ever known, but it did so in 1998 in Kentucky, after a macabre single-truck crash involving University of Kentucky football players. Two passengers, ages nineteen and twenty-one, died. The intoxicated twenty-one-year-old driver survived and served four months in prison for reckless homicide.

In the week after the accident, the driver's parents came from Florida to visit their hospitalized son, and they attended the funeral of the nineteen-year-old victim. The victim's parents, in turn, asked these virtual strangers to join them in the front row, so they would not feel ostracized.

You witness these things, you attend the funerals of sport figures, you stand in stadiums for moments of silence, and you just hope people won't get so embroiled in life as to forget. That's where, to an outsider, Liverpool fans seem to have taken something unbearable and implemented it into their fandom as a way of giving homage.

So, fully eighteen years and three weeks down the line in life, Anfield's Hillsborough memorial teemed with fresh flowers and careful attention. I found myself gazing and reading until I had no idea how much time had passed. At the Vietnam War Memorial in Washington, the wall with 58,000 names, I always try to read the notes from soldiers' family members or friends, and at Anfield I found myself reading a poem typewritten on a full sheet of 8½-by-11 paper.

It came from the family of Adam Spearitt, who died that day at fourteen, less than the number of years that have passed since his death. The poem went along for two or three stanzas about the day, April 15, 1989, and about the fans going to Sheffield for the FA Cup semifinal:

Some got there early
Some arrived late
Hard to say more
Pain's too great

Even as a foreigner who spent the spring of 1989 living in Los Angeles and hearing about Hillsborough only vaguely, those last two lines just staggered me.

34

ELVIS AND THE BEATLES

I knew a great soul named Dick Fick, who died at fifty of alcohol-related illness in 2003 after I'd lost touch with him, which I'll regret only for as long as I live. He coached basketball at Morehead State University in Kentucky during the 1990s, and one famous night in a game at Kentucky in Rupp Arena, he objected to a referee's call by lying supine on the floor and looking straight up to the rafters as if dead of shock. He was outstanding company at lunch in Nashville or at coffee in Seattle or walking down Bourbon Street in New Orleans. When he'd tell of his baseball treks to Chicago, he'd wax about how he'd tell his wife April he had to go, and she'd reply that she knew he had to go, and he'd drive and fly to Chicago, and he'd take his seat in the stadium with his newspapers and—I can hear it now—"I've got my *Sun-Times,* I've got my *Trib,* and I've got my beer, and I'm livin'!"

I thought of him on Sunday, May 6, 2007, because I had my *Times* (of London, a technicality), and I had my train schedules, and I had my scenarios for promotion among the second-division clubs, and I was livin'. After a misspent childhood roaming the barren lands of relegation-less sports, I would see some promotion or some relegation.

As of dawn that morning, the top of the second-division table looked thus:

1. Birmingham . . . . .86 points
2. Sunderland . . . . .85 points
3. Derby County . . . . .81 points
4. West Brom . . . . .73 points
5. Wolverhampton . . . . .73 points
6. Southampton . . . . .72 points
7. Stoke . . . . .72 points
8. Preston North End . . . . .71 points

I decided that with Derby County safely into the playoff involving the third-through-sixth-place clubs, I'd try a place whose fate teetered in the balance that day. I'd never been to Preston. On a dismally dreary Sunday afternoon, May 6, 2007, in the heart of the English May winter period, I disembarked at Preston and walked through the empty streets until I found Sir Tom Finney Way and the stadium, Deepdale. I passed the sculpture that replicates a prize-winning photograph of Sir Tom Finney, the great player sloshing through water during a match at Stamford Bridge, which to me looked like all Torquay. I'd read that Finney grew up right next to Deepdale and that he remained so loyal to the club that he turned down big offers such as one from Italy, an act that would've led to his incarceration in the United States for failure to engage in remorseless capitalism.

I felt curious to see how people would look if their club did or did not leapfrog into the four-team playoff. As it happened, I did not see much of anything, because they would not sell me a ticket: I lacked a ticket-buying past at Preston, and in fact I also lacked any sort of past in Preston. I did love the name Preston, though, because I'd had a great-uncle Preston with big arms and a big voice and a penchant for not saddling his recollected stories with the fussy dullness of the truth. I had read that Preston North End won the very first soccer title, in 1889, when they became the only team to go unbeaten in both the league and the FA Cup, which must've gone over well in their Internet chat rooms. I read that the club had almost bobbed into the Premiership in recent years but had kept getting trammeled in the four-team playoff thicket and hadn't cracked the top level since 1961. The stadium apparently has the remarkable capacity of 22,222, as well as a gaping open end, so I went over and stood there on the sidewalk in front of somebody's row house. Police presence seemed heavy. I could see large blocks of fans inside, and at times they held their scarves above their heads en masse in that way Europeans do that we never do but should, with the caveat that we don't have team scarves, which we also should. The stadium seemed somewhat metallic; the fan noise echoed this tinny sound.

I tried to follow the match by the fans' reactions, and I thought maybe I could threaten the all-time record for most games unwitnessed from just outside a forbidden stadium. When Preston scored at eighty-three minutes, that sustained din seemed obvious. When Preston finished its 1–0 win, though, the fans leaving seemed reasonably merry but not giddy. I suppose their midrange expressions could've told me that Barnsley had not been able to beat fourth-place West Brom (uh, no: 7–0), or that Leicester City couldn't beat fifth-place Wolves (4–1), or that Southend couldn't beat sixth-place Southampton (also 4–1), and that Preston North End had finished seventh, leapfrogging only Stoke.

But what blew me away in the dying moments of a Preston North End season that I had not witnessed was the song that blared out of the stadium speakers as the players must've been making their thank-you parade. Again in the world, Elvis Presley crooned "Can't Help Falling in Love." As an American, I just couldn't help falling in love with the concept that Elvis, raised in that two-room house in Tupelo, Mississippi, materialized thirty years posthumous in northwest England on the grayest gray Sunday in May. If you ever toured Graceland, Elvis's home in Memphis, they'd tell you that Elvis lined up those three televisions in the living room because he liked to watch three football games at once, yet here he adorned that other kind of football as a crowd thanked its players.

I felt pleased we Americans could make a contribution and I watched people head off into summer down Sir Tom Finney Way, and I saw a group of the most astonishing Birmingham fans walking up a sidewalk singing, to the tune of the Village People's

"Go West," "Bye Bye to the Championship." One was dressed as a waitress in pink, one as a detective in sunglasses, one as a doctor, one as a nurse, and one as, improbably, a can of Spam. For just a moment, some young Preston fans, maybe eleven or twelve years old, railed at these gloaters, and a brief sidewalk-to-sidewalk shouting spree ensued, but we all moved on, and I watched children mass for autographs outside the Preston dressing room before leaving.

On the way back to the train station, I ran across a group of Birmingham fans surrounded by police and those scary police horses that might just feel the urge to kick you at any moment. I wondered what these fans had done, but it dawned on me that they'd done nothing except attend the match, and that this would be their police escort back to the station. So I inadvertently wound up walking alongside the police, and even though I had no affiliation save for a club so far south it's just shy of France, they seemed to have a surfeit of officers, so I had six protecting me while traffic stopped and drivers might've seethed.

I, dumb American, had my own police escort out of Preston. To me, it defied all known logic, and I enjoyed it utterly.

I even felt amazed anew at the train platform, where they steered the Birmingham fans into their own segregated cars, and one of the police officers said I could sit anywhere by explaining to another—no, really—"He's normal."

Having seen no promotion from the second division, I rode off down the spine of the country in search of relegation from the Premiership, potentially available way down in the Valley to the east of London. On Monday night, May 7, Charlton would play Tottenham hoping to elude Hades' grasp. On Monday morning, May 7, the Premiership's cellar dwellers went thus:

16. Sheffield United . . . . .38 points
17. West Ham . . . . .38 points
18. Wigan . . . . .35 points
19. Charlton . . . . .33 points
20. Watford . . . . .27 points

That meant that if Charlton did not defeat both Tottenham and Liverpool, it would neither catch West Ham nor spend an eighth straight year in the Premiership, this after gaining frequent note as a model lower-money operation. In the last twelve months, Charlton had switched managers thrice, employing one manager for twelve matches and another for eight. Fans had booed the club off the pitch after a League Cup loss to the Wycombe Wanderers of League Two, the fourth division. Back in February, though, Charlton had drilled West Ham 4–0 in the Valley and looked like the survivor of the two. Come late April, though, West Ham had started hogging wins with the Herculean help of a player whose presence rather defined the misgivings of watching modern-day sports. Back in September 2006, with abundant fanfare, West Ham had acquired two Argentine players, Carlos Tévez and Javier Mascherano, but had done so improperly by Premier League rules. Liverpool snatched Mascherano in late January, and in April, the Premier League fined West Ham a record £5.5 million ($11 million) for the Tévez-Mascherano transaction, but crucially docked West Ham no standings points and allowed the twenty-three-year-old Tévez to stay on. Lauded by no less than Diego Maradona as a twenty-first-century Argentine supernova, the short, stocky Tévez almost single-footedly dragged West Ham toward survival while observers cringed over the injustice. As West Ham suddenly won six of eight matches to spring from twenty points to thirty-eight by May 7, Tévez scored goals against Blackburn on March 17 (penalty), Middlesbrough on March 31, and Bolton on May 5 (two goals).

Meanwhile, Charlton had not exactly decomposed, but sort of sailed sideways.

I saw that tickets remained available, so I called up Monday morning, but they would not sell me one because I lacked a ticket-buying history. I tried the idiot-American-tourist-from-New York routine, but they did not buckle. I refrained from asking if it counted that I stood outside the stadium during a match with Wigan one Saturday in August 2005 eating fish and chips and cursing myself.

I decided to go anyway, hoping to find another ticket angel

whose father could not attend. I had no such luck, even given forty-five prematch minutes of milling around, and I doubled my lifetime total of matches spent just outside the Valley while people absorbed a match within. I spent the first half of Charlton versus Tottenham in a pub a good walk away, and the second half outside the stadium under the statue of Sam Bartram. The statue depicts the Charlton great with wavy hair, smiling and holding a ball in his right hand, palm upward, and I worried that in his very statue Bartram might be committing a handball, but I checked it out and learned that Bartram had been a goalkeeper. Whew. As the second half opened with Tottenham ahead 1–0 on a goal from the fabulous Dimitar Berbatov, I could hear the public-address imploring the fans, "Forty-five minutes left in the Valley this season! This is the moment when we really need your support!"

I could see the action through a window on a lounge TV screen, and I could see that Charlton strained mightily, but that things looked bleaker by the minute because even a draw wouldn't suffice. It grew clear I would experience my first relegation, even if tangentially, and so I listened for the sounds. I've never been a Beatles sort—it was the Clash that moved me and rattled my brain—but I had to credit the wisdom of playing the Beatles' "Let It Be" during the eighties minutes.

I've never heard it sound better. And in this pregnant moment that called for worthy songs, a clever sort in Charlton employ played "Always Look on the Bright Side of Life" from Monty Python. Whimsical. Magical. As the minutes drained off and some of the crowd drained out, an usher let me run into the stadium for the closing, the 2–0 final score, the player parade, and the chants, featuring "We'll Be Back" to the tune of "Stars and Stripes Forever." I had seen relegation, and again I felt astounded by that buoyant creature, the English fan. In the top row, a little band played and people danced. The season had waned and then croaked, but this populace we Americans associate with a crusty realism engaged again in a deathless optimism. I don't want to say all the fans exulted, but many smiled. Many looked like people going home after a regular old 2–0 loss to a big club. Some

stopped and did interviews with TV crews. Relegation had occurred, and I saw not one ten-year-old boy crying his eyes purple
like I did after the Dallas Cowboys upset the Los Angeles Rams
37–7 in the 1976 NFC Championship game at Los Angeles.

In fact, I saw something downright marvelous.

On Floyd Road coursing out of the Valley toward the train
station, I saw a boy not all that much younger than I was on my
purple-eyed day when my mother came to my bedroom and tried
to console me even as she must've felt baffled. He skipped along,
somewhere in the vicinity of his parents, and even though the
Monty Python heyday had long preceded his birth, he sang, solo:

> *Always look on the bright side of your life,*
> *Always look on the bright side of your life . . .*

I'd seen relegation for the first time in my life. It was wonderful. In the train station, throngs waited on both platforms. The
opposite platform, headed away from London, suddenly broke
into a chant to the tune of "Stars and Stripes Forever":

> *We'll be back, we'll be back, we'll be back,*
> *We'll be back, we'll be back,*
> *We'll be baaaaaaaaack.*

A train arrived. The doors opened. They boarded, left behind
an empty platform, and rode off toward the second division, and
I had to say that I hoped their ticket was round-trip.

35

ONE GOAL FROM EUROPE

Consider all the farewells accorded people as they retire. Some get an office party. Some hear other people singing "For he's (or she's) a jolly good fellow. . . ." Some listen to original songs penned by coworkers and chockablock with dull or callous inside jokes. Some get a big company lunch. There seemed to be a twentieth-century American tradition about getting a watch, although I never knew anybody who actually got one. Some get cards, genuine presents, or gag gifts such as laxatives. Some get something practical, like a laptop.

My own father got . . . happier.

Some, if professional coaches or managers, get the cheers of a grateful stadium or coliseum. Some, if professional coaches or managers, get a contract buyout and a figurative kick in the rear end. Some, if professional U.S. congressmen, get an indictment or a matching set of same.

And some, if American professional athletes, make farewell tours through their leagues, receiving gifts in every city, looking mildly embarrassed, and reminding us all that we belong to a ludicrous species that will spot somebody exponentially wealthy and then all but foam at the mouth in the act of lavishing more stuff on him.

Well, on a chilly but clearing day on the southern edge of England, on Sunday, May 13, 2007, some 20,187 of my dearest friends and I may have witnessed an unparalleled send-off.

An English fellow from Tring named Graham Poll, aged forty-three at the time, may or may not have refereed his last Premiership match as Portsmouth played Arsenal. Many suspected yes. Others suspected no. Many didn't care. Others cared deeply, and those hoped for yes.

And so, in fond farewell, the distinctive crooners of Fratton Park serenaded Mr. Poll for a solid minute at least. They serenaded him with still nineteen minutes plus added time remaining in his Premiership career. They sang a song I'd somehow never heard even though I'm sure I'd seen Poll do a Portsmouth match before. Toning down their usual tempo, they went all Celine Dion, all Streisand, opting for a ballad and for overall lyrical majesty:

> *Oh, Graham Poll,*
> *He's a f——ing a——hole,*
> *He's a f——ing a——hole,*
> *He's a f——ing a——hole . . .*
> *Oh, Graham Poll,*
> *He's a f——ing a——hole,*
> *He's a f——ing a——hole,*
> *He's a f——ing a——hole.*

As this opus, so much more memorable than a watch, wafted out over the Fratton End, then across to the other stands, I did not participate because I felt too much awe. I thought I'd exhausted my supply of awe at the world's most popular sports league, but apparently I had not. Forgive my rawness, but I had just never had the experience of standing in a stadium listening to people warble about an alleged f——ing a——hole.

Mr. Poll had just treated the audience to a turn of refereeing seldom seen on the numerous pitches of earth, for in the sixty-eighth minute of a goal-less draw, he had shown us a black swan, a white alligator—a retroactive offside call. I confess to having no previous idea that anyone on earth, not even Nelson Mandela, had the authority to make a retroactive offside call. I also confess to a lack of guilt over my lack of knowledge of the retroactive offside call, for those seasoned sorts around me seemed similarly flummoxed.

They stated their flummoxed-ness in such words as: "f——," "c——," "w——," "mother——," and "dis——."

(Oh, sorry, that last one's printable: "disgrace.")

It had taken me only about thirty live matches to learn how to greet possible offside infractions by swiveling my head to see whether the linesman raised that gaudy little checkerboard flag. So it came as a jolt in the sixty-eighth minute of Portsmouth versus Arsenal to see the linesman's flag arm remain down, then see a bunch of Portsmouth players in the corner of the pitch hugging and celebrating their shiny new 1–0 lead, then see almost the entire Arsenal squad protesting, then hear the public-address announcer confirm Niko Kranjcar's rebound goal . . .

Then realize the play had not ended.

Here's how it had begun: LuaLua had maneuvered to his right just outside the corner of the box and loosed a shot. It had skittered all the way to a reserve goalkeeper with the great name of Mart Poom, then ricocheted off Poom. It had bounced to Richard Hughes right in front. Hughes had swept it left-legged but not well enough, and Poom had stopped it, whereupon it had bounced back toward Hughes like a diabolical pinball while Arsenal's Philippe Senderos had hopped over Hughes to help Poom. From there, it had caromed off either Hughes's body or Senderos's leg, but almost certainly Senderos's leg toward the left, where Kranjcar stood and swept it in. If it touched Hughes's body but not Senderos's leg before it caromed to Kranjcar, it should have been offside. If it touched Senderos's leg after or instead of Hughes's body before it caromed to Kranjcar, it should have been a goal. But if you could see any of that from the crowd, you must have been, as the great *Los Angeles Times* sportswriter Jim Murray once wrote while trying to watch ice hockey, part hawk. I had little idea of the details as I hopped up and down celebrating the goal in front of four seats, including the three to my right, weirdly vacant. I thought we might've just finished quite possibly beating Manchester United, Liverpool, and Arsenal within five Saturdays. Had I really experienced that in my nascent season following this game?

As I came to rest with my heart still scraping my ribs and all Pompey plugged in and supercharged, Poll began scurrying over toward Darren Cann, the linesman and assistant referee with the flag still pointed downward.

They conversed, and this might not have been exactly the conversation, but I think I lip-read most of it:

POLL: Did the ball come off blue or yellow?
CANN: Green.
POLL: Green?
CANN: Well, green is what you get when you combine blue and yellow.
POLL: Is it?
CANN: Yes, but if I had to guess, I thought yellow.
POLL: Why?
CANN: Well, it might just be that when I look out on the pitch and see you, I see yellow, because you gave those three yellow cards to a single Croatian player in the Australia-Croatia World Cup match last June, when it's almost humanly impossible to give three yellow cards to one player in one match given that two merit ejection, so I see you and think yellow.
POLL: Oh, well, then, I say blue.

In truth, the conversation did seem somewhat shorter than that, but no less substantive. Poll waved off the goal—well, didn't actually wave it off, but just pointed to some spot on the pitch that indicated Arsenal should start from there and the score should remain 0–0.

As a whole stand's resentment showed great endurance for a solid minute, then two minutes, then three, I began to time the unmitigated derision of Poll that overran any attention to the continuing game. The contempt went strong for six minutes. It began with the vehement remark "You're not fit to / You're not fit to / You're not fit to referee / You're not fit to ref-uh-ree," but that seemed tame and impersonal given that nobody in the human race has ever really been fit to referee, and given that this was quite possibly the guy's last game before moving to another division or out to pasture.

Gathering itself, the crowd dipped into its reservoir of lyrics, and "The Ballad of Graham Poll the F——ing A——hole" swept up apparently from a soul just two seats to the left of one blue bear, proving that one man and one voice indeed can make a difference. Thereby could Fratton Park supply Poll with a more personalized farewell, a send-off that would ring across the fields of time.

The song sustained itself through several verses, each oddly identical to the last, and it seemed to emanate from deep in Fratton's collective diaphragm. I've seldom heard such mission attached to a song since Whitney Houston famously sang "The Star-Spangled Banner" before Super Bowl XXV in 1991 as the United States commenced a first war with Iraq. I'd always heard of the English unpopularity of a Poll tax, and this Poll tax had been severe. At last, the ballad faded, and through the final twenty or so minutes, including the mere two minutes of added time, there remained only residual insults, heckles, and bad vibes directed at Poll. That, and zero goals. When the final whistle blew, Linvoy Primus began by hugging Poll, a lovely gesture. I thought of one of the cleverer tabloid headlines of the 2006 World Cup: "Exit Poll."

Now, that very morning I had feared tenth place, again. I had walked in the English May winter to the Brighton train station hoping against tenth place. I understand it's madness for a Portsmouth fan to dread tenth place, Portsmouth never having finished higher than thirteenth in a Premiership season, and tenth in the top level still representing the best season in the last half century. But, bloody hell, I'd spent my entire Portsmouth tenure in single-digit places, and I'd gotten used to those single digits, and I just did not want a defeat to Arsenal coupled with a Blackburn victory against Reading consigning ninth-place Pompey to the double-digits. That's right: Pompey had stayed at fifty-three points after Everton, while Blackburn had crept up again to fifty-one, and it dawned on me again that fans often travel to the stadium in fear, and that fear is an integral part of fandom that helps make fandom so appalling. Sure, sportswriters travel to the stadium in fear, but it's a vaguer fear; it's a fear of a stringent deadline, or a fear that somebody might've taken down the buffet already, or a fear that the press parking lot might've filled and we might have to walk an extra ten blocks. Fans have deeper fears, such as tumbling into an undue tenth place after spending eight months in third and fourth and sixth and seventh and ninth.

Well, turns out, some scenarios can turn out even worse than your club falling blithely into tenth. One example: Your club could begin the last day in ninth place. It could have fifty-three points. The club just ahead, in eighth—call it "Reading"—will have fifty-four. The club just ahead of that, in seventh—call that one "Bolton"—will have fifty-five. Then, as this nightmare grinds away, the final day will have Bolton drawing 2–2 with Aston Villa, reaching fifty-six points. It will have Reading drawing 3–3 with Blackburn, reaching fifty-five points. That means that if your club wins, it really will go on a European tour, the UEFA Cup—amazing—because its plus-five goal difference betters Bolton's minus-five goal difference. A European tour for your club, by the way, would be only the first one ever. It's not like you've been awash in European tours and can shrug off the UEFA Cup as would, say, Arsenal.

So as the nightmare hits its spin cycle and your eyes start wiggling, your club also will draw, 0–0, with Arsenal, but not just any 0–0. This will be that special kind of 0–0 that happens to include a goal, and a goal celebration before a jubilant crowd, and an announcement of the goal over the stadium public-address. Then, a referee in his final match will run over to the assistant referee, and you'll just know the goal you saw is about to vanish, and the Pompey fans will feel a profound state of powerlessness as he who has all the power rules it's still 0–0. And sport just teems with these things, these near misses, or near makes, these narrow passageways of exhilaration or excruciation. Some never abate. Chicagoans lament a single basketball call in New York from 1994—they still can name the referee—and St. Louisans lament a single baseball call in Kansas City from 1985—they still can name the umpire—and here comes Poll over to Cann, and while this one's not so significant because it costs seventh place and not first place, well, still, imagine Fratton Park beholding a shock seventh place.

Imagine that life experience.

And so as your body starts to heave and you start shouting unintelligible things in the REM hours, as sweat droplets start to materialize, a song will career around the head, some sort of chant you've never heard in your life, something like:

Oh, Graham Poll,
You're a f——ing a——hole . . .

In this unquestionable nightmare, you'll hear some people singing "He's" a f——ing a——hole, and some people singing "You're," just for variety. Then somebody in the dream will run up to you and give you the other scores, activating the dreaded what-if gland as you hanker for Reading or Bolton to have won so as to render this Poll tax less punishing. Your avuncular manager will tell of how much he wanted Europe, and he'll try to bite his lip to avoid a fine from the league, and he'll say of his summer plans, "If I say anything, Sandra and I will end up on a caravan on Canvey Island when I want to go to Mallorca." And you'll have never heard of Canvey Island, but you'll learn it's an estuary off the coast of Essex, once fashionable, then not, now somewhere in between in the airplane age when people tend to vacation in Spain or Portugal, and you'll learn it's the home to the Chapman Lighthouse of Joseph Conrad's *Heart of Darkness*.

And finishing ninth, with seventh so accessible, might have some people waking yelling, for no apparent reason, Conrad words: "The horror. The horror."

36

THE WHOLE MEAT
RAFFLE OF IT ALL

Final days haul some pretty heavy emotions that grip even that insouciant creature, the sportswriter. I remember feeling wells of emotion, preposterously, on Sunday nights after Super Bowls, on Monday nights after March Madness, on Mondays after Olympics closed, especially in Sydney, when I felt very nearly debilitated. How could they just . . . stop?

The last exam has finished; it's time to say good-bye to all your fellow pupils. Have a good summer. See you next year.

"Have a good summer," the Fratton Park public-address blared as everybody filed out. "See you next year."

Before that melancholy farewell, before Graham Poll received such an eloquent serenade, before the match even started, the day had begun with a sigh. May 13, 2007, Portsmouth versus Arsenal, the last game of the season, and one last turn at rail replacement. One last time that morning, I had entered "Fratton" into a train-station ticket machine, and one last time I learned my route would halt for rail replacement. Again, I would sacrifice mightily for my blue squad.

The train from Brighton to Angmering along the southern coast of the great country stopped eleven times. Then about twenty assorted passengers boarded a rail replacement bus, and we waited as the bus driver conducted an amiable conversation with one of the train supervisors. Minutes later, after the jovial conversation ended, thank you very much, on we went.

Thereby did I lose another fifteen minutes off the end of my life, for my club.

Like most of the other rail replacement double-decker bus drivers, this one knew his machine intricately, but that didn't alter my sensation that the bus might well topple given the speed with which he took turns off of roundabouts as he seemingly impersonated Juan Pablo Montoya. We stopped in Arundel, with its lovely castle perched on the hill. The passenger total thickened, and next to me sat an adorable little boy from India with a Chelsea bag. We proceeded bruisingly along the roads, peering out at the open pastures of the real, green England, until we reached Barnham after seemingly several hours. From Barnham, the train stopped eleven more times before Fratton.

There went another profound sacrifice for my club.

On a gray day on the southern edge of England, at about a quarter to three—a quarter to kickoff for so many heavy English Saturdays through the years—the train finally rolled to where the left-side window availed a view of the ancient and majestic light stanchions of Fratton Park. There they sprouted from their neighborhood of warehouses and storage facilities. I noticed the big B&Q store and marveled at my knowledge that it was not the same B&Q from which Glen Johnson had tried to steal a toilet seat.

The things I'd learned.

I still didn't quite pronounce "Pompey" correctly, sometimes stressing the latter syllable rather than the proper former, and I still waited for referees to blow the whistle for a five-second violation, à la basketball, whenever players took a long time to throw in a ball. But by the season's game number thirty-eight I did know a gem when I saw one.

One: In the seventh minute, Arsenal's Gaël Clichy fashioned a shot that deflected off Noé Pamarot and flew past goalkeeper James, yet seemed awry and unthreatening as it neared the far post. But just as it passed its last swatch of available goal mouth, it seemed to slow. It seemed to activate its left blinker light. It definitely curled antagonistically to the left. It seemed to hang there. I heard a woman shriek. Just then, a guy wearing Portsmouth number 6, who turned out to be Djimi Traoré, contorted himself and kicked it back over his own head for a save.

Another: Any sight of Arsenal's Cesc Fàbregas with a soccer ball.

And another: When Poll awarded a penalty shot to Arsenal in the thirty-eighth minute, and when Julio Baptista lined up to take the penalty, I thought again of how I'd seen James try to stop penalty shots at Watford and against Newcastle and at Everton, but none successfully. Here's an athlete with buckets of decency, I thought. Here's a one-man threat to lower the world's athlete narcissism ratio. Here's Portsmouth's player of the year, just awarded in pregame. So Baptista struck. And James flew to his right. And James met the shot, which flew up over the corner of the goal. And the Fratton End erupted. And so did the other stands. And the place seemed almost to sway. And I joined with my fellow humankind in a vociferous chorus of "England's number one! England's, England's number one!" And I long since knew what that meant.

As will happen in this world, Arsenal seemed faster than Portsmouth, and the idea of winning seemed far-fetched, but time ground on, still 0–0. No Sol Campbell (injury), no Matt Taylor (injury), no Kanu for a while (didn't start), and no Pedro Mendes until near the end (recovering from injury), but with Arsenal similarly depleted, and the season on its dying fumes, we in the Fratton End implored the Pompey players at about fifty minutes with "Guantánamera:"

> One goal from Europe,
> We're only one goal from Europe,
> One goal from Eurrrrroooopppppe . . .

Pretty soon came the heartfelt song to the retiree, a genteel signal of courtesy and esteem. We all drifted into the late seventies, into the eighties, on past eighty-five. In the final five minutes, the Blue Army chant seemed more urgent than ever, the Pompey Chimes felt harder. Even in added time, another "One Goal from Europe" went up.

Then it all stopped, another thirty-eight games in the books, still one goal from Europe, and the applause sounded like rain on a roof. The sky had blued, the sun had come out, the players cleared the pitch, and seemingly half the 20,000 cleared. I stayed, of course, for the kind of lap of honor I'd seen at Everton and even relegated Charlton.

As the players reemerged and began their lap by walking to their right, there came none of the major din of the last home match at Everton or even the last home match at Charlton, no boom, no catchy loud song with only the single lyric. They came around the pitch in a little blob, sort of a ragtag parade, no frills, and I found it fitting, the subtlety of Fratton as compared with other places, rather emblematic of what first drew me to this old rodeo ground. Sol Campbell walked in jeans and a coat, and Matt Taylor, dressed in jeans and a shirt, carried a tot. The lap so lacked pomp and the stadium fell so shy of posh that if you'd just landed from a trip to Mars you might've presumed this the second division or the third, when not for one moment in the whole marathon, from Blackburn's visit in August to Arsenal's visit in May, had this team felt the floor of the first division so much as shudder. I'd sought the relegation tightrope, and I'd found a club that surpassed its previous season by sixteen points, the largest improvement within the Premiership, plus a club that had its best season in fifty-two years.

So as they came by my corner of the Fratton End, I felt a hint of eye mist at the sight of James, leading the pack, and Campbell, tucked in behind, as well as for the whole last day of exams, school shuttering for summer, Sydney closing down its Games. I made sure to remember that I was an interloping American applauding a Nigerian, a Congolese, a Croat, and at least five Englishmen, and that that might be the best you can say of sport, that somehow we'd all converged from all these places on the south edge of England, and we'd all got along, save for a few referees here and there. I even had a moment of lunacy when I suspected we'd all been through something together, though neither the Pompey players nor the people who sat around me would know me if I bumped into them at the B&Q the next day. It can be such a pain to follow sport, so full of the mental gymnastics of rationalizing, so immersed in the hideous business pages, that at least we can value the shared experience.

That and, of course, the company of a blue bear and some chums.

Charlie and Dan and Hopkins and I met up by the player parking lot and walked the walk to the final-exam pub for the season-closing "pint," which, when translated into England's English, means "pints." Children beamed out car windows at the blue bear, reaffirming the intrinsic value of a blue bear, especially one that beams right back at them and waves, about which they probably prattle on until bedtime. We entered the Devonshire Arms, where the patrons' expressions reaffirmed the intrinsic value of walking into a bar with a blue bear. We ordered our familiar array of pints, myself and my adoptive Premiership parents. We got a table and watched footage of Carlos Tévez's marvelous goal for West Ham at forty-five minutes at Manchester United, even while we unanimously agreed that it bothered us that any club could stay up because of a light penalty for an illegal contract with the very player who scored their survival goal. We even felt for old Neil Warnock, the blunt manager at Sheffield United, admired his sincerity in life, and wondered how that tortured face must look freshly relegated. We talked about the previous night's Eurovision song contest, a hugely watched competition in which amateur musicians from each European country submit new songs, on which the continent votes. We discussed the brilliant BBC commentary that undercuts it, which I learned came from Terry Wogan. Who knows, another year, I might even approach cultural literacy.

We sat through an astonishing pub event, something I'd never imagined upon the face of the planet. A fold-up table materialized, and on that table appeared plastic bags bloated with bloody stuff that looked very much like the venison sausage we ate for months in 1978 after my little brother nabbed a long-sought

four-point buck. Astoundingly to myself, a woman began reading off winning raffle numbers. So I saw my first meat raffle. Who
knows, another two years, I might even obtain cultural literacy.

My three parents shocked me with a birthday present, the
sight of which shocked me further: a 2006–2007 Portsmouth
shirt, replete with the Oki Printing Solutions corporate logo on
front, but when I flipped it, wondering if it'd be a Campbell or a
Primus or a James, I saw a number 7 on the back and a CULPEP-
PER. Overwhelmed, I said I did not deserve the shirt because I
had not suffered sufficiently and had never been lower than the
top ten in my entire Pompey tenure.

You never know. Get out of the house, board the train, and
go to the stadium, and you might end up knowing some of the
best souls you ever met.

Good thing too, as fandom grows tougher across time, never
having been easy in the first place in its woolly, exasperating history. As the news programs showed Sheffield United fans in tears
and Charlie sang, "Cry on the telly / I saw you cry on the telly,"
it seemed four clubs might sue the Premiership because of West
Ham. What a lovely closing day, a closing day in which you can
hit the post, as did Sheffield United, and lose £35 million ($70
million), a closing day promising . . . lawyers.

Jaw-dropping money, resentment, lawyers: why, it seems
downright American.

Sometime in that early evening still lit up outside with northern latitude, the larynxes of Pompey reactivated, the pub sang a
rendition of the Pompey Chimes, and either before that or after
that, the pub rediscovered the ballad of the day:

Oh, Graham Poll,
He's a f——ing a——hole,
He's a f——ing a——hole . . .

Moments later, I went to get the round that turned "pint"
into "pints"—two Fosters, one London Pride, one Stella (that's
mine)—and as I waited in front of the taps, I suddenly heard a
man in a Portsmouth shirt to my left on a bar stool. He stared at

the screen on his cell phone, as if checking texts or surfing the Internet or something. And as he looked down, he warbled softly to himself, "Graham Poll / He's a f——ing a——hole / He's a f——ing a——hole. . . ."

This floored me utterly, and later, on the dark-of-night rail replacement bus from Barnham back to Angmering, as the monstrous vehicle raged through the southern edge of England threatening to topple, and as a young couple maybe eighteen years old sat across from me and licked each other's faces, and as I tried to decide whether I found them grotesque or sweet, I thought about that guy warbling into his cell phone. Sure, I thought about buoyant Portsmouth fans and buoyant Charlton fans and buoyant Brentford fans and deafening Aston Villa fans and soaring forty-five-yard goals and own goals that trickled in enchantingly, but I also thought about stolen toilet seats and Ben Thatcher and scary stories about favorite players and the big four and Carlos Tévez and money, money, money, money, money.

I'd fled my homeland for the motherland, fled the staleness for some freshness. I'd run across new legacies and new protagonists and new thugs, as well as beery trains and untold goose bumps and even a blue bear. I'd left behind all my misgivings about sports and found . . . some fresh misgivings about sports. After a year following the biggest league on earth, I may know a little about a little and not much about much, but I do know one thing.

I think it's hard being a fan.

Chuck Culpepper is a two-time Pulitzer Prize nominee and a former sports feature writer and Sunday columnist for *Newsday*. He covers European sporting events for the *Los Angeles Times* and has written for ESPN Books. He lives in London.